Globalization Revisited

Written by one of the leading scholars of global politics, *Globalization Revisited* is a major new book for students of globalization. It describes and explains the challenges to liberalism and the global order as a result of globalizing forces – from financial interconnectedness to the growth of religious fundamentalisms.

The text:

- provides a detailed analysis of the economic and financial aspects of globalization;
- examines the changes to global power and governance created by globalization, including its effect on the sovereignty of the nation state;
- discusses recent trends such as the increased use of networks and social media;
- assesses the rise of globalizing fundamentalism; and
- analyses the challenges to globalization posed by contemporary events such as the global financial crisis.

This book will be essential reading for all students of globalization, and will be of great interest to students of global politics and global governance.

Grahame Thompson is Visiting Research Professor at the Department of Business and Politics, The Copenhagen Business School, Denmark, and Emeritus Professor of Political Economy at the Open University, England.

Critical issues in global politics

This series engages with the most significant issues in contemporary global politics. Each text is written by a leading scholar and provides a short, accessible and stimulating overview of the issue for advanced undergraduates and graduate students of international relations and global politics. As well as providing a survey of the field, the books also contain original and groundbreaking thinking that will drive forward debates on these key issues.

Globalization Revisited

Grahame Thompson

Routledge
Taylor & Francis Group

LONDON AND NEW YORK

First published 2015
by Routledge
2 Park Square, Milton Park, Abingdon, Oxon OX14 4RN

and by Routledge
711 Third Avenue, New York, NY 10017

Routledge is an imprint of the Taylor & Francis Group, an informa business

© 2015 Grahame Thompson

The right of Grahame Thompson to be identified as author of this work has been asserted by him in accordance with the Copyright, Designs and Patents Act 1988.

British Library Cataloging in Publication Data
A catalogue record for this book is available from the British Library

Library of Congress Cataloging in Publication data
A catalogue record for this book has been requested

ISBN: 978-1-138-78289-1 (hbk)
ISBN: 978-1-138-78296-9 (pbk)
ISBN: 978-1-315-74648-7 (ebk)

Typeset in Baskerville
by Out of House Publishing

Printed and bound in Great Britain by
TJ International Ltd, Padstow, Cornwall

Contents

Illustrations

Figures

Table

Acknowledgements

Many people have contributed to my writing this volume over many years. But in particular I would like to single out the following who have made a special effort on my behalf, or closely supported the production of the book in various ways: Eddie Ashbee, John Campbell, Ciaran Driver, Ismail Eutek, Paul du Gay, Lars Bo Kaspersen, Oliver Kessler, Kasper Lindskow, Photis Lysandrou, Glenn Morgan, Mike Pryke, Jakob Vestergaard, Gary Wickham, Duncan Wigan and Karel Williams. In addition, the participants at numerous 'Work in Progress' seminars held at the Department of Business and Politics, Copenhagen Business School, deserve special thanks for listening to many of the chapter presentations and providing a rich feedback to me in the subsequent discussions.

The chapters that appear in the volume are heavily reworked versions of a number of my published articles. These are as follows: Chapter 2, 'The fate of territorial engineering: mechanisms of territorial power and post-liberal forms of international governance', *International Politics*, 44 (5), pp. 487–512 (2007). Chapter 3, 'Exploring sameness and difference: fundamentalisms and the future of globalization', *Globalizations*, 3 (4), pp. 427–43 (2006), and 'Religious fundamentalisms, territories and globalization', *Economy and Society*, 36 (1), pp. 19–50 (2008). Chapter 4, 'Financial globalization and the "crisis": a critical assessment and "what is to be done?"', *New Political Economy*, 15 (1), pp. 125–43 (2010). Chapter 5, 'The global regulatory consequences of an irrational crisis: examining "animal spirits" and "excessive exuberances"', *Globalizations*, 7 (1), pp. 85–100 (2010). Chapter 6, 'Sources of financial sociability: networks, ecological systems or diligent risk preparedness?', *Journal of Cultural Economy*, 4 (4),

October, pp. 405–21 (2011). Chapter 7, 'From artisan to partisan: what would it mean to be an artisan of finance?', *Journal of Cultural Economy*, 7 (1), pp. 95–120 (2014).

Grahame F. Thompson, Copenhagen: 1 May 2014.

Abbreviations

AC	Alternative Currency
ASEAN	Association of Southeast Asian Nations
B2B	Business to Business
BIS	Bank for International Settlements
BND	Bank of North Dakota
BoE	Bank of England
BoJ	Bank of Japan
BP	Bristol Pound
BS	Balance Sheet
CB	Central Bank
CDO	Collateralized Debt Obligation
CDS	Credit Default Swaps
C-GEM	Computable General Equilibrium Model
CoVaR	Covariance of Value at Risk
CRA	Credit Rating Agency
ECB	European Central Bank
EMH	Efficient Market Hypothesis
EU	European Union
FDI	Foreign Direct Investment
Fed	US Federal Reserve Bank
FS	Financial System
G-20	Group of Twenty Nations
G-C	Gaussian Copula
GDP	Gross Domestic Product
GiQ	*Globalization in Question*
HFT	High-Frequency Trading
HRE	Holy Roman Empire
ICT	Information and Communication Technology
LOLR	Lender of Last Resort

MERCOSUR	Mercado Común del Sur (Southern Common Market)
NAFTA	North American Free Trade Agreement
OECD	Organisation for Economic Cooperation and Development
OMO	Open Market Operations
PBoC	People's Bank of China
PLO	Palestine Liberation Organization
PNAC	Project for the New American Century
QE	Quantitative Easing
TARP	Troubled Asset Relief Program
TB	Treasury Bill
TPP	Trans-Pacific Partnership
TTIP	Transatlantic Trade and Investment Partnership
UHFT	Ultra High-Frequency Trading
UK	United Kingdom
US	United States of America
VaR	Value at Risk

Laocoön and His Sons (excavated in 1506, attributed to between 27 BC and AD 68, Vatican Museum, Vatican City, Rome)

1 Introduction

What is at stake in revisiting globalization?

Introduction

The issue of 'globalization' refuses to go away. In the early 1990s when I began investigating this category, and the trends in the international economy it purports to describe, many of my academic colleagues assured me that it was only a passing phase and like other fashionable concepts of the day it would be short-lived. They have been proved wrong. Globalization has endured: both as a conceptual formulation and as an analytical description of the current condition. Indeed, if anything it has expanded its range and content way beyond economic analysis. In late 2008, for instance, my attention was drawn to a symposium on globalization at the Kiel Institute for the World Economy where the following were among the scheduled topic sessions: energy demand and supply; climate change and the environment; water management and waste management; the ageing population; corruption; big cities; terrorism; immigration; health care/epidemics/pandemics; social fragmentation; and more besides. And this was an event organized by an economics' institute. If one were to enter the world of politics, technology or culture an even wider range of topics would be squeezed under the umbrella term of globalization. The category has become the ubiquitous indicator of a claimed epochal change in the modern condition, something enthusiastically embraced by politicians, journalists, management gurus, commentators and academics alike. And it is something that unites the political left and the right (and almost all those in between), even as the former are suspicious of it or condemn it while the latter welcome it or think its effects benign. It is with us and must be accepted as a valid analytical or descriptive device whatever might be one's normative attitude towards its determinants or its consequences. It has become the common-sense and taken-for-granted mantra of our times.

One of the most fascinating features of globalization is its ability to inflate. More and more aspects of social existence are taken under its wing – as indicated by the list from the Kiel Institute just mentioned. The umbrella of globalization continues to expand, gathering an increasing number of features within its analytical embrace. So, as a result, it rather ends up trying to explain everything. Just like its intellectual cousin and prior meta-conceptual category – 'modernization' – globalization inherits the mantle of epochal change agent with a ubiquitous systemic consequence. But this presents a problem. Anything that tries to explain everything ends up explaining nothing. And rather like a balloon that is continually inflated, it becomes vulnerable. To try to include everything means the boundary around the edifice becomes stretched and thinner and thus is easily punctured: intellectual compromises and looseness become the rule, leading to a lack of precision and focus. While an inflating balloon eventually bursts, a similar fate awaits globalization. Any currency that inflates eventually devalues itself. Thus, in trying to explain too much, the outcome is for globalization to collapse as a successful analytical device.

I have been a consistent critic of these positions, and continue to be one, though now from a somewhat different vantage point – one explained at length in this volume. Originally with my colleague Paul Hirst (and later with Simon Bromley) we mounted a sustained investigation into the strong claims made about globalization, and found them wanting (Hirst and Thompson 1996, 1999; Hirst *et al.* 2009). In the early debate about globalization we were designated as the traditionalists and sceptics, in contrast to the enthusiasts or agnostics (Goldblatt *et al.* 1999; Held and McGrew 2002; Martell 2007). Our initial project was to criticize globalization in the name of the continued salience of domestic political capacity to manage economies and organize their effective governance. The strong globalization thesis disarms politicians and citizens alike. It characterizes national economic policy-making as pointless, and political resistance as counterproductive to economic success. But what if globalization was not as pervasive or totalizing as it might seem? This we wanted to explore with an eye to its political consequences. So there was a political project of sorts behind our initial investigations: to combat exaggerated claims about globalization and its tendency to inflate. This accounts for the focus of our early work and, indeed, the chapters that follow in this volume.

In these chapters I revisit globalization, but mainly within the limited scope of its economic and political dimensions. Where these directly abut cultural or technological aspects some attention is devoted to these features, but they are not the main focus. This is because, as indicated above, I remain suspicious of attributing too much to globalization. I think the category works best when it is limited and focused, and the politico-economic domain provides the most productive terrain for its exploration and is central to the debate about the other aspects. This is not an argument for the economy being somehow structurally 'determinant-in-the-last-instance', but it is about how economic and political forces serve to shape cultural and technological ones. As far as I am concerned culture is the least globalized aspect of globalization, particularly popular culture. While there is a lot of talk about the Americanization of global culture – so-called 'McDonaldization' – and the ubiquitous reach of ICTs and social media etc., when it comes to it who is willing to fight and get killed for the chance to watch *Robocop III* (or whatever number it is now!), or any other Hollywood film and its like, or indeed for the chance to consume a McDonalds' hamburger? Admittedly these films are watched, and no doubt enjoyed, around the globe, but their impact is limited. Similarly with cuisine. When it comes to it, people will only fight and die for deeply held and embedded cultural values and beliefs, ones they have adhered to for a long time. This arises most forcefully in the book with the analysis of fundamentalisms, centred on Chapter 3. Fundamentalists want to defend their beliefs and values in a situation of perceived threat and turmoil. Of course some have argued that it is precisely globalization that is responsible for this hardening of attitudes and reactions. Globalization exposes cultural differences and fragments continuities. But this is an argument that both wants to have its cake and to eat it at the same time. Cultures were fragmented and remained segregated long before the advent of globalization (see, in particular, Chapter 3). But what about the much vaunted social media revolution? The problem is that, although used by a broadly middle class intelligentsia to initiate several pro-democracy movements in Arab countries – for instance – it failed to alter the political landscapes there because already well-entrenched and organized political forces (such as the Muslim Brotherhood and the Army in Egypt) took advantage of the situation to advance their own agendas and marginalize the original protesters. If one refuses to yield to a Kantian-inspired myth of an enlightened global cosmopolitanism the result is a non-homogeneous global culture: it remains fractured and often antagonistically poised. We still live in a cultural pluriverse, not a cultural universe. There is no 'globe' to which globalization can be the adequate response as far as culture is concerned. And, as we will see, this may also be the case for the economy.

The chapters in this book derive from several of my publications, many of which have appeared since the last edition of *Globalization in Question* (*GiQ*) was published in 2009. They represent an advance on the argument of that book, taking up new issues and reformulating others as responses to new developments and arrangements in the international political economy. It was never the argument of *GiQ* that 'nothing had changed', despite the fact that the book was highly sceptical about everything changing with globalization. We were always attentive to innovative developments and dynamic adjustments. Our working motto was 'always expect the unexpected'. That has been taken forward into the present volume. So I have tried to come to terms with both changes in the intellectual environment of debate about globalization, as well as what has happened to the international political economy on the ground, so to speak. This means that a new set of issues are taken up in this book that were not the concerns of my previous ventures into examining the nature of globalization. Things have moved on and so have I. Nowhere is this more so than in the context of the financial system and the economic crisis that developed in its wake after 2008. So there will be much to say about this in the chapters below.

But I remain sceptical of globalization nevertheless. The sources of this continued scepticism will become evident later in the chapter, and those that follow. However, this is now a milder scepticism. I have learned to be somewhat more nuanced about my attitude towards globalization, more attuned to the criticisms made of the original formulations advanced in *GiQ*. For instance, I accept now that there has been a certain loosening of sovereign power, but without this in any way destroying such power. What is the point of taking up a hard sceptical position yet again if, as a result, no-one listens to it anymore? It may indicate an intellectual disappointment or failure on my part but the attempt to persuade others that globalization was, at its simplest, exaggerated, and at its most complex, a myth, seems to have failed. Anyway, that is how it has turned out. There is even more 'globo-speak' nowadays than ever before. So one has to be pragmatic and realistic as well as sceptical – at least that is my intellectual disposition. In the early 1990s there was a case for taking up a hard position, to differentiate oneself from both the novel hype around globalization at the time and the developing positions of others. My feeling now is that a different strategy is needed. The hype has turned into the norm. This requires a review of the characteristics of the debate, a subtle reassessment and possible adaptation of the argument, and a sober revisit to its terms. That is what is offered in the chapters that follow.

Setting the scene

This section raises some general issues about globalization that will inform the more specific analysis contained in the chapters that follow.

It provides an opportunity to clarify the type of analysis being offered and its methodological protocols. Here I differentiate the approach adopted in the book from other ways of dealing with globalization, indicating the range of issues tackled and, importantly, what is not dealt with in the book. As will become clear, my interests and concerns are particular and directed at a set of rather specific aspects of the global order: territorial formation and its politics; fundamentalisms and their connection to globalization; financial calculation, model-building and the 'irrationality' of much financial activity; domestic and international financial relationships; and Central Bank activity.

The reasons these particular areas are focused upon is that they represent key themes in current debates about globalization. As discussed later in this chapter, territory (and along with it, sovereignty) continues to be central to conceptions of how the international system might be being transformed under contemporary conditions. Second, fundamentalisms have perhaps rather unexpectedly appeared to galvanize forces that are challenging a broadly liberal domestic and international order. These fundamentalisms are not just confessional but also secular in character: newly invigorated meta-enthusiasms, for which there is little that cool heads can do to counter. And fundamentalisms are vigorously trans-territorial: they recognize no national boundaries to the embrace of their enthusiasms. The significance of these should not be exaggerated but, nevertheless, they also represent a threat that should not be easily underestimated either. Third, financial matters have become central to any analysis of the international economic system, so three chapters are devoted to this aspect of globalization. Finally, Central Banks have emerged as the major managers of their economies in the wake of austerity politics after the 2007–8 financial crash. But the way this activity is configured has served to bring sovereign debt, and its associated risks, to the fore in international relations and economic policy-making.

But do all these issues add up to comprise a meaningful whole that can be subject to a single theoretical endeavour? I am often asked about my 'theoretical position', and whether I have a theory of globalization or whether I am trying to develop one. The rest of the chapter will show why I am reluctant to conceive the project of analysing globalization as fitting into a single specifiable theoretical framework, or of trying to find such a framework. The social sciences are saturated with theories. Many of these are over-elaborate, too complex for their own good, and never quite up to the task at hand. But the response is not to insist on yet further elaborate theorizing but to be modest about the scope of theory. Surely we do not need yet another grand social theory, this time about globalization? In fact this is both unnecessary and impossible. Even if globalization existed in the manner the enthusiasts for it insist, it would be too complex to be encompassed within a single theoretical endeavour. So, in contrast to an overly theoretical approach ('theoreticization' much for its own sake), the emphasis here is on a political arithmetic that is parsimonious in terms of theory but generous in terms of empirics. Instead of making wild and unsubstantiated a priori claims about the ubiquity of globalization, I have always been sensitive to providing empirical evidence for the trends identified. Thus this approach is more sympathetic to an emphasis on 'thick description' (Geertz 1973) than to a stance where a preferred theoretical framework is announced in advance and the subsequent analysis merely elaborates on that or fills in the empirical detail. But such an approach is not blind to theory: quite the contrary. It is highly sensitive to theory but does not defer to a single theoretical model (see Thompson 2012). As will become clear, theories are mobilized throughout the analysis – how could it be otherwise? But these are pragmatically assembled as suits the purpose, not imposed from without or in advance. Different theories suit different parts of the analysis and they are treated in that context. Theory is mobilized in the interests of a *strategy*, not the other way round.

In a moment I turn to various approaches to globalization that are either *not* the centre of attention in this volume, or which are taken up in it in a rather limited and particular manner, or for specific purposes. Outlines of these positions – what are termed below 'analytical stances' – are presented as a prelude to distinguishing between these and the one that informs the analysis in the subsequent chapters. There is a voluminous literature on globalization, which it would be impossible to summarize adequately so I concentrate on some rather generic characterizations, ones that have proved enduring and important in the general debates about globalization since the 1990s.

Approaching globalization

Independently of explicit theories of globalization – where these tend to mirror general theories of socio-economic affairs – there is a series of what might be termed 'analytical stances' directed towards its description. These analytical stances have themselves proliferated: another aspect of the inflationary process associated with globalization. They represent *analytical claims* of what globalization is, how it is organized and what to do about it. By and large these positions take globalization as an accomplished fact, though they all hedge this in various ways and with various degrees of reservation. And as will become clear, these alternative positions are not totally exclusive of one another: they overlap and merge into one another. The rest of this subsection outlines these different analytical stances (and draws on Hirst *et al.* 2009: Chapter 1). It is worth reiterating these here so as to further clarify and differentiate the approach of this volume from these other stances.

From 'globality' to 'planetarity'?

The first influential position on globalization is one that links it to a 'post-colonial' discursive approach. Often based around avant-garde anthropological and post-structuralist intellectual trends, this position works with a number of complex concepts, stressing aspects such as different spatial levels in the global arena and their manifestations, which involve multiple connections, relationships, flexibilities, flows, etc. (Ong and Collier 2004; Tsing 2004). These 'assemblages' are argued to be continually evolving: dissolving and reforming, producing new and often surprising terrains of activity. In this case globalization is viewed as the consequence of these multiple flows and connections – and a state of affairs that now needs to be transcended. One of the objectives for this perspective is to disrupt this conception of 'globality', and even replace it by that of 'planetarity'. This concept is designed to describe a possible world 'above' the North–South divide; 'beyond' the colonial and the Other; 'outside' of the national and the global (Chakrabarty 2000; Spivak 2004: Chapter 3). The project associated with 'planetarity' involves the development of a certain new language and discourse to express this possible world that lies 'beyond globalization'.

And although not directly aligned with the post-colonial discourses, there is a closely associated conception that perceives the global as a series of 'camps' – zones of indistinction typified by the suspension of the rule of law – that infect the rest of the social order (e.g. Agamben 1998, 2005). One rather pessimistic consequence of this conception is that such zones of indistinction embody the final expression of a degenerate modernity: 'bare life' reappears as the characteristic modality of global existence. It can lead to a rather hopeless and disarming attitude: the global is beyond control, management or regulation. As should have become clear, neither of these variations on a logic of 'transformational globalization' suits the analytical protocols of this volume. If – as argued below – globalization in this sense does not exist, there is no need for its transformation in such a radical manner.

A new empire?

A second characterization of globalization is one that does not so much offer a critique of it as such, but rather a critique of a particular political appropriation of it. In this case, current globalization is expressed as the emergence of a new empire centred upon the hegemony of the USA (e.g. Hardt and Negri 2000). The USA is considered the only truly global power, and it is using this status, aligned with neoconservative political ideology and neoliberal economics, to construct a world order very much in its own image. In doing so, it has thrown off the mantle of proceeding through multilateral agreements and compromises with its partners. Instead it has adopted a new strategy of unilateral action, building transient 'coalitions of the willing' under its leadership, and varying in composition dependent upon the objective at hand. In the economic field this position manifests itself as a rampant expression of Anglo-American neoliberalism. Neoliberal economic ideology and practice has become synonymous with economic globalization as a totalizing agenda for economic reform that undermines public activity, nation states and independent economies alike.

Somewhat aligned but adjacent to this position is one that views the global arena as made up of a 'clash of civilizations' or as a 'clash of fundamentalisms' (e.g. Huntington 1996, 2004a, 2004b). The USA is seen as the central defender of Western civilization, thus it is at the forefront of constructing a coalition to reinforce its hegemonic leadership. But in this case the global is fatally fractured, something alluded to earlier and which will be raised again in comments on the cosmopolitan position reviewed in a moment. As will become apparent in Chapter 3 – where the issue of fundamentalisms and their relationship to globalization is analysed in detail – there may be clashes along these lines in the international arena, but these are not clashes between such large aggregations as civilizations or fundamentalisms. The problem is whether civilizations or fundamentalisms exist in any seriously homogeneous way such that there could be an organized clash between them. Rather, there would seem to be as many clashes *within* civilizations (whatever these may be) as between them. And fundamentalisms do not exist as unitary entities either, but are already always riven with rivalries, disputes and indeed armed clashes (as in the case of religious fundamentalist-driven insurgencies in many Middle East contexts, where Sunni and Shia religious extremists are fighting each other, for instance). And fundamentalisms are not just religious-based; there are also secular fundamentalisms such as neoliberal market fundamentalism, extreme animal rights activism and so on.

The (K)Cant of cosmopolitanism?

A third influential position on globalization would stress the emergence of a new international cosmopolitan order in the wake of the complex interdependency and integration that characterizes what is seen as the break-up of the Westphalian international system. In this case, new political responses are required to address the deterritorialization of authority in the global system. Very much developed in the shadow of Kant's pamphlet *Perpetual Peace* (Kant 1919 – first published in 1795), which itself was a call to arms for a new world order, this position stresses the role of transnational civil society actors in the formation of global democratic accountability and political responsibility. The most incisive and insistent advocate of this position has been David Held and his co-authors (e.g. Held 2004, 2010; Held and McGrew 2002: Chapter 9). It is characteristically embodied in his call for a 'new global covenant' among the 'democratic peoples' of the globe, designed to address the growing democratic deficit he sees as resulting from the leaking of power from sovereign states towards what is at present a highly problematic and unsatisfactorily ungoverned but nevertheless coordinated international *market-driven* order (Held 2004).

This position is itself closely aligned to the more sociologically oriented approach to globalization exemplified by Robertson (1992) and Scholte (2005), who introduce such concepts as 'glocalization' and 'supraterritoriality' into the lexicon of globalization. Glocalization refers to the simultaneous immanence of 'the global and the local', and their reciprocal interdependence in the field of culture in particular. Supraterritoriality is one of a number of similar concepts (extraterritoriality, trans-territoriality) expressing relationships that go beyond territorial space. It is designed to capture the way globalization is supposed to have fatally undermined the possibility of nationally based territorial governance. It requires new transnational and transformational institutions of governance, rather similar to those proposed in the context of cosmopolitanism. Below, and in Chapter 2, we tackle the issue of territoriality as viewed from the perspective of this volume.

No doubt, again, there is a nuanced and elaborate defence to be made of these positions, but I would stress that they are underpinned (at least implicitly) by an acceptance of the full globalization story; otherwise why is there a need for such a radical and new international political order? But if – as is argued in the chapters later – there is no complete globalization of the international system, then the 'global' of globalization does not (yet?) exist in this form: there is no single 'cosmos' for cosmopolitanism to address, for instance. Against this, it is suggested, we are still caught in a 'pluriverse' rather than in a 'universe' (e.g. Latour 2004): there remains a set of heavily competing voices in the international order that do not necessarily address one another in a 'common language', and without such a universal language for all to lock into these voices will continue to speak past one another to a great extent (as in the case of fundamentalism briefly mentioned above). Thus, we are not in a position to forge such an ambitious global covenant or a global cosmopolitan order. Rather, we will have to continue to learn to live with – and within – a certain *durable disorder* (see below and Thompson 2012: Chapter 6) where the best that can be hoped for is ad hoc and limited governance responses to emergent problems, combining firefighting 'crises' as they arise and the installation of (usually ineffective) prudential regulation in their wake.

Networks of jurdification?

A fourth take on globalization is to see it as involving the development of networks of cross-cutting relationships in various domains that straddle national borders (Castells 1996; Teubner 2011). In part, this conceives of the system in the context of the role of ICTs and social media in stimulating locational disengagement, and the move towards global standard setting and norm generation. Global standard setting not only involves the traditional public bodies of international governance, but also increasingly private or quasi-private actors that both claim and exercise a public power (Claire-Cutler 2003; Claire-Cutler *et al.* 1999). An added aspect to this development is the way 'international governance' is being increasingly rendered into various networked legal forms, something stressed (and celebrated) by Slaughter (2004), but also involving the progressive juridicalization and constitutionalization of the international sphere without a clear single sovereign presence or legitimating authority to sanction them (e.g. Gruber 2000; Joerges *et al.* 2004; Thompson 2012).

Additionally, this position could be loosely tied to the global conceived in the image of a Luhmannesque-type system and subsystem (non-)integration (Albert *et al.* 2001; Albert and Hilkermeier 2004). For Niklas Luhmann – the spiritual father of this position – the social order is made up of a series of autonomous spheres of meaning, displaying different 'logics of observation'. These systems may be economic, political or legal systems, organizational entities or even individuals. Each of these systems orients itself according to its own distinctions, its own constructions of reality and its own observational codes. Here the global system is characterized by overlapping relatively enclosed systems, which poses the problem of their macro-level coordination and governance. But the constitutive differentiation of society into (sub)systems means that they all operate according to their own distinctions, thereby continually reproducing new differences as they abut and collide with one another. The best that can be expected from this is loose couplings between different subsystems. This frustrates any attempt at overall coordination or governance by a competent authority. Only 'self-governance' is possible, driven by the enclosed inner logic of each (sub)system. One consequence is that new perturbations, differentiations, irritations, provocations and unexpected events continually arise in this world. This enables Gunter Teubner – a related and leading figure in this style of analysis – to align it with an understanding of the global as a radically differentiated 'polycontextual' space, where territories and national sovereignties are broken apart as contingent events produce a 'global law without a state': a transnational legal order for global markets that has developed outside of national and international law, strictly speaking. In turn, this connects to the question of the surrogate juridicalization and constitutionalization of the international sphere as mentioned immediately above (Teubner 2012).

Since I have discussed this very stimulating approach at length elsewhere – and criticized it – I do not say anything further about it here (Thompson 2012: Chapter 2).

A world system?

Another, and fifth characterization of the global system, places this in the longer historical tradition of Marxist and quasi-Marxist 'World Systems Analysis' (WSA) theories. Originally associated with the names of Andre Gunder Frank (Gunder Frank and Gills 1996), Immanuel Wallerstein (2004) and Giovanni Arrighi (Arrighi and Silver 1999), this position has advanced along several related trajectories, some of which no longer pay particular heed or explicit homage to their historical tradition. The first of these, and the one that continues to pay most respect to its intellectual lineage, is the 'global cities' approach (Sassen 2002; Knox and Taylor 1995; Taylor 2003). Here the global is viewed as the continuation of a structured 'centre–periphery' set of exploitative relations involving the emergence of a network of global cities that becomes the new 'centre' of the international system. This network of cities in turn exploits the hinterlands of their locations, which become the new 'semi-peripheries'. And in turn there is a periphery of non-global cities and their hinterlands that are also structured into these relationships as the ultimate source of surpluses appropriated by their more powerful neighbours or cousins.

The difficulty with this approach is that it views global cities as almost autonomous entities independent of their national states. But when it comes to it there would be little such cities could do to forestall their subordination to sovereign states if those states chose to exercise their authority over them. With few exceptions (Singapore, Hong Kong?), global cities are part of the fabric of larger sovereign entities and beholden to them in political, legal and economic terms.

Another variation of this logic, though one that has now somewhat lost its close connection to the original WSA approach, is 'Global Value Chain' analysis (GVC). In fact, there are a number of alternative formulations of this basic position that address the global economy, including 'Global Commodity Chain' (GCC) and 'Global Production Chain' (GPC), and now 'Global Wealth Chain' (Seabrook and Wigan 2014) analyses. For those involved in this type of approach these differences are highly relevant (Gibbon *et al.* 2008; RIPE 2014), but for our purposes they can be treated similarly. Within this perspective, the global is conceived as a series of linked stages in various discrete chains of production, distribution or wealth. These chains involve production units, wholesalers, markets, shipping companies, retailers, banks, consumers, etc., all of which serve to link several remote stages into a global production network. This particular position is concerned with how such chains are organized and governed (by producers or retailers in the main) and how this establishes who gets what in the chain of value distribution. The difficulty here has been to systematically show exactly how surpluses and value are moved along these chains, or from the periphery to the centre. With very few exceptions that I am aware of this problem has never been properly confronted by these analyses (a notable single exception is the case of the Finnish mobile phone supplier Nokia – see Ali-Yrkkö 2010).

Supranational regionalization?

The sixth development discussed here would stress the emergence of supra-state regional economic and social configurations or blocs. Typical examples of these would be the EU, NAFTA, MERCOSUR, ASEAN or the more recently proposed and presently-being-negotiated pacts between the USA and the EU (TTIP) and by 12 countries around the Pacific rim (TPP). This position involves both *de facto* and *de jure* aspects, which do not necessarily advance at the same pace or in coordination with one another. Thus for our purposes supranational regionalism involves the development of geographically contiguous areas composed of the territories of those nation states that have either combined in an integrative economic or monetary union, or whose economies have evolved into a closely interdependent entity through normal market-based trade and investment integration. This imagery is a forceful one and signals an alternative conception of the international economy, somewhat in distinction to that of its strict globalization.

Still a multilateral system?

The final position discussed here is perhaps the most conventional. It stresses the continuation of multilateral interdependency and integration between essentially independent national economies or societies. This involves dealing with flows of resources across space and time in an international context. As should become clear later in the book, this position is still partly endorsed by its analysis, though it emphasizes the limits to the process and perhaps its exhaustion under current conditions. The analysis here remains committed to its basic imagery without thinking this is the end of the matter. Thus, while this account is compatible with growing and deepening international connectedness in trade and investment – with an open world economy of interlinked trading nations – it is also sceptical of the continued pertinence of this as the *single* dimension along which the international system is progressing. The financial system and the productive economy, for instance, might be evolving at quite different temporalities, and there is a similar differentiation within the financial system itself. So those who see extreme globalizers as one pole of the debate, and people who deny globalization as the other – putting themselves conveniently in the sensible middle ground – are doing the issue a disservice. The point for this book is to 'trouble' both of these conceptions.

So, to conclude, although this brief sketch of analytical stances does not cover all the ground marked out by the globalization debate, it sums up a broad range of the most important positions. The last two of these represent the main ones in contention in current *politico-economic* debates about globalization, and they raise important issues about their compatibility and governance. Broadly speaking, the issue is whether the development of trading and investment blocs is complementary to the 'multilateralism' of the global system (as embodied in the final position just described), or whether these two processes are in some sense in competition with one another (de Lombaerde 2007; Cooper 2008). Such competition could manifest itself in the trade and investment diversionary aspects of these blocs as opposed to trade or investment creation aspects, in terms of alternative and discriminatory regulatory initiatives, and in terms of their potential political rivalry. Disputes concerning these issues occupy several chapters in the later part of this book.

Contours of a global political economy

What, then, emerges from this description of various positions in the globalization debate, and the emphasis on the latter two positions in particular? It suggests that there are now four fairly separate (though connected) senses in which the term economic globalization is commonly used in the academic globalization literature that connects to these positions:

(1) To refer to the growth of interdependency and integration by way of the movement or flows of economic resources and activity across distance, space and borders. This is the traditional usage, concentrating upon international trade, investment and migration patterns.

(2) To refer to an increase in the sensitivity of movements of key economic variables in any given place to those in another place. The movements of prices of goods, services and assets, rates of change of real variables such as output and employment, and factors such as preferences and technologies may become increasingly aligned across territorially distinct economic spaces.

(3) To refer to the growth of processes without a fixed territorial location or with little regard to distance. Here it is the emergence of information and communication technologies (ICTs) that is focused upon, particularly the World Wide Web and Internet, but also involving such things as telephone traffic, broadcasting and social networking.

(4) To refer to the growth of interdependency and integration by way of the adoption or harmonization of common standards. Clearly, in this case, globalization does not need to involve the flow of resources across borders since if all agents adopt a common global standard and operate within it, globalization has emerged surreptitiously, so to speak, from behind our backs without anyone necessarily noticing it.

It is fair to say that in the current phase of the globalization debate the emphasis has shifted from the first of these to the fourth, as issues around global standard setting have come to the fore, and as questions of trade and investment integration recede into the background. But the second sense of globalization obviously invokes the financial system in particular, where 'price setting' might seem to have gone global on a huge scale. We examine in more detail these senses of economic globalization as the main chapters unfold. But the overall position is to problematize these and show how in the present phase of globalization an uncertain and unstable juxtaposition emerges between global forces, on the one hand, and supranational regional ones on the other (cf. Hirst *et al.* 2009).

Of course, in principle it would be possible to run the international system as an imperial project, so there is at least a reasonable *prima facie* case for examining the links between globalization and empire. At issue is whether the USA (or any other state) does – or indeed, could ever – resort to this in the modern world. Two obvious major constraints on any return to imperial rule are the rise of 'nationalism', on the one hand, and 'democracy' on the other. Both of these political ideologies and movements effectively destroyed the imperialisms of the nineteenth and early twentieth centuries, condemning them as failed political movements of a past era. Unless these ideologies could be completely displaced, under present circumstances it is very unlikely, therefore, that 'imperialism' could return. In addition, the USA has been unable to seriously mobilize local support for its efforts at direct rule in any but a very few parts of the world, possibly in the Middle East; but even here such support is weak and highly unstable. Thus, on this account alone, it would be more or less impossible for the USA to be described as a new imperialist, or for it to become one. Might it not be wise, therefore, to quickly forget all those many books and articles that combine 'Imperialism' or 'Empire' with 'the USA' in their titles?

Thus we are left with various forms of hegemonic project or multilateralism as the only alternative and seemingly viable and realistic mechanisms for organizing 'global governance'. As argued elsewhere (Thompson 2012: Chapter 6) the first of these has proved hideously expensive for the hegemon, and eventually almost bankrupts it, while the latter represents a cheaper option but suffers from the great difficulty of organizing ongoing agreement and maintaining coherence. But some form of multilateral intergovernmentalism looks the most likely and least-worst outcome under current conditions.

Given this, however, the actual form it would take might well be as a semi-permanent *durable disorder*, as mentioned above. This

would involve a patchwork of overlapping often competitive jurisdictions and territories, where there are few public goods provided
and only minimal collective endeavours. It is typified by the preva-
lence of unruly 'warrior' politics and ad hoc interventions. It leads to
the 'enclavization' of public and private life. This could also see the
emergence of a 'leopard spot' type economy – where small, isolated
patches of prosperity and wealth are set among a more generalized
inequality and economic failure. In many ways this strikes a chord as
an image for the present international condition, though, as hinted
at above, still set – at best – within the contours of a weak multilateral intergovermentalism. The main point is that there is no single
logic to the international system that adequately captures its hetero-
geneous complexity.

Rather the international system is made up of varying aspects existing in multiple sites of operation and overlapping configurations,
even though its basic architecture remains dependent upon nation
states. Whether we like it or not, there are only nine countries that
really matter in the world, and what these countries decide to do will
determine what happens in it – despite all the chatter about globalization. These countries are the fairly obvious ones, and they are listed in
a rough order of their importance: the USA, China, India, Germany,
Japan, Russia, France, the UK and Brazil. There are clearly a few more
that – on a different day, so to speak – one might additionally include:
South Africa, Korea (North and South), Pakistan and Iran. These latter are there mainly for geopolitical reasons rather than for strictly
economic ones. Obviously one could quibble about this list, but the
point is to emphasize the reality of global power as it is actually configured rather than how modern Kantians or others might wish it to be.
But this argument is controversial and raises its own critical response
from those who see the end of the nation state and the end of territorial integrity as the key ingredients of globalization.

So, based on the above discussion, the next section draws these two
issues out for further reflection: the nation state and territory. These
are intimately connected so they are largely treated together. In addition, the discussion takes a particular trajectory through these concepts. It concentrates on issues that are most pertinent from the point
of view of the analysis of the chapters that follow.

The fate of the state and territory

There are two senses of the state in play here: the state as an apparatus of order and rule, and the state as a national entity, a territorial

jurisdiction exercising a claim on sovereignty over that territory. Clearly these involve separate but overlapping considerations.

While the issue of territory has a long history in the context of discussions of IR theory and globalization, it was the accusation that the discipline had succumbed to a 'territorial trap', which prevented it from stepping outside a realist framework of the international state system, that propelled the current debate about 'state and territory' (Agnew 1994, 2009; Shah 2012; Sassen 2013; among many others). Most of this literature makes the perfectly reasonable points that:

- issues of 'territoriality' are not confined to the nation state but involve other types of borders, border regions and border crossings (e.g. Elden 2009; Strandsbjerg 2010; Rumford 2010; Anderson *et al.* 2002; Vaughan-Williams 2008);
- there is a long historical evolution of the concepts that illuminate territories and borders, which has transformed meanings given to these terms, and such an evolution continues into the era of 'globalization' (Branch 2011; Elden 2013; Ruggie 1993);
- the words territory, terror, 'life' (bios), violence, force and strength are either etymologically close or equivalent in many languages, so this opens up a consideration of the linkages between such terms and their consequences for the notions of state and sovereignty in particular (Foucault 1980, 2008 – 31 January and 7 March 1979; Elden 2009; Hindess 2006); and
- as a consequence, territory is a contested complex capability, national borders are not necessarily barriers to economic flows, state power is being 'reconstructed and reconstituted' not necessarily diminished, and spatial ordering and fixing are newly problematic and unstable.

While I have nothing necessarily against any of these formulations I choose to concentrate upon the continued existence of nation states and of territorial politics. But the problem with those authors who wish to deny the continued central pertinence of nation and state to the international system is that they are suspicious and even fearful of the state. And this is something that typifies and unites 'critical scholarship' on the one hand, and 'neoliberal scholarship' on the other. This tradition of anti-statism in the social sciences arises from the liberal and democratic ideal afforded to civil society. In liberal discourse, civil society is foregrounded *against* the state, acting as a check on its expansionary dynamic and authoritarian tendencies. This gets embodied in the romantic notion of a pure and meta-political sociality, often one radicalized by Marxist designs for a society without a state. It lives on in the tradition of emancipatory 'critique' and those calls for a plural cosmopolitan international order where 'transnational civil society' actors replace an order constitutionally dependent upon the rule of law. Instead of this we have a loose configuration of networks, campaigning organizations and informal institutions of cross-border 'governance' (for a critique of these formulations see Loughlin 2014).

But rather than seeing the state as the antithesis of society, Kriegel, for instance (1996), views it as the major vehicle for human liberty, for social peace and security, and, paradoxically, as providing sanctuary for those very political critics who attack it; in other words, the state plays a crucial and ongoing role in the formation and maintenance of 'civil society' (see also, in a more politico-philosophical register, Skinner 1998). It is not its antithesis. It is not an anachronism in the modern world. Indeed, while most of the emerging economies that are challenging 'the West' are busily building strong states, critical scholarship in the West strongly condemns the territorial state there as an anachronism.

So, almost everyone is critical of the state: worried about its growth, the stranglehold it has over welfare paternalism, its legacy of an attachment to authoritarianism and fascism, and so on. These criticisms tend to highlight that the state has an intrinsic tendency to expand as it targets an assumed autonomous 'civil society' in particular (as in Habermas's account of the 'juridification of the lifeworld', for instance).

And this form of 'state phobia' in the modern era (du Gay 2012; Villadsen and Dean 2012) was something first drawn attention to by Foucault in the 1970s (Foucault 1980, 2008). But Foucault was himself hesitantly ambiguous about the state. He does not take it up directly, but rather in terms of *governmentality*, a concept subsequent followers have used as part of their own critique of the category of the state (Mennicken and Miller 2012). ('The state is nothing else but the mobile effect of a regime of multiple governmentalities' – Foucault 2008, p. 77.)

This discussion also takes Foucault into the emergence of neoliberalism as a reaction to the generalized mistrust or anxiety regarding the state. Neoliberalism is classically state-phobic; never more so than with Hayek's writings about money and government. Like so many other things for neoliberalism, the state issuance of money and the exclusivity of its use was a defining feature of their state phobia: the misuse by governments of their control of money has been a constant refrain.

But, contrary to the sentiment of the globalization enthusiasts – neo-liberals and the governmentality school alike – the state continues to *exist*. It cannot just be wished away or treated as a fading reality. And this is equally the case in a domestic setting as it is in an international one. The modern state is a political apparatus that minimally delivers the governmental capacity needed to protect the members of a territorial population from each other, and from external enemies. Of course this is controversially enacted under contemporary conditions, constrained by an international matrix of connections and relationships. But when have things been different?

Ultimately, whether or not the state can be said to have fundamentally altered in its basic characteristics, components and capacities is an empirical issue. It is noticeable, for instance, how such a lot is claimed for the globalization thesis with little resort to empirical evidence: it tends to rely on purely a priori assertion. For example, in a recent special issue of the journal *International Political Sociology*, on territorialization (*IPS* 2013, which contains eight articles dealing with various aspects of globalization), there was not a single evidential table or diagram showing empirical material to back up the various arguments. It is as though 'empirical verification' is looked upon with disdain: it has been transcended by an over-theorized a priori argumentation and a series of assertions. Of course, this is not to say that some of the articles in the *IPS* special issue were not of interest: they were. And evidence does not necessarily have to appear just in the form of empirical data. It is quite reasonable for it to appear in the form of an argument, a description or a polemic. But these cannot serve as the sole criteria of assessment. They need to appear alongside some hard evidence, empirically verifiable and justifiable, rich enough to exemplify the argument. The chapters below are therefore highly sensitive to the empirical nature of globalization, particularly as they deal with its economic and governance aspects.

The state is not an *ideal* institutional form. It is what it is: sometimes a disappointment, sometimes mendacious, sometimes a menace even. But it is the only institution capable of corralling passions, delivering fundamental rights and demanding effective obligations. Sovereign state backing is needed for all of these. It deals in civil liberties and it delivers these more often than not. What more can be practically expected? As Geuss (2001) suggests, it is important to have an independent power that could intervene in the economy to prevent it from self-destruction, as recent events since 2008 have amply testified.

Thus we remain a long way from the idea of a world where countries protected by patriotism and highly defended borders are succeeded by competing commercial city states or transnational civil forces fuelled by an open and borderless international free market in economic resources. While continuing to stress the key role of national states in the international architecture, this is not a 'territorial realism'. States are foregrounded because they still dominate the other dimensions and aspects of international economic activity; not because they are somehow the only rational actors in a system of national interest protection. The analysis is realistic but not an example of intellectual realism – nor is it 'critical realist'.

So what is it? The next subsection develops the methodological protocols that underpin the analysis: that show from where it comes and to where it goes.

Methodological responses and criticisms

One of the main critical methodological points made in relationship to the original formulation of globalization provided in previous analyses concerns the nature of globalization as a 'process', and globalization as a 'state of affairs'. In the discussion by Goldblatt *et al.* (1999) and Perraton (2001) the approach adopted in *GiQ*, for instance, was categorized as a 'traditionalist' one – which became the main way that approach is now understood. But these authors also suggest that the approach adopted a single 'end-state' conception of globalization, a single 'equilibrium outcome'. In contrast to this it was suggested that the only proper way to understand globalization was as a *process* with no single outcome, but one with several possible trajectories dependent upon the dynamic of the various conflicts and struggles that drive the momentum of an essentially 'open system'. Indeed, this has become a defining motif for many of the claims made about globalization discussed in the previous sections.

In the first instance, what a response to this criticism requires is a discussion of the nature of the concept 'process' in social analysis, and second, whether the Held *et al.* point is a valid one in respect to the discussion of 'globalization' in those previous formulations. I begin with a rather general discussion of 'processes', which, it is suggested, has some wider methodological significance. This would stress *five* aspects to the concept of process, which in a skeletal form at least operates in the analysis of the book that follows.

The first of these aspects is that processes need some conceptualization of a *structure* that articulates them. This would involve as simple a structure as possible to express the elements involved and the relationships between them. The elements are features such as entities, agents, components, levels of analysis, their relationships and the like. Such a structure need not be a traditional 'depth structure', however, but could be a structure of affiliations operating 'all on the surface', so to speak, in the spirit of the discussion above: a kind of assemblage. Second, all processes require some means or conception of their *periodization*. This involves such aspects as the nature of events, the ideas of turning points, break points, phases and contrasts. Third, there is a problem about how *change* occurs. This involves questions of whether the process is conceived as a slow evolution or one with rapid discontinuities, the nature of disjunctures, or smooth transformations, the agency involved in change, etc.

Fourth, it seems necessary to add two further aspects of processes to the more conventional ones just outlined. Without these I do not see how the idea of a process can do much intellectual work and lend itself to a political analysis. The first of these is to ask 'Where are processes going?' This is not so much to ask a question about a necessary 'end point' but rather to pose the issue of towards what social formation or order the trends are pointing. What is the direction of travel? Thus, this conception of a process is definitely not one that favours a view of it as a completely 'open system' – one that is always in a complex state of flux and being continuously 'formatted, enacted and performed'. In a way, then, this differentiates the approach of this book from those claims on globalization that precisely celebrate this analytical style, as outlined earlier in this chapter, particularly in connection to the first and fourth characterizations outlined there (see also Thompson 2004b and 2004c for a more developed critique of these kind of open-system methodologies). Finally, there is a need to ask the question 'Where are we now?' Where are we in the unfolding process? And this, in a way, does require at least a temporary conception of something towards which the system or process is tending, as just outlined. But this aspect of processes involves the injunction to 'stop time', as it were; to interrupt the ever-unfolding movement to generate some conceptual stability. And it concretely demonstrates the basic difference between evolutionary time (which does not stop, of course) and analytical time, which has to be brought to a temporary halt for any analytical work to be done in relationship to processes.

The primary consequence of these remarks is that it is a notion of the *conjuncture* that represents the key to the analytical stance adopted here. Capturing the relationships between the elements in play at any time is the central message that emerges from this approach to globalization. It is not that 'historical' trends or processes are ignored, only that they are considered in their current manifestations: they operate as

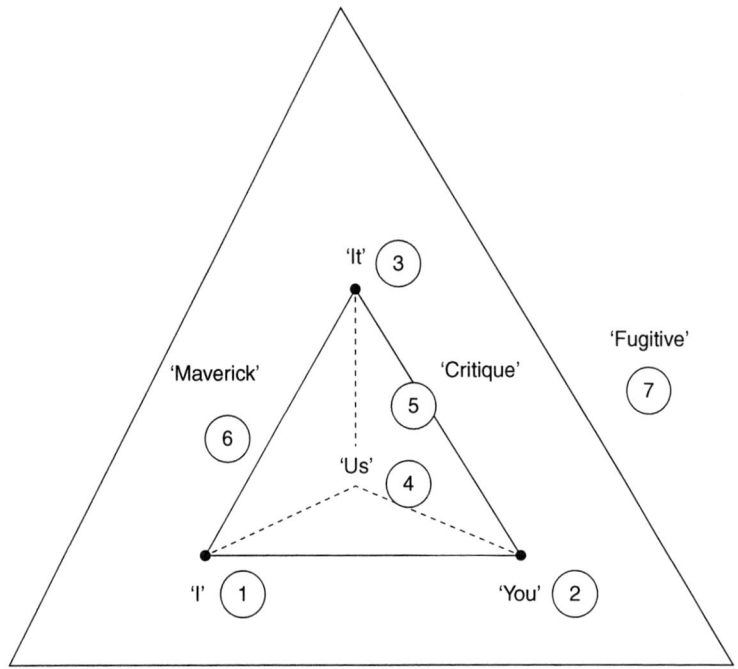

Figure 1.1. The methodological protocols in general

features locked into the present conjuncture. The diachronic appears there as part of the synchronic, underpinning its current characteristics and helping to frame its features. But this can be captured in the 'now' without the necessity of resorting to a long historical narrative.

Finally, we can sum up the overall analytical stance adopted here in terms of Figure 1.1, and the frontispiece to this chapter. Figure 1.1 represents this overall conceptual framework as involving a series of numbers, and a certain type of persona attached to each of them. This is a purely illustrative figure, designed to invoke a style of reasoning, not a tight theoretical framework. It conjures up a sentiment and a disposition that indicates how a sceptical, pragmatic, anti-romantic and realistic approach would ideally work. At first glance this may seem somewhat unusual in terms of its terminology and substance, but that is needed to express what is at stake.

We can begin with the main triangle inscribed in the centre of the diagram, fixed there by the numbers 1, 2 and 3. The features here are the Subject 'I' (1), the Object 'You' (2), and the Transcendental

'It' (3). Between these operates the 'Us' (4). This complex defines a neat and comfortable analytical terrain. And once these – what are known as Ogden–Richards' triangles – are opened up, they proliferate (Ogden and Richards 1949; Eco and Sebeok 1984). How many times does one see such triangular formulations appearing in intellectual work (e.g. Albert *et al.* 2001; Pollitt and Bouckaert 2004: 45, 183; see also Thompson 2008b)? The number 3 – and the division of things into three – is ubiquitous. But this leads to a thoroughly ecclesiastical form of thinking, ultimately dependent upon a quasi-religious trinity. It is intellectually convenient, comfortable, but also highly constraining. Within the boundary of the numbers 1–3 lurk all those analytical approaches that announce a theoretical framework in advance, or appeal to and adhere to a particular intellectual tradition: that know where they are going and, as a consequence, what they will conclude – almost in advance. So the ultimate challenge is to avoid the restraining impulse of the number 4.

Situated directly on the boundary of this analytical terrain sits the figure of 'Critique' (5), an uncomfortable position of both acceptance and non-acceptance, inclusion and exclusion, etc. (almost one of 'us', but still not quite). So the 'practice of critique' (but not necessarily of criticism) sits uncomfortably on the edge, but does not fully escape the embrace of the triangular framework. However, beyond the inner triangle, but not completely beyond the conventional analytical terrain, lies what I have termed the persona of the 'Maverick' (6). This figure expresses or invokes the radical expulsion or the exteriority of a thought. It would be exemplified by such figures as Slavoj Žižek, Giles Deleuze and Gayatri Spivak: those that are 'beyond' but never quite separate. This is about as far as conventional analysis can take us, I suspect.

What I wish to invoke, however, is another figure – which I call, for want of a better term, the 'Fugitive' (7). As shown in the diagram, this figure is genuinely 'outside' the terrain of conventional thought. It is in flight from the triangles, desperately trying to escape their analytical embrace. Note that to illustrate its position, I have felt obliged to construct a 'boundary' around the inner triangle of conventional analytical thought and its margins, which also takes the form of a triangle in Figure 1.1 but which could in principle be of any shape. On the other hand, I have drawn this rather deliberately as a triangle so as to focus attention on a problem that cannot be easily overcome, or indeed probably not overcome at all. It is almost impossible to completely undermine, or escape from, the traditional analytical logic if one wants to remain at least in touch with, and to comment upon, 'conventional' approaches. Thus, I am not sure that there is a position completely and utterly beyond this terrain if one is to continue to engage with traditional intellectual work in any meaningful way. A Fugitive remains 'tethered' to its terrain by the mere fact that it is exactly a Fugitive from something. It cannot completely escape the embrace of its imagination, for instance. The position (7) is thus probably at best on its own boundary with respect to the traditional combination of the conventional logic and its margins.

And this 'struggle' with the number 7 is well illustrated by the frontispiece to this chapter: Laocoön and his sons are fighting to throw off the serpent's constraint. So the attempt to defeat 'logocentrism' is not a modern concern. It is something that has haunted Western intellectual endeavour since the Greeks.

Thus, from the point of view of this volume and its analytical approach to globalization, the intellectual challenge is 'How to be the number 7?' So how to methodologically live and think this position as Fugitive is the problem taken up in a moment in a concrete manner and expressed in rather more mundane analytical and descriptive terms. And although Figure 1.1 expresses the spirit of the approach outlined so far, as with any methodological protocols these are inevitably compromised when it comes to any actual concrete analysis based upon them. They represent a reference point that will never be completely or truly activated in practice. Methodology can never quite live up to its pretensions. As is all too evident in intellectual and, indeed, practical life, principles are seldom sufficient to the moment or the task; rather, they are most often overwhelmed by the moment and the task. So empirical demonstration is always under-determined by principles or theories. Indeed, that is the fate of a non-dogmatic approach to anything, I suspect.

The chapters in outline

In this section I outline the content of the book, describing the issues discussed in each chapter and providing a rationale for the manner of their treatment.

The next chapter – 'The fate of territorial engineering in an era of "durable disorder": mechanisms of territorial power and post-liberal forms of international governance' – assesses the issues first of the rise of territorial power, and then of its fate in a period of globalization and the revival of religious intolerance. The twin concepts of sovereign power and bio-power are deployed to investigate the emergence of territorial engineering in the seventeenth century. The chapter then goes on to address whether there is a genuine threat to the continuation of a broadly liberal international (and domestic) order, driven by the re-emergence of religious and secular fundamentalisms. A key feature of modern fundamentalisms is that they promote and trade on the deterritorialization of social, political, cultural and economic activity. It is argued that this is a manifestation of a new form of 'spirited martial power'. The risks associated with these developments should not be over-exaggerated, but they exist nonetheless. If this is the case, the problem becomes one of how to reterritorialize the activities and disputes engendered by this reappearance and re-emergence of spirited martial power in the international system, with all its attendant links to religious fundamentalisms. Here the argument is that this requires a re-examination of the nature of international borders, and indeed a re-emphasis on their role – not just in respect to containing disorder and restoring the capacity for governance, but also as a way of reconfiguring international toleration and of righting a wrong.

The issue of fundamentalisms is developed in Chapter 3 – 'Exploring sameness and difference: fundamentalisms and the future of globalization'. The emergence of fundamentalisms – both secular and religious – has become a key element in the functioning of the international system and threatens to continue shaping it over the coming decades. But what exactly are fundamentalisms? This chapter provides a response to this question by taking up the relationship between sameness and difference, arguing that fundamentalisms are predicated on a deep desire for sameness. This desire for sameness becomes all the more potent in a period of rapid change and dislocation, and with the loss of ideological certainties. In the light of this, the implications for the emphasis on sameness are pursued in terms of what fundamentalisms make of the international system and globalization. The chapter then goes on to analyse what the two main monotheist religious fundamentalisms – Islam and Christianity – have had to say about the international system, and in particular their attitudes towards, and visions of, 'globalization'. The chapter concentrates upon the fundamentalist position in respect of the two religious doctrines discussed, while fully recognizing that the non-fundamentalists and mainstream traditions in each case do not necessarily share the sentiments announced by – or pursued by – their fundamentalist co-religionists. But it is the fundamentalist variants of the two doctrines that are having the greatest impact on the international situation, so the emphasis is upon these (though there are also some shorter reflections on Jewish religious fundamentalism). In addition, the chapter concentrates upon the attitudes of these positions towards the idea of territory, since this is a category that is widely at stake in the general discussion of globalization and its consequences. Finally, the chapter assesses the impact of these doctrines on the conduct of international relations, the likely success or otherwise of their impact, and the nature of the international system that is being forged in the wake of the re-emergence of fundamentalist activity in the domestic and international spheres.

In Chapter 4 the book moves away from examining territory and religion as important framing features of the international system, to investigate the role of finance and the economic crisis of 2007–8 and its aftermath in shaping the contours of globalization. In 'Globalization, finance and the "crisis": a critical assessment', the analysis challenges the strong notion that the recent financial crisis was global in scope. In so doing, it asks what a truly global financial system would look like, and whether we as yet have such a genuinely global arrangement. The chapter argues that international financial relationships are quite differentiated, being made up of domestic-national, supranational, regional and international aspects, and this imagery does not conform to the typical idea of globalization. The system is characterized by contagion, however, and the chapter goes on to consider the role of this in generating spillovers into the wider economic mechanism. Given this characterization of the financial system, the implications for how to organize a regulatory response are preliminarily pursued. Here the argument is that the principle of 'distributed preparedness for resilience' should guide this response, not a new set of top-down global rules and norms organized once again by the institutions of global economic governance. This principle is examined and developed at greater length in the following two chapters.

Chapter 4 is the first of several chapters that delve into the nature of economic calculation, dealing with the notions of rationality and irrationality and their consequences for specifically financial matters. This takes the discussion into several analytical and theoretical areas that are not immediately linked to globalization, but which deal with underlying assumptions, mechanisms and behavioural characteristics of financial agents and their activities. But this investigation is necessary, I would argue, to uncover what is wrong with modern-day finance as a prelude to suggesting sensible reform policies. That the financialization of the international economic system is upon us with a vengeance is hardly disputable. However, if we are to avoid the complacent return to a 'business-as-usual' mentality in respect to international financial management and governance, there is a real need to understand the underlying causes of financial crises and why they seem to regularly reoccur. In addition, it has been the state that has come to the rescue of this financial system in the post-crisis period: it has tried to 'corral the passions' unleashed by financial excess, which itself is partly a result of the irrationality found in aspects of individual decision-making, model-building and the organizational structure of modern finance.

Understanding all of this, and developing a response to it, is the task begun in Chapter 5 – 'The global regulatory consequences of an irrational crisis: examining "animal spirits" and "excessive exuberances" as features of the financial system'. What would it mean to describe the financial system as 'irrational'? And what would be the global regulatory implications and consequences for the financial system if it were thoroughly, or even partially, irrational? These are the issues pursued in this chapter. It sets out to explore the nature of both the financial system and the economic models deployed to price the main products that are traded in the system – such as options, derivatives and collateralized debt obligations (CDOs). The underlying assumptions associated with these economic models are examined, and the failure of the markets to track risks assessed. The chapter moves on to review several alternative and radical theoretical approaches that draw attention to the nature of the potential irrationality of markets and decision-making in the financial sphere – such as 'excessive exuberances' and 'animal spirits'. Finally, the chapter assesses the consequences of this kind of analysis for regulation. A key claim is that the financial system might be more profitably considered as one that works in a similar way as do natural disasters like earthquakes, tsunamis or volcanoes. Natural disaster planning is thus an intellectual resource that needs to be brought into play to manage and regulate the international financial system. This is linked directly to the issue of irrationality, considered in its existential forms as highlighted by the radical philosophical literature reviewed earlier. Thus, a completely new and different framework for considering financial regulation is suggested, in contrast to the current emphasis on rational top-down initiatives emanating from global calculation centres such as the BIS, the IMF's Financial Stability Forum or the G-20.

We continue the investigation of the underlying characteristics of financial calculation in Chapter 6 – 'Sources of financial sociability: networks, ecological systems or diligent risk preparedness?' This chapter investigates the sources of sociability in modern-day financial systems as another component in picturing the characteristics of contemporary finance. Four sources are identified: sociality dependent upon contract, upon relational interdependency, upon routines, habits and norm, and finally upon the operation of will and passion. Each of these would provide its own rationale for regulation, but it is the fourth that is stressed here as a radical conception, one that needs to be more fully addressed than has so far proved possible in an analytical context. And it is this conception that connects most closely to a second overall theme of the chapter, which is to explore further the nature of irrationality as manifest in financial crises. When the contours of both these aspects of financial calculation have been elaborated, the chapter moves on to consider how they might shape further the regulatory responses to the seeming inevitability of financial crises in modern capitalist economies.

With Chapter 7 – 'From artisan to partisan: what would it mean to be an artisan of finance?' – the examination of things strictly financial in a rather abstract way comes to an end. It sums up much of what has been argued before, by situating this in the context of the twin concepts of 'artisan' and 'partisan'. Thus, it asks the question of what a revitalized financial sector might look like if this were to be reconfigured so as to reproduce, first, an artisanal-like persona for the financial analyst and craft-like organizational structure for financial businesses; and second, if this were to be reterritorialized so that it acted like a partisan rather than, as at present, like a disembedded footloose structure of 'global finance'. Although the analysis is initially pitched at a rather abstract and theoretical level – pulling together artisans, nomads and partisans, and tracing their intellectual lineages – the chapter ends with three very concrete illustrations of actual financial relations in practice that meet some of the criteria for being artisanal and partisanal. The chapter connects territory with governance in the concrete context of actual, locally based, financial dealings and structures that point towards a different and more resilient financial sector.

Chapter 8 examines the evolution of Central Bank (CB) activity since the financial crisis of 2007–8. In 'Creating credit and rating it: Central Banks in post-crisis global finance', the huge expansion of the CB's balance sheet is analysed and assessed. It is argued that this presents new problems of managing the unwinding of those positions, as innovatory policies like quantitative easing are scaled back. This poses problems of institutional credibility and the resilience of the CB as a manager of financial systems and of sovereign debt. A consequence of these events has been a renewed focus on exactly how sovereign risks are assessed in the new era of Central Bank-led capitalism. The chapter explores the institutional reaction by the traditional credit ratings agencies and a series of new organizations that are trying to muscle in on the credit ratings business, with new metrics of calculation and sovereign credit risk assessment. Finally, how long the present phase of low global interest rates might continue is examined, and the prospects for growth considered.

2   The fate of territorial engineering in an era of 'durable disorder'

Mechanisms of territorial power and post-liberal forms of international governance

Introduction

This chapter explores the fate of 'territorial engineering' in respect to both the discourse and practice of globalization. While the nature of production engineering and financial engineering are by now quite familiar, that of territorial engineering is less readily appreciated. This concept is explored in the context of first the construction of territorial power, and then in regard to its possible fate in a period in which territorially based authority seems to be under some threat. Thus the chapter represents a first attempt at dealing with the idea of a durable disorder as characterizing the international system, something broached in the introductory chapter.

The framework adopted in the early part of the analysis is to deploy a Foucauldian-inspired intellectual apparatus involving the twin concepts of sovereign power and bio-power, arguing that these have been central in organizing the construction of territorial power. But beneath, or perhaps better, behind such territorially engineered power, has always lurked another form of power, which is termed here a 'spirited martial power'. Spirited martial power has to do with the struggles formed in the context of 'blood, toil and soil', heroic virtue and legendary combat. Its connections to 'race', ethnicity and religiosity are investigated, and its place with respect to 'warrior politics' and terror explored.

The main issue pursued in the chapter is to examine in what forms such spirited martial power are reappearing in the current international context and how these are affecting the traditional understanding of territoriality (Chapter 1). First, it is argued that the conventional sense of territoriality rested on the formation of religious toleration in the seventeenth century. The forging of religious toleration enabled the modern territorial state to emerge and consolidate, as spirited (and in this case, perhaps spiritual) martial power was dissipated or harnessed in the interests of state-building.

In the current era, however, where such nation states are thought of as being undermined by 'globalization', we have also seen a re-emergence of religious intolerance and new forms of spirited martial power in its wake. Territoriality in its traditionally understood sense is under threat, or so it seems (as discussed in Chapter 1). We may be in a period of reverse (territorial) engineering and the creation of a non-durable disorder.

But how are the new modalities of spirited martial power now appearing in an explicitly international context to be contemporarily understood? Is this still a question of re-establishing a new form of religious toleration, or has the axis of toleration shifted? In this context, the chapter outlines the contours of a new regime of international toleration, one designed to contain the newly emerging spirited martial power within the confines of a broadly liberal form of international arrangement for governance, and thereby to establish and maintain the *durability* of any consequent potential disorder.

The notion of 'territorial engineering'

The idea of production engineering is a well-established one. It involves all those material processes and technologies that go to make commodities and services that are on offer in the marketplace. In addition to this, there is by now a well-established discourse addressing financial engineering. This concept is perhaps less familiar than that of production engineering, but it has to do with how firms conduct a parallel activity to production engineering so as to reproduce themselves financially. It involves such activities as the raising of funds for investment, merger and takeover strategies, chasing subsidies of various kinds, approaches to pricing and marketing, the monitoring and manipulation of company share prices, practices of accounting for profit, etc. Often such financial engineering is associated with less-than-transparent or-honest dealings, though there is no necessary connection to this aspect of company activity. This chapter extends the idea of engineering – in the form of a deliberative activity of forging together a disparate set of mechanisms, processes and practices – to that of assembling a territory: hence the term 'territorial engineering'. To set the discussion going, Figure 2.1 introduces two key considerations that are argued to have been crucial in the historical construction of the notion of a territory: those of sovereign power and bio-power.

Foucault argued that sovereign power was an 'invention' of the early eighteenth century (Foucault 1981). This is not to say there was no discourse about sovereignty well before then. After all, Bodin was writing in the late sixteenth century, and Hobbes in the mid-seventeenth

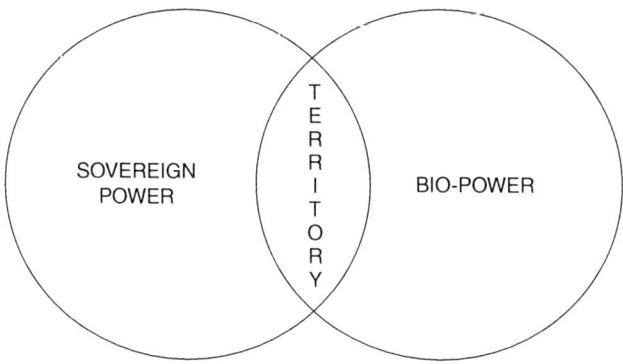

Figure 2.1. Constructing territory I

century, and several of the key treaties involving modern notions of sovereignty that are discussed in a moment were signed in those two centuries. But as a formal system of power – one consolidated and practised on the ground, so to speak – by which a mutually established and matured state system was operative and recognized by all the main parties, this happened somewhat later. Such sovereign power has to do with the consolidation of authority and the law into a single unambiguous pinnacle of power. Fundamentally, 'sovereign power' involves the issue of who (or what) has 'authority' to decide over life and death. It poses in an acute way the politics of life and death (Agamben 1998; Schmitt 1998). For instance, suicide is always a crime from the point of view of sovereign power because it challenges the right of the sovereign to have the decisive authority over death. Terrorist acts of various kinds similarly contravene sovereign power for the same reason. They both directly challenge 'sovereign power'.

Bio-power involves the politics of vitality, of 'man' and 'the body' – indeed of the 'body politic'. It is concerned with all those 'techniques of government' associated with the notion of a population (Foucault 2007, 2008): how to manage a population, how to nurture its health and hygiene, how to ensure its IQ, how to attend to its nutritional requirements, how to establish and ensure its safety and security, its welfare, its reproductive capacities, its fighting capabilities and so on. All the moral, ethical and economic techniques classically associated with what Foucault called the 'pastor and his flock' as a mode of power are involved here (Hindess 1996). Like the notion of sovereign power just discussed, there was a long lead-in time to the consolidation of this form of power, as aspects of its modalities were developed from the seventeenth century onwards, but in its formal sense, as an operationally consolidated system of power, this was an 'invention' of the late eighteenth century.

As these two forms of power became fused together, we have the formation and consolidation of both a concern for and the capacity to establish and preserve a territory in the modern sense of the term, particularly the territory of the nation state.[1] It provided the space for the emergence of what is termed here 'territorial engineering'; that is, exactly how space is engineered into a territory that can be organized as such, managed and regulated. In the modern period this is in part reproduced from definite material instruments and processes such as the issuing of passports, visas, social security numbers, driving licences, identity cards and screening of physical features, establishment and scrutiny of biometric data, the uses of radar, electronic eavesdropping, defensive fortifications, rituals of border meetings and crossings, and involving various forms of classification and identification of people and things so as to secure those borders (see, for instance, Kearney 2004 and the references cited therein).

But how was territory first shaped and formed in the shadow of sovereign power and bio-power? One of the most interesting and ambitious books to pose this issue is Chandra Mukerji's *Territorial Ambitions and the Gardens of Versailles* (Mukerji 1997). In this book she argues that the gardens of Versailles were emblematic of the formation of the French territorial state. As Louis XIV stepped out on to the terrace at the back of his palace at Fontainebleau, he saw France laid out before him. The gardens were a metaphor for the whole of France. And their construction involved the assemblage of a vast array of design skills and techniques, emergent technologies, discourses and expertise of various kinds, practical skills, instruments and equipment, artistic conceptions, craft endeavours and so on – all marshalled for the explicit purpose of creating 'France in miniature' as it were, which could be surveyed and enjoyed from the vantage point of the terrace by the sovereign. It assembled and involved those very practical techniques that were themselves being used at the time to develop and consolidate the French territory as a whole; the collection of data, surveying, planning and mapping techniques, construction of earthworks, the raising of finance, the construction of fortifications, canal- and bridge-building, the planting of forests, the erection of symbolic architectural motifs, drainage and water management, aesthetic deliberation, establishment of transport thoroughfares and so on were all brought to bear in the construction and laying-out of the gardens. At the centre of this was the *tapis vert* – the lawn that runs down the centre of the gardens, an open flat space that allowed the sovereign to write his own particular part in this endeavour, and confirm the spectral authority of a single point of reference for sovereign power. This is an ingenious, telling and largely convincing story as to how to think about the concept of territorial engineering.[2] But it is not the total story. And both these forms of power now seem to be being put into question …

'Spirited martial power' and territorial engineering

For instance, sovereign power no longer seems fully able to determine the decisions over life and death – to have quite the same grip on governmental power as it used to. In a wider register, national sovereignty is thought to have been undermined by the growth of international trade interdependency, investment integration and new forms of 'global' political authority. And in the case of the narrower definition of sovereign power associated with life and death, this is being usurped by a new religiosity and ethics of the self, where, for instance, suicide becomes an instrument of religious conscience and operates as a potential technique for establishing governmental power. In addition, the same is the case with terrorist activity and assassination. These are a crime in the era of sovereignty, but now they are increasingly being employed as a way of – if not exactly usurping that power then of strongly challenging it – offering an alternative claim to legitimacy. Furthermore, is bio-power such a strong element in the current configuration of governmental arrangements, as the concern with – and the ability to foster and preserve – a coherent population fades? It is often claimed that migration is so pervasive that a clearly defined and managed population associated with a specific territory is no longer a viable political category. These points thus serve to raise questions over Figure 2.1 as both a sufficiently general explanatory representation of the nature of 'territorial engineering' and the fate of such a conception in the contemporary era. What is needed first, then, is a further elaboration of the nature of territorial engineering. This is undertaken in the context of Figure 2.2.

Regarding the twin forms of power argued to articulate the notion of territory in Figure 2.1, the case of Figure 2.2 illustrates that there has always been another type of power lurking behind these two. For want of a better term, this is called 'spirited martial power'.[3] There are two aspects to this spirited martial power: its discursive foundations and its practical organizational forms. These are now dealt with in turn. In a discursive sense this conception of power is wrought from struggles formed in the context of 'blood, toil and soil', heroic virtue and legendary combat. It involves sagas and stories providing canonical images

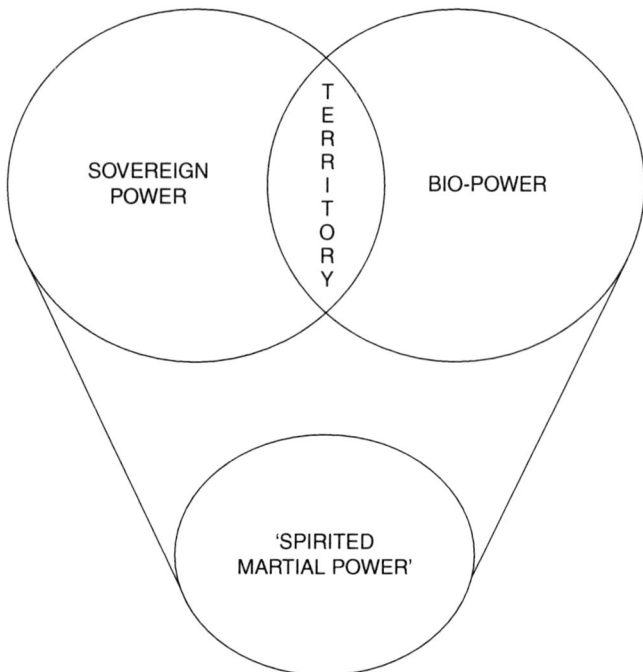

Figure 2.2. Constructing territory II

of patriotic virtue and extreme self-sacrifice, glory rooted in a moral-ity of consequences and actual results, episodes in an endless drama of momentous stakes whose plot is never determined in advance but always the outcome of intervention and fate. It trades on the renewal of honour and virility, the triumph of will, and a politics of superstition.

A further feature of this martial power, but also its spirited ethos, is that it carries a heavily romanticized vision under which the nihilistic craving for violence and turmoil overcomes and overwhelms any form of stable social arrangements, civil order or governance. It celebrates extreme passion in combat, continual gladiatorial contestation. It can also foster an attitude of martyrdom and an aesthetic sense of terror (even an aesthetic of death). But it also implies a certain form of self-mastery needed to secure its drive.

So the power associated with this set of attitudes and actions is termed 'spirited martial power' – a power that celebrates valour, endurance and suffering. This is an active power – or rather a 'power of action', a power that invokes heroic effort above all else, the achievement of glory, and the formation of a warrior culture.[4]

What are some of the practical modalities of this form of power? A number of these are outlined that are not meant to be directly linked either historically or in terms of similar overt sentiments. Rather they are registers of a common but underlying conceptual ferment.

During the English Civil War radical elements of the New Model Army developed a critique of English history as it had unfolded since 1066. They argued that the Norman king, William the Conqueror, had destroyed the authentic lineage of Saxon warrior kings and their knightly valour (Foucault 2003: 63–84). In their eyes the result of this was the sorry state of the monarchy by the early seventeenth century – against which they were fighting. They wanted to restore this corrupted tradition (corrupted by 'a foreigner' of a different 'race') and reinstall the former glorious era of what is termed here, spirited martial power.

This also had (and continues to have) its echoes in popular culture. The classic example would be Sir Walter Scott and his tales of daring deeds in *Ivanhoe*, or in the Arthurian legends, of the crusades of Richard the Lionheart, and in the contemporary interest in the *Lord of the Rings* saga and even the Harry Potter stories. What is more, it is not unconnected to E. P. Thompson's quest for the authentic expression of the noble English working class, seen as something of a down-trodden and submerged social category, denied its proper place in history and ignored by bourgeois historiography (Valverde 2007).

Furthermore, it could be argued to appear in the form of Hardt and Negri's concept of the 'multitude' that needs to rise up against the exploitative forces of globalization and empire (Hardt and Negri 2000; Thompson 2012). For them the multitude is a deterritorialized mass, an underclass awaiting its moment of emancipation (in some ways very much akin to Thompson's English working-class heroes).

Finally, probably the boldest expression of such a martial power in the contemporary period would be the image or figure of a nomadic and deterritorialized warrior culture – not just involving the depoliticized terrorist or fundamentalist, but also to some extent expressing what some traditional armed forces are argued to increasingly look like (Ignatieff 1997). Was someone like George Bush the exemplary warrior politician? (Berman 2003 – see also Chapter 3.)

To some this may all sound an exaggeration, but it captures a certain currency of the present period. Thus, instead of the liberal and rational determinants of territorial engineering establishing classic nation states and a state system, we would have blood, toil and soil as the determinant moments in the struggle for political control over a territory – often, though not exclusively, driven by religious conviction and confessional organization. And this has become trans-territorial in form. It is the attachment of religious and other fundamentalisms to martial power that gives them – and martial power itself – their current spirited potency.[5] While the 'ordinary' politics of religions (even of their fundamentalist variants) may be philanthropic and involve charitable welfarism – in the main religious organizations work in the fields of the mass media (newspapers, TV, radio, magazines), in education, through charitable work and voluntary work – fundamentalisms are 'orthoprax' rather than orthodox; that is, they stress the conformity to many practices of the self and codes of conduct beyond strict exegesis of the scriptures, and this emphasis on confessional practices above scriptural disputation provides the space for martial power to attach itself neatly to religious fundamentalism (though such a systematic observance of ritual practices does not necessarily come at the expense of belief, of course). The mobilizatory nature of martial power feeds into its warrior-like status with its emphasis on action. One further manifestation is the 'mass mobilization' and the 'mass protest' of post-ideological politics, though in large part fundamentalist religious terrorist groups work through secret underground networks for obvious reasons.[6] This is the explicit subject of the next chapter.

Finally in this section, although one might want to be very sceptical of the *Clash of Civilizations* thesis advanced by Samuel Huntington (Huntington 1996, see also Huntington 2004a and 2004b), he does tap into several contemporary moments in the operation of spirited martial power. He argues that the two main monotheisms in contemporary theocratic dispute – extremist Christianity and Islam – are deterritorialized in their modalities of operation. They operate with the idea of a dynamic moving frontier of conversion, impervious to national or any other borders. He also points out that the boundaries between these – where his clashes are most acute – have been very bloody ones. This theme is taken up again in the next chapter.

Toleration

Given the emphasis placed on the revival of religious extremism in accounting for the re-emergence of spirited martial power as a threat to the sovereign power/bio-power couple that lurks behind territorial engineering, we now turn to the way religious toleration was established at the end of the seventeenth century. This will open up a route for analytically confronting (and responding to) the rise of religious fundamentalisms in the present period (explored in detail in the following chapter), which, it should be stressed, is a quite different one to that of the seventeenth century. Nonetheless, there are some important parallels that are worth exploring. The history of sixteenth- and seventeenth-century state-building is a contentious and disputed one. What is emphasized here is the complex interaction between the development of absolutism and religious toleration. Prior to the age of absolutism, subjects were placed in a loose configurative structure of responsibilities: as members of churches, of guilds or other political institutions, dependent vassals, or as members of the feudal order of estates.

By the late sixteenth century the traditional plural order based on these subject-forming positions was in disarray, undermined by acute religious strife and antagonistic sectarian conflict, which threatened the disintegration of the nascent European political system. However, these European religious wars were progressively brought to an end during the seventeenth century, as religious toleration emerged and absolutist regimes consolidated political power in the nation state.

A further key element in the progressive rationalization of the social order during the seventeenth century was neostoicism, which provided a practical guide to the art of living that was not inspired by theological disputation (Oestreich 1982). This secular 'philosophy of life' stressed the ethical virtues of frugality, dutifulness, obedience, self-inspection and discipline, toleration and moderation, while at the same time it recognized the need for a powerful and efficient state and the acceptance for the central role of force and the army in centralizing such control. This neatly chimed with absolutism's claims for exclusive sovereignty and *raison d'état* (that nothing should harm the state, while conscience and morality should be subject to the dictates of politics).

To a large extent it was the combined modality of neostoicism, absolutism, *raison d'état* and Christian reconciliation that 'pacified' the warrior-like spirituality of martial power in Europe during the seventeenth century. It grafted onto the extant martial power a passive form of suffering, servitude and deference. Or perhaps, better expressed, it remoulded warrior martial power into a more precise and clinical form of martial power, one where passivity becomes heroic. This initially opened the way to the attachment of civic virtue to martial power, and then to the undermining, undercutting and eventually the dilution of warrior-like spirited martial power, with a new heroic attachment to civic virtue and state-building.[7]

A key determinant to this pacificatory role afforded by Christian reconciliation was the ending of the religious wars in Europe, where, until then, Christian had fought – and slaughtered – Christian. This itself was predicated on the emergence of toleration between the fratricidally rivalrous religious communities. So it is the category of toleration that needs to be brought more squarely back into the discussion and, as will be argued in a moment, into the international sphere more generally. However, the point is not that spirited martial power represented an exclusive component of the religious wars, only that these provided a context in which it was able to flourish. So, as a consequence, the ending of those wars did not destroy it but rather cut away the space for its particularly virulent mode of expression.

To a large extent toleration in its traditional sense has been seen as a supreme liberal virtue. And as a liberal virtue it is connected – closely connected – to individual conscience and private reflection (see in particular the next chapter). So the history of toleration is closely associated with the rise of religious toleration in particular, and with the rights of individuals to profess, practise and maintain whichever confessional doctrine they wish. Their adherence to this confessional doctrine became a matter of their private opinions, deliberations and consciences. Importantly, the original political struggles to establish religious toleration within the context and boundaries of the nation state were not entirely divorced from 'international issues'. After all, the Treaty of Westphalia (1648) – which began moves towards ending the religious wars and intolerance in Europe – was an international treaty between what were at the time princely proto-states. And it was an international treaty that established probably the first-ever human right – religious freedom of a sort. The treaty of 1648 built on and consolidated many of the provisions first announced by the Peace of Augsburg in 1555. The 1555 peace settlement allowed the right of subjects to emigrate, the ability of princes to reform religion in their territories, and the right of institutions to foster and preserve confessional parity within the Holy Roman Empire (Saunders 2006). The treaty went on to allow the confessional character of a state to be determined by its ruler, with the agreement that other states should not interfere or intervene in the internal religious affairs of that state; they should respect its confessional character and refrain from inciting trouble or supporting domestic religious strife in other states (in fact this religious toleration was only extended to those of Catholic, Lutheran and Calvinist faiths). Member states of the Empire were bound to allow at least private worship and liberty of conscience. A key clause in the treaty was one allowing emigration for those who did not wish to adhere to the confessional character of the state in which they lived – extending this to all religious minorities and dissidents within their domains. In effect, this clause established the right of individual religious conscience – as suggested above, probably the first-ever 'civil right' – which could legitimately exist alongside the different confessional characters of the state in which such individuals lived. The Treaty of Westphalia thus established the principle of religious toleration (if not always its practice, of course). It also showed how an international treaty was of key importance in establishing the rights of individuals within their domestic territories, individuals who, potentially at least, could claim these rights against certain powers of the ruler him/herself. This treaty also enabled the modern nation state to rise and consolidate, since the sovereign power was able to enforce sole rule over a given territory, with this ability being legitimated by recognition from other powers. Before that, this rule had always been open to challenges from abroad.[8]

The advent of religious toleration in the seventeenth and eighteenth centuries involved a two-step process.[9] The first was to disengage the state from the Church, asserting the former's independence from any confessional appropriation by the latter. The second step was to turn religious experience into a matter of the holding of opinions. It was in this way that radical spiritualism could be recast as a matter of private conscience. Thus – in terms of religious belief in this case – these two moves at one and the same time served to both 'depoliticize' the Church and create a 'public sphere' of state activity in distinction to a 'private sphere' of individual conscience or opinion. 'Domestic religious toleration' followed, by being confined within the civil sphere over which the state would adjudicate and guarantee by providing a legal framework in which the competing, but now private, interests were recognized. In addition, in the name of its neutrality, the state wanted to curb the enthusiasm of secular forces as well as religious ones.

And here is a key point in the argument. These moves – enshrined in the Treaty of Westphalia and in the rise of religious toleration via the separation of Church and state – represented a genuine political event. Political events are those events that declare a radical equality (Rancière 1999).[10] They announce an equality where there had previously been a deep inequality. They right a wrong. By announcing the essential equality of religious beliefs and confessional practices, an inequality and a wrong were attended to in a practical context of some significance. This is why the events surrounding these moves have endured for so long. They were a genuine and fundamental political event.[11]

But the question this raises is what would such a political event look like in the present period, a period that is also to some extent typified by a radical inequality involving religious disputation? Before tackling this issue, further clarification is called for on the particular approach to toleration being outlined here. A key element is to differentiate it from an influential conception that sees toleration as an essentially repressive act (Marcuse 1965).[12] In the case of the Marcusian approach, the extension of toleration to one's adversaries serves only to temporarily placate them in the interests of maintaining authority over them or to bolster an existing inequality in favour of the more powerful party. As against this approach, the working definition adopted here is to suggest toleration as the cultivation of a style of behaviour that embodies a studied indifference towards difference. This is what expresses its commitment to a radical equality of treatment. In this sense, toleration is a genuinely mutual act, one that does not necessarily favour either party. Rather, while explicitly recognizing differences between groups, however defined, its objective is to accept these differences for what they are, share a (mild) interest in them, even to learn something from these differences, but to leave it at that and not to continually interfere. Now, this might seem to precisely license gross inequalities and deny the existence of fundamental disagreements. But it need not necessarily lead to this. As argued below, while it might provide a mechanism for tolerating the intolerant, it does not necessarily mean tolerating the intolerable. These distinctions are clarified in a moment (see also Ricoeur 1996).[13]

But exactly what is it that is to be tolerated in the international sphere under present conditions? In the historical case of religious toleration it was, of course, confessional choice that was at stake. In the contemporary period, it is suggested, toleration has mainly to do with some very difficult issues associated with the existence of disputed international borders that define distinct territorial jurisdictions. This is the main difference between toleration in the seventeenth century and toleration in the twenty-first – the axis of toleration is different: religion then, national boundaries now. Whatever current religious-based disputes exist, they are over-determined by boundary disputes, it is suggested. If we are to resist the unpicking of the territorially engineered state system by unpalatable trans-territorial groups newly inspired by a contemporarily invigorated spirited martial power, this is a key lesson.

And this will involve a very different type of political event to address it. It is controversially suggested that this political event involves the declaration of a fundamental equality with respect to all existent and extant international borders in the first instance. This is controversial since it might seem to involve a clear 'inequality'; existing international boundaries are often arbitrary and were imposed by occupying powers and colonial administrations. In many contexts they are fiercely fought over as a consequence, or at least the subject of a constant disputation. Be that as it may, the point is that there are two sides to every border dispute, and both these positions have to be respected if practical political toleration is to take hold. This is the nature of the radical equality to be announced here – it is to accept the necessity of a mutual recognition of the current status quo before anything more can be done. How this might be operationalized will be discussed a moment. And this position is bolstered by a further recognition that peace and peaceful coexistence are very conservative objectives. Peace cannot be associated with radical change or with a serious breach of the status quo – the redrawing of political and jurisdictional boundaries, for instance. People have to feel safe and that their positions are not to be compromised if they are to agree to peace (rather than having peace 'imposed' upon them).

These considerations might provide the necessary prerequisites for the reterritorialization of the emergent spirited martial power, preventing it from getting out of control and completely overwhelming a broadly liberal international order – which it is threatening to do – and thereby preventing a process of reverse-territorial engineering.[11] Thus, the claim here is that only if the 'inequities' associated with borders are attended to in a practical manner will it become possible to deal with contemporary religious intolerance (which I will explore in a moment). The issue confronted in the following analysis is how to foster the conditions for a reterritorialization of social and political activity – and by extension of economic activity as well. There are some real advantages, then, to a Westphalian system of states. It is easier to secure governance and order under such circumstances than to celebrate the emergent trans-territoriality of political and social forces that are thought to herald the advent of a new cosmopolitan era. Under contemporary circumstances, this latter is more likely to degenerate into an anarchy of warrior politics driven by the spirited martial power associated with religiously inspired ideological disputes.

Boundaries

But how are the boundaries so in dispute to be thought about and constituted?[15] Boundaries exist as linked sites of difference and local oppositions. Differences and local oppositions are 'connected up'; yoked together to form entities. Thus, boundaries exist (in our case national boundaries) 'before' entities. Entities – the 'thing-ness' of social space (in our case national territories) – are thus constituted by boundaries, not the reverse; thing-ness is an enduring entity, it has the quality of 'entiness'. In principle, then, boundaries could exist without entities – they are simply sites of difference, neighbourhoods of oppositions. From this perspective, 'space' only comes into existence when a border is established. This enables scrutiny of both sides of the border as well as of the border itself. Thus, while there is no space without a border, space has no borders of itself. Indeed, it is the border that brings into existence an observation of it; observation (or the 'relevant observer') does not exist prior to the border. Members and strangers only exist in relationship to boundaries, as several dimensions of difference are linked up, connected to form a boundary. Members are placed 'inside' the entity-to-be; indeed, members are made up by the establishment of that boundary. For instance, there cannot be the category of a 'citizen' without the idea of a national boundary with a certain jurisdictional capacity and competence. And there cannot be an illegal immigrant without this either.[16] Similarly, there cannot properly be a 'dehumanized' camp occupant without there being a camp of a certain type first.

Plans and scripts are some of the ways this yoking is achieved; it is the action of scripting and narrating that pulls together a set of boundaries into a social entity with the quality of thing-ness (hence the importance of religious ideology in reconstituting new boundaries that ostensibly cut across existing national ones). Zones of difference are proto-boundaries that are yoked together to produce enduring entities. Of course, new differences are always being set up or emerging within groups, so how do (1) old entities endure, and (2) new ones emerge? Old ones endure inasmuch that cleavages are overlapped and compacted into a cohesiveness; an assemblage of various sides and sites of difference. Thus the boundary around a corporation links up various transactions and markets to create an entity – the firm (Holmström and Roberts 1998). The border around a territory is created by linking up various localities of difference, various frontiers of opposition. Neither space nor time can exist without boundaries from the point of view of this topological logic (Walzer 1981). As soon as an old boundary is broken, a new one is formed. In the case of territories, new jurisdictions are formed. In fact, the history of the twentieth century is one of a growing number of territorial boundaries around nation states, which is illustrated in Figure 2.3.

As shown in this figure, there has been a quickening of the pace of national boundary formation since the end of the Second World War. So there are many more boundaries over which there could be disputes as we move through the twenty-first century. Note also that this increase in the number of countries has been accompanied by an increase in economic openness (as measured by the trade to GDP ratio, for instance). And as shown in Figure 2.4 there is a close correlation between these two features.

Alesina and Spolaore (2003) argue that 'globalization' – in the form of increased international trade interdependency and investment

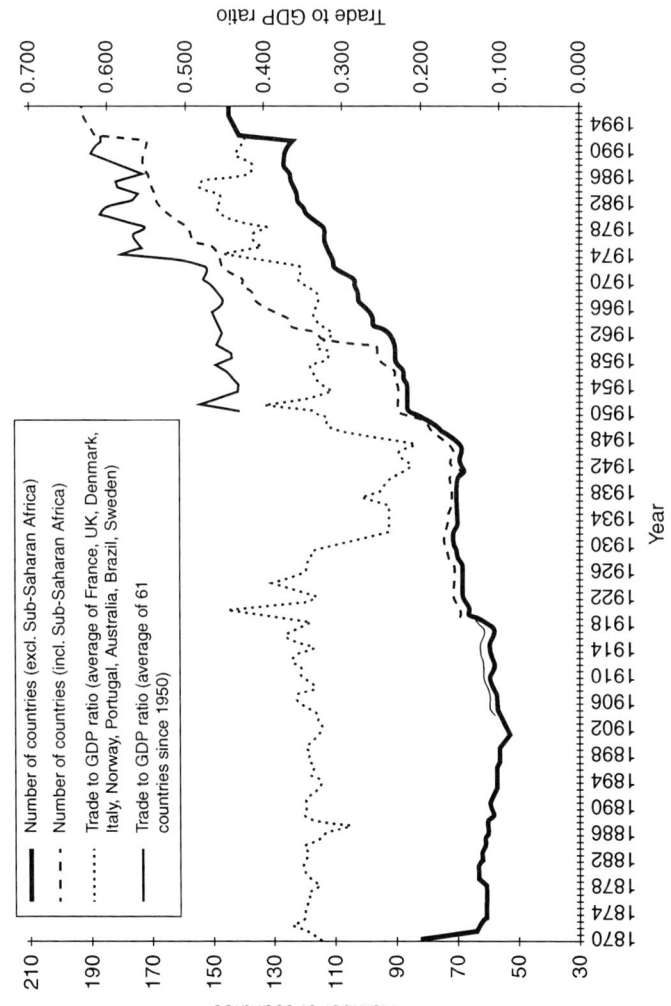

Figure 2.3. Number of countries and trade openness

Source: Alesina *et al.* 2003, Figure 2.

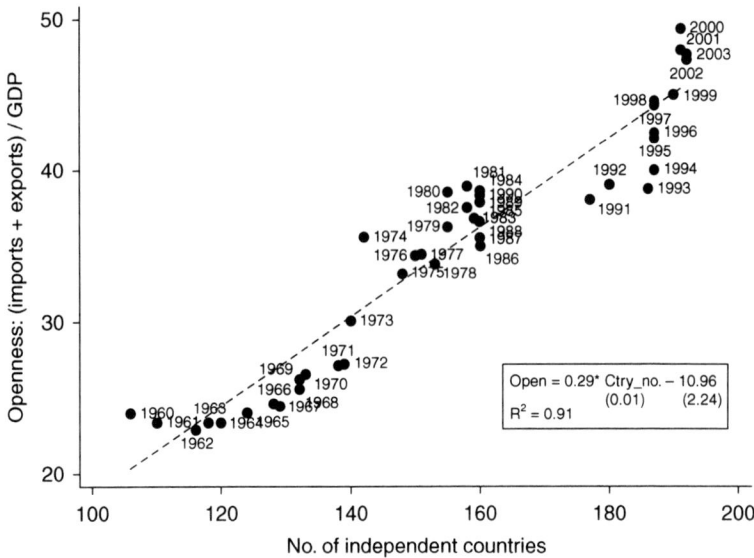

Figure 2.4. Correlation between number of independent countries and trade
    openness
Source: Lavellée and Vicard 2010, Figure 1.

integration – has encouraged the formation of 'smaller' states: in
terms of population or GDP, not necessarily in terms of spatial area.[17]
But it is only as long as populations and territories feel economically
and politically secure that this trend will continue, they suggest (see
also Rieger and Leibfried 2003).

International toleration

In the face of these developments – where territorial-based authority is
under threat from the emergence of new forms of trans-territorial spirited martial power, and where there are more borders over which there
could be dispute – what might be the response? The problem is that
the 'territorial engineering' so carefully crafted to provide a key mechanism in establishing a liberal international order could be undone.
The suggestion pursued in this section is to outline a form of *modus
vivendi* – a regime of acceptable compromises and norms – that would
bolster the commitment to peaceful coexistence at the international
level.[18] In large part this represents a series of suggestions only. But in
an increasingly fragmented and antagonistically poised international

system, there is a need to think creatively about a relatively robust complex of mutually reinforcing commitments designed to establish a tolerant and peaceful coexistence. Such a system would be part of the construction for a 'durable disorder' as discussed in the previous chapter. This section experiments with a list of conditions and principles that might begin to offer a vocabulary for thinking about this. The concrete conditions under which these might operate as principles, or how they might be deployed in specific circumstances, are not developed here (though see Thompson 2012). At this stage the analysis remains discursive. We start with the most obvious of these conditions, the availability of financial resources and their deployment.

Finance and money

A practical regime of international toleration requires a great deal of money to be devoted to it. The current state of disorder in the international system is not unrelated to the gross inequalities that continue to exist within countries (indeed they are growing in the advanced industrial economies), or between the rich and the poor economies (Auvinen and Nafziger 1999, 2003 – though there are some signs that international inequality between countries may be declining slightly – see Thompson 2006 and Milanovic 2012). But, without a radical redistribution of income, the prospects for long-term peaceful co-existence look bleak.

However, there are issues closer to hand that could be more immediately addressed. In particular there would need to be much more emphasis on peacekeeping activities of various kinds and intelligence-gathering. Military action is very expensive but so too is peacekeeping. Peacekeeping is a growth industry, and the military know this. Some 'armed forces' have a comparative advantage in peacekeeping over war-making. In many ways this is true of the British armed forces, and a large number of military personnel recognize this.[19] The UK armed forces, for instance, could not prevail in any conflict overseas without the assistance of the US forces, as was demonstrated in the Falklands Islands/Islas Malvinas and Iraq; and the more astute commanders and managers realize this. If 'training for peace' were to be taken seriously by armed forces, there would be much less emphasis on hardware and more on software. However, the strategic decisions taken by successive UK governments have moved against this. They have gone for the hardware option (two new aircraft carriers, support for the Euro-fighter) and a watered-down version of the revolution in military affairs. In a situation where 'personnel-on-the-ground' are needed for peacekeeping activities, with skills more like those of an Oxfam field officer or an armed constabulary, these high-tech hard equipment options are the wrong ones. However, for whatever purpose or objective, peacekeeping will remain an expensive business, and there is a need for more of it if international toleration in the sense defined here is to be fostered.

Truths and truces

Second, a further way to revive the lost virtue of toleration in international affairs is to emphasize the principle of 'truce seeking' above that of 'truth seeking'. Our social order is one in which truth seeking is the deeply embedded and widely accepted one. It appears in the form of the discourse 'I am right and you are wrong', which animates so many aspects of daily life and intellectual culture. Finding who is to blame as things go wrong, and attributing guilt to those responsible, are the supreme objectives of both our legal system and that of common justice. The finding of a true cause for things also lies behind the commitment to an interventionary political order and economic culture.

But truces are interesting situations, perhaps more interesting than truth situations, if we have in mind the fostering of toleration. Truces are positions – often only temporary – in which no party is fully satisfied or has secured all its objectives. They are situations neither of continued conflict nor of outright victory or resolution, so they avoid celebratory gloating or humiliating defeat. They are 'in between' and thus uncomfortable. Nevertheless, they are truces; what more can be asked for in a world where outbreaks of conflict of some kind seem inevitable? They offer periods for reflection and trust-building. They provide an occasion to seek compromise and consensus, an opportunity to build cooperation and reconciliation, an opportunity to turn *détente* into a more enduring *entente*. In this way, truce seeking behaviours and mechanisms represent an important way of defusing potential and actual antagonistic conflicts. They are a prime example of establishing a more tolerant framework for social order.

Sieges as stalemates

If the conditions for truces cannot be found, it might be possible to develop the mentality of sieges, perhaps better expressed as 'stalemates'. Like truces, sieges/stalemates are interesting states of affairs. We are accustomed to think of the 'decisive battle' as the key moment in any war, and particularly in bringing about the conditions for the enemy's defeat. But historically, most wars ended 'peacefully' in the context of sieges or stalemates. In fact, until relatively recently, most wars were rather leisurely affairs. There were few actual battles, and the ones that there were, were quickly over anyway. Most wars took the form of long marches – endless wanderings about the countryside looking for the enemy – and long sieges of towns and fortifications. The (re)activation of a 'siege/stalemate mentality' among modern-day antagonistically poised combatants provides another opportunity for the 'temporary' interruption of conflicts. If such sieges/stalemates could be turned into semi-permanent states of affairs, in effect the equivalent of 'toleration' would have been established.

Appeasement

Perhaps more controversially, there remains something to be said for resurrecting the heavily discredited concept of 'appeasement' as a principle for the strengthening of toleration. Appeasement is a tougher category than a truce or a siege/stalemate because it requires the stronger party to genuinely give up a potential advantage that it could exercise if it wished. It thus requires the stronger party to be magnanimous; to forgo or suppress its own interest in the name of the common good of both interests. It can also be considered as a way of tolerating the intolerant (always a problem for more conventional conceptions of toleration). This category is a 'dangerous' one, because it requires suppression of an advantage, which could backfire. But the taking of such risks is a necessary feature of any system that has as its ultimate objective the strengthening of peace overall.

Separation

Finally, however, there may be a need to face afresh the fact that agreement on an 'integrated' toleration is not possible to achieve. The conventional liberal wisdom is that integration and multiculturalism are the ultimate virtues for a tolerant society.

An important salient feature of liberalism is its presumption that there exists a political community that is homogeneous enough to be governed, regulated or managed. In this case, sovereignty is able to exercise its effective control because a generalized consent is possible in principle. But without this presumption the juridico-legal notion of sovereignty is undermined. A number of centres of political capacity can exist, among which there is no necessary presumption of social passivity and consensual agreement. Any such agreement must be negotiated or struggled for, and will only ever be contingently established.

Under these circumstances it may be necessary to reinstate physical separatedness as a realistic criterion for toleration. This would echo points that could be made about such international orders as the Ottoman Empire, where physical separation between confessional, cultural, legal and ethnic groupings was common, even as they existed in close proximity to one another. De facto separation has tended to arise in cases of extreme antagonistic pluralism anyway, so there may be occasions to embrace this more formally, and organize for it, rather than maintain the pretense of integration and multiculturalism. Properly organized and supervised, such an approach might actually enhance toleration rather than undermine it, as is often argued. It is not necessarily a 'failure' of toleration to recognize the necessity of particular communities to live apart if they cannot live together. This involves a (reluctant) substitution of 'mutual extraterritoriality' by 'separate territoriality'.

What is to be tolerated?

After this brief discussion of separatedness of combatants it is useful to raise once again the issue of what all this toleration is about. In response, and to reiterate: the problem is that the legacy of nation state-building and imperialism has left some uncomfortable, or grossly unfair and often unjustifiable, 'territorial boundary problems', the inequities of which are understandably the objects of struggle for those disadvantaged by the arbitrariness of those processes. The 'hand of fate' involved in nation-building and imperialism has left many with an outcome that does not at all suit their purpose or expectation. Existing nation states are nothing more than 'communities of fate' but ones forged by the practices of territorial engineering discussed above. Why should those disadvantaged groups not challenge the existing boundaries of the international system and upset any carefully crafted toleration built around them?

   The response to this is, of course, they will. The regime of toleration suggested here does not justify the intolerable. Nor does it unconditionally guarantee peace. There will always be conflict. The conception of politics deployed in this analysis perceives it as constituted by, and constitutive of, 'disagreements' and 'antagonisms'. It is difficult to see how these could be escaped. They cannot all be neatly 'negotiated' out of the system for all time, as a generalized 'tolerant' consensus, and agreement, emerges. We are thus dealing at best with a temporary settlement; one, nevertheless, that deserves support for what it can deliver in the medium term. But this suggested regime of toleration requires as a minimum that all sides accept in the first instance the existing boundaries of the system as a legitimate aspect of its existence, and a basis for negotiation. This does require a certain compromise, a certain appreciation that the legacy it embodies carries its own legitimacy, that these boundaries cannot be destroyed at will, since they have constituted their own 'new' sets of expectations and commitments, whether this is fully appreciated or not.

As suggested above, perhaps unfortunately, peace is a very conservative objective. It requires parties to feel that they would be less threatened than with the existing status quo. It is risky since it might put any party at a disadvantage, making it reliant on the goodwill of others and at their convenience. This is why peace cannot be associated with radical change. It cannot be part of a major reorganization of the social order. It requires a 'de-escalation' of conflict and turmoil rather than any potential 're-escalation' of it.

In addition, it should be remembered that international peace can only be made by states. Peace movements are important and all very well – they have their place – but they do not make peace and have not been able to put serious pressure on governments if they are intent on conflict. For instance, although anti-Iraq war peace movements were highly active in the USA, the UK and elsewhere, and the majority of the populations in these countries did not initially support that war, this made little difference. The problem is, states are not 'moral agents'. They are political and strategic actors who calculate the possible advantages and disadvantages of policies according to their perceived interests, survival instincts, 'hard' choices and so on. This makes peace above all a political calculation, where moral considerations will always be secondary.

Conclusions

By way of conclusion consider Figure 2.5. This sums up many of the arguments of this chapter. In the top half, two scenarios for the international system are sketched: antagonistic pluralism[20] and tolerant pluralism. The suggestion of this chapter is that the issue is broadly one of moving from situation 1 to situation 2 in the top half of the figure – not by replacing 1 with 2, but by 'surrounding' 1 with 2 so that 1 is 'squeezed' and finally 'dissolves' into situation 2 (thereby 'changing the regime').[21] The direction of movement thus goes from 2 to 1. But perhaps there are other considerations and positions indicated by situations 3 and 4, shown in the bottom half of Figure 2.5. If we are actually in the position of situation 3 – one that might be termed 'unilateral antagonism' (and this may be nearer the present case given the role of the USA) – then it is going to be doubly difficult to move

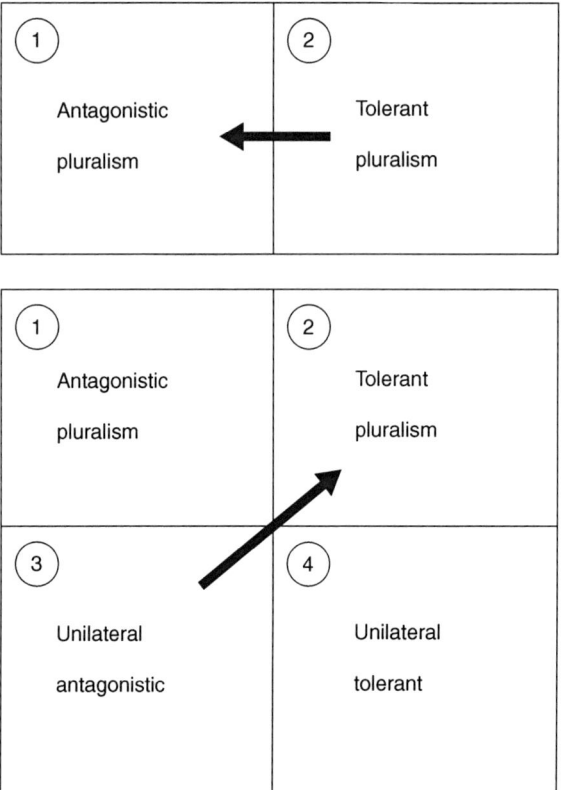

Figure 2.5. Scenarios of the international system

to situation 2. But is a move from situation 3 to situation 2 likely to be more difficult than a move from situation 1 to situation 2 (by which 2 'enfolds' 1)? At this stage I leave a response to this question open.

What has been argued in this chapter is that there exists a genuine threat to the continuation of a broadly liberal international (and domestic) order, driven by the re-emergence of what has been termed spirited martial power, aligned to the rise of religious and secular fundamentalisms. This risk should not be over-exaggerated but it exists nonetheless. As discussed in the next chapter, a key feature of such fundamentalisms is that they both promote and trade on the deterritorialization of social, political, cultural and economic activity, which is seen as a feature of contemporary globalization. In the case of 'warrior politics' in particular, such a deterritorialization represents a serious danger. If this is the case, the issue becomes how to reterritorialize the activities and disputes engendered by this reappearance and re-emergence. There is an urgent need to reterritorialize the extraterritorial in the case of this aspect of politics at least. Here the argument was that this requires a re-examination of the nature of international borders, and indeed the re-emphasis of their role, not just in respect to containing disorder and restoring the capacity for governance, but also as a way of reconfiguring international toleration and righting a wrong. One should be suspicious of further positive claims about, and celebration of, deterritorialization. And while the issue of reterritorialization has been discussed here in terms of it political dimensions, in later chapters we take up the same issue in terms of economic matters, particularly in the case of the financial system (Chapters 6 and 7).

Notes

1 The relationship between sovereign power and bio-power is clearly more complex than I can go into here. For instance, there is a strong case for arguing that bio-power redefines sovereign power; after the eighteenth century, bio-power becomes newly constitutive of sovereign power. Of course, for Foucault, sovereign power was always something of a problematic category since it spoke exclusively to the juridico-legal aspect of power that he was at pains to criticize. In addition, bio-power itself has gone through a number of mutations and transformations; from a concern with managing a population, to managing only those at risk for instance. However, despite these well-taken points, I want to preserve the basic architecture of Figure 2.1 for analytical convenience and clarity. It is complicated in a moment. Also at this point, perhaps it is worth recalling Max Weber's classic modernist definition of the nation state as 'the legitimate monopoly over the use of violence within a recognized and bounded territory' (Weber 1978: 904–5). Thus, modern statehood is based upon the coupling together of the principles of territoriality, jurisdictional or administrative capacity, and military monopoly, including the use of violence and the legitimacy to do so (which is itself crucially based on recognition by other states).

2 For a more conventional story about how the notion of a territory emerged in a politico-philosophical theoretical register, see Baldwin (1992). To avoid misunderstandings, the emphasis on the idea of 'territorial engineering' and the stress on technologies of power, material practices and processes in this chapter is part of a deliberate attempt to avoid situating the analysis in the framework of political philosophy. See also Geuss (2002) for similar sentiments directed at circumscribing excessive philosophically inclined claims for liberalism. He stresses that early liberalism was more concerned with 'order' than with 'justice', a sentiment echoed here. More on the consequences of this approach later.

3 This conception of a 'spirited martial power' is derived from a rather liberal reading of the lectures in Foucault (2003). Inasmuch as sovereign power is associated with the term 'demos' and bio-power with that of 'ethnos', spirited martial power would be associated with the term 'credos'. Originally it

was Tom Osborne (Bristol University) who suggested to me the term 'spiritual' be added to the term 'martial' in this formulation. However, further thought suggested this might be better termed 'spirited' than 'spiritual'. The term 'spiritual' is too exclusively associated with religious experiences, whereas 'spirited' better captures the dynamic of both religious and non-religious forces designated by the current formulation.

4 Importantly, the etymology of the word 'territory' is to be found not only in the form of an area of land under a particular jurisdiction but also from 'terror' – which has to do with 'one who frightens' or a 'place from which people are frightened off', which itself is further etymologically linked to the term 'terrorist' (Baldwin 1992: 209–10). See also Chapter 2 above.

5 The relationship between fundamentalisms (and not just religious ones) and martial power in the current period is a complex one, which is yet to be fully explored, though an analysis of fundamentalism is the specific object of the next chapter. On the general issue of what fundamentalisms stand for, see Sim (2004) and Marty and Appleby (1991–94, 1993). For recent analyses of religious fundamentalisms, see Ali (2002) and Ruthven (2004). On the issues of religious fundamentalism and terror, see Berman (2003), Juergensmeyer (2003) and Stern (2003). A number of these books are what might be termed 'popular potboilers', but they are instructive nonetheless and should not be dismissed out of hand. In the analysis that follows in the main chapter not much more is said about secular fundamentalisms such as extreme neoliberal economic analysis and policy prescriptions, or animal rights liberationists – this is saved for Chapter 3. But, although operating in a completely different register, as Chapter 3 demonstrates, there are connections between religious and secular fundamentalism in terms of martial power, particularly in the discursive drive that typifies both of them.

6 On the organizational nature of fundamentalist terrorist networks, see Gunaranta (2002) and Sageman (2004).

7 I would suggest that Machiavelli operated as a crucial intermediate step in the transformation and move from full-blown martial power to its civilizing pacification. For Machiavelli the morality of an action is determined by the excellence of its outcome; if it is effective it is virtuous. His morality is illusion free, where honour, self-interests and fear are managed for a 'well-governed polity'. Primitive necessity rules, but an enlightened self-interest is a key feature of his political outlook. Note, however, that Machiavelli is concerned with the power and preservation of the Prince, not necessarily the state (as in 'reason of state' theory).

8 The Treaty of Westphalia has been afforded an exalted status in the establishment of the international system of states, one that it perhaps does not fully deserve. It is certainly fashionable nowadays to dismiss the treaty as a significant event in the formation of the international state system. But while there is now a well-established critique of this status (see for instance Teschke 2003; Rosenberg 2005), as Chapter 1 argued, the continued existence of nation states is a reality that cannot be ignored, as will be argued at length later. The burden of the argument to come is that the 'institutions' of the nation state and the state system need to be strengthened and its deterritorialized activity reterritorialized.

9 These paragraphs draw upon Thompson (2002–5), and also Asad (2003), Creppell (2003), Walzer (1997) and Zagorin (2003).

10 I thank Claudia Aradau for drawing my attention to this rather precise definition of a political event. But I take this 'ethical' moment in the foundation of politics to be a consequence of politics being about conviction, and therefore always involving an ethos.

11 Again, there is a much more nuanced story to be told here about the nature of this 'event'. To start with, it was centred on the Holy Roman Empire (HRE), so France and England were at the margins. And who was actually arguing for a radical equality of religions at the time? Certainly some Brandenburg political philosophers such as Pufendorf and Thomasius (see Hunter 2002: Chapters 4 and 5). Also, the Calvinistic dynastic rulers of Lutheran proto-nations such as the Hohenzollerns had little choice in putting it forward, but they also kept Catholics very much in their place. As mentioned in the main text, it was the Peace of Augsburg in 1555 that actually first proposed this equality, but it was consolidated in relationship to the so-called *Normajahr* of 1624 (standard year). This established the moment of religious distribution in Europe and the benchmark for religious standing among 'states': the dominant religion in a territory at this time became the 'state religion'. The Treaty of Westphalia further consolidated this, as the three religions (Calvinism, Lutheranism and Catholicism) became legitimate bodies under Imperial (HRE) law (although the Habsburg princes were afforded some exceptions to this – the measures of toleration did not extend to non-Catholics in the hereditary lands of the House of Habsburg). An important provision in the treaty was that a prince should forfeit his lands if he changed his religion, which placed an obstacle in the way of a further spread both of the Reformation and the Counter-Reformation. However, the situation in England and Ireland was more difficult, and France continued to kill or drive Protestants into exile. The point being made about the treaty of 1648, however, is that it marked a kind of watershed event in the establishment of a certain religious equality, not that it fully or immediately secured this in the practice of religious toleration throughout Europe.

12 This is alternatively termed the 'permissions' approach by Forst (2004).

13 Such a definition will not satisfy everyone. For many, toleration is absolutely not an issue of 'indifference'. Rather it requires the active dislike of something but at the same time the capacity (or 'value') of tolerating such a dislike (e.g. Williams 2006). And Forst (2004) wishes to see it in rather similar terms as requiring a reciprocity of mutual respect and justice. Both these authors discuss the kind of 'practical toleration' of indifference defended here, but dismiss it as not quite meeting the philosophically correct protocols of true toleration. As far as possible I try to deal with the political aspects of toleration, not its ethical or philosophical aspects.

14 Paul Hirst posed this nicely in one of his last published contributions before his death (Hirst 2003). He asked what the limits were to the accommodation of non-democratic, fundamentalist and religious governmental organization to the continuation of a liberal international order (pp. 55–8). A similar issue is posed by Rawls (1999) in his discussion of exactly who the 'acceptable peoples' to be included within the 'law of the peoples' at an international level are. This is not the place to discuss these

issues at length (though see Tan 2005), but the comments in the rest of this chapter provide my initial response to this question. I have discussed the Rawlsian formulations at length in Thompson (2012).

15   The discussion relies heavily on Abbott (2001) and Walzer (1981).

16   Thompson (2014) justifies these statements in the context of a discussion of constitutionality and the everyday life of citizenship, in distinction to the contemporary emphasis on 'acts' of citizenship that suggests that any political act can be considered a citizenly one. I do not subscribe to this position.

17   They do not suggest that there is a strong causal mechanism operating here – from globalization to smaller states – only that the former has allowed the latter to develop, and there tends towards a reciprocal relationship between the two trends (Alesina and Spolaore 2003:192–9). This is further illustrated by Figure 2.4 where correlation should not be confused with causation.

18   See Gray (2000) for a defence of the idea of *modus vivendi* as a key aspect for liberalism.

19   These comments are based on my observations and conversations with military personnel while teaching at the UK Joint Services Defence College for several years. Some of the most ardent 'peaceniks' that I have met are from the army. They know that to orient themselves towards 'peacekeeping' is necessary if they are to, first of all, continue to attract funds and secondly, not lose out to 'private' peacekeeping initiatives/intelligence-gathering organizations that also see this as an opportunity and as a growing market. In addition, some of the most 'dovish' voices in US foreign policy come from the military. If the anti-war movement was more intelligent it would try to capitalize on this dilemma for the armed forces, and try to strike up an 'alliance for peace(keeping)' with the armed forces (and against moves towards the unaccountable privatization of peacekeeping).

20   To be precise about this, antagonistic pluralism is a system in which the pluralization of interests and social forces intensifies to such an extent that it becomes increasingly difficult to organize compromises and agreement between these interests and forces, and in which the usual channels of democratic activity begin to look increasingly suspect and lose their legitimacy. This new period is one often accompanied by an increase in the extent of ungovernable manic capitalism. Manic capitalism is a frenetic economic system embodying an intense and uncontrollable dynamic of competitive activity driven as much by corruption, marketeering, speculation, profiteering and mismanagement as by genuine ordered economic exchange.

21   'Changing the regime' is not the same as 'regime change'. Regime change involves an intervention from 'outside' to change the political leadership, government or administration. Changing the regime implies a process of the application of pressure or negotiation to reform, adapt or change the structure, peacefully and with consent.

3 Exploring sameness and difference

Fundamentalisms and the future of globalization

Introduction

What are we to make of the rise of fundamentalisms for the future of the international system?

This is the issue confronted in this chapter, and it develops remarks made about the rise of fundamentalisms in the previous chapter. In most people's eyes 'fundamentalism' is associated with religion and particularly with the rise of militant Islam. Clearly, Islamic fundamentalism is an important issue and one that could threaten the future of a broadly liberal domestic and international environment if it were ever to seriously take hold as a global political force. But religious fundamentalism is not confined just to Islam. It represents a strong feature of contemporary Christian doctrine as well, particularly in the form of the 'born-again' movement in the USA and elsewhere (Northcott 2004). In addition, we should not ignore secular fundamentalisms (Ruthven 2004; Sim 2004). One of these with a strong ethical underpinning is militant animal rights activism. This has engaged in a series of harassments, intimidations and bombings. Another would be fundamentalist nationalism: the kind promoted by extreme right-wing political groups such as the Front National in France and the BNP in Britain (though at the moment the BNP may be something of a spent force in the context of British politics). This fundamentalism is often associated with overt racism. But the one that has had – and continues to have – the greatest potential impact at the international level is extreme neoliberalism, or, as it is better known, 'market fundamentalism'.

Later I analyse in detail the specificities of the main monotheist religious fundamentalisms that are most active in the international sphere and assess their likely political impact at the global level. I leave 'market fundamentalism' for a more thorough treatment in later chapters. The previous chapter provided an analytical framework for considering the nature of contemporary deterritorialization under the impact of 'globalization' into which fundamentalisms of various varieties neatly fit. In the chapter here we first step back a little from these specific investigations to ask a key question of all fundamentalisms: what do they mean from the point of view of those committed to them, and why are they so compelling? I will argue (among other things) that fundamentalisms can be very productively thought around the distinction between 'sameness and difference'. Indeed, I will argue that this is the key relational aspect to the individual's commitment to fundamentalisms, as well as to fundamentalisms' collective aspirations. The chapter then goes on to discuss the likely impact of the rise of fundamentalisms for the future of the international system, dealing with the three main theocratic fundamentalisms, each in turn: Islamic, Christian and (to a lesser extent) Jewish. Finally, the consequences of these fundamentalisms for the politics of the international system are explored, and their impact on recent US foreign policy is highlighted in particular. The chapter ends with a summary and conclusion.

What does fundamentalism mean?

Sigmund Freud's reflections on religion in *Civilization and Its Discontents* (Freud 2004 [1930]) provides an important entry point into thinking about the rise of modern fundamentalisms, as does Georg Simmel in *On Individuality and Social Forms* (Simmel 1971), which explores the relationships between groups and individuality. I exploit both of these fairly freely in what follows.[1]

What, then, is meant by religious fundamentalism? As a preliminary specification we could say that it is a militant form of piety that amounts to a rebellion against modern secularism. Or so it at first seems. In fact, as argued later, religious fundamentalisms are a very 'modern' phenomenon. They operate precisely to facilitate an engagement with modernity, and are thoroughly intertwined with secularism as a result. Thus, I prefer to treat religious and secular fundamentalisms as parallel projects, both of which meet the conditions outlined in a moment. For religious fundamentalisms, the claim to be such is based upon the demand to take the word of their God entirely literally. For the secular form it is usually based upon some doctrine or text that is similarly thought to be canonical and beyond dispute.

Why are we interested in – indeed at some level fascinated by – fundamentalisms and fundamentalists? I think they are fascinating to us because of their certitudes, which 'we' cannot quite match. Fundamentalists are absolutely certain about their beliefs and destinies. 'We' cannot quite grasp or achieve this level of certitude or of self-meaning or self-belief, though we would dearly like to do so. Thus they have achieved things that are always just beyond the grasp of the rest of us. In this respect, fundamentalists trade on a very modern pathology, or perhaps better, a modern syndrome. This can be termed 'meaning deficit disorder'. This we all experience, and suffer from. For most of us 'life' is so complicated and things so difficult to fully grasp that we give up in 'despair' about making complete sense of it all. In addition, this syndrome arises from the basic uncertainties and risks that are pervasive throughout the modern experience, something often summed up rather crudely under the title of a 'risk society'. On both counts, fundamentalists 'cure' this disorder. They neither lack understanding nor remain uncertain.

Thus, I would suggest, fundamentalists represent an idealized version of ourselves; they are like 'us'. Indeed, in some ways they are more like ourselves than we are because they are even better than we are, since they have the certitudes that we lack but continue to desire and pursue. This then relates to some remarks about sameness and difference that I would like to make, which are important for: (1) understanding fundamentalism, and (2) understanding what is said about (national) borders and frontiers in the analysis of deterritorialization and globalization that I take up in a moment.

A basic proposition for this approach is that what divides 'us' are the things that 'we' share.

What divides us are thus not so much differences, as such, but similarities – the things and attributes we share. Humans are ambivalently alike and different simultaneously. This is the basic relational aspect to things, which needs to be stressed in connection to fundamentalisms. And while it is more difficult to acknowledge sameness than it is difference, fundamentalists work against the notion of differences and their displacement on to others (and the 'Other') that the difficulty of acknowledging sameness promotes. Fundamentalists disavow difference in the name of sameness. They offer a retreat from, or a withdrawal from, difference in the name of sameness. They want, indeed insist, that everything and everyone should be the same – the same as them (and many of them are prepared to die to achieve this). Thus we should all conform to their way of life, worship their God (who is the only true God), conform to their beliefs, to their ideals, etc. This is connected to what Freud called 'the narcissism of minor differences' (Freud 2004 [1930]: 64)[2] – we are narcissistically fascinated with minor differences because fundamentally we all desire to be the same.[3] Thus the point to emphasize is that fundamentalists are an idealized version of 'us'. They are like ourselves, if not better than ourselves. This is why at some level, at least, everyone is a potential fundamentalist, though often only reluctantly so.[4] What fundamentalism works with, then, is the classic triangular formulation of 'I' (1), 'You' (2), 'It' (3 – 'God' in this case) and 'Us' (4) as sketched in Chapter 1. It is deeply inscribed within the inner triangle of Figure 1.1 (see earlier), where it provides a comfortable and secure place: an enclosed world protected from the vicissitudes of a complex configurative disorder that lies beyond (embodied in the numbers 5–7).

But this is the site of a genuine problem. 'Idealization' is closely linked to 'intolerance'. Indeed, intolerance is predicated on idealism. Chasing an 'ideal' or believing in 'principles' forms the basis for extremism and intolerance. It promotes 'blind faith' in distinction to pragmatic reason. When these ideals and beliefs are embodied in a 'leader', which for fundamentalists they often are, extremism closely follows. Those close to the leader, those existing in the neighbourhood, the shadow or the proximity of the leader – let us call them the 'nobility' – who have respect for the leader, offering deference to the leader, who understand the leader, are the ground troops for fundamentalism and extremism. Those not proximately close to the leader are the same, but ignoble. They need to be converted to actually become the same and become noble. Thus we should be more suspicious than we generally are about the role of ideals and principles in the conduct of politics. Principles can be the harbinger of extremism and fundamentalism. They are the basis of overt enthusiasms that undermine considered judgement.

And this in turn relates to the practice of 'sacrifice', which is such a strong feature of (particularly, though not exclusively, religious) fundamentalist thought, rhetoric and activity. Here the issue of 'meaning deficit disorder' arises again. Meaning needs to be sacrificed so as to realize the potential to go forward and to improve. What is true of intellectual meaning is also true of the 'meaning of life' – hence the reason that the practice of sacrifice (suicide/martyrdom) is so central to fundamentalist activity. There is a need to give up something for there to be progress. For the most extreme fundamentalist, of course, this also means the giving up of someone else's life; those of hostages, passers-by, trapped victims, etc. But, once again, they are not that different to 'us'. Under extreme circumstances we could do the same thing.

So what about the often noted 'aggression' and violence associated with fundamentalism? Well, perhaps fundamentalists are actually terrified of aggression and violence, again just like everybody else, but in their case in a peculiarly acute form. In wanting to deny difference or displace it and reaffirm sameness they also want to eliminate what they see as the basis of aggression. For them the only way to eliminate violence is for us to all be the same. Aggression arises where there are differences.[5]

Here arises the basis for two senses of the term 'respect'. Respect has a positive connotation in the sense of an active interest in, a wish to engage with, learn from, get to know and enrich oneself by the encounter. On the other hand, there is the negative sense of respect; respect deserved by adherence to the leader, indeed earned by closeness and deference to the leader. This also offers a basic support for fundamentalism and extremism. Thus the street slogan 'Respect!' (invoked in the form of a demand) is not always one to be taken as lightly or as positively as it often is.

Finally, suppose we define tolerance in the sense of the ability to endure pain. This is also a feature of intolerance. Fundamentalists tolerate pain – endure it – in the name of their intolerance. They pride themselves on tolerating pain and suffering in the name of their intolerance of other attitudes or aspirations. How might this connect to the issue of sameness? For fundamentalists, tolerance and intolerance become the same in that they can both pertain to the endurance of pain and suffering.[6]

Preliminary implications and consequences

Since the 'cultural turn' in analytical matters from the 1980s onwards, the issue of *difference* has come to dominate cultural analysis. Indeed, it is a range of 'D words' that are in play here: 'différence' (Derrida), 'différend' (Lyotard), and 'difference' (Deleuze) and others, none of which have quite the same meaning as the word 'difference' in English.[7] So while there are important contrasts between these 'D words' from the point of view of cultural analysis, I remain with the English version in what follows and, as should be clear from what was written above, this eventually needs to be contrasted to the much neglected 'S words': similarity and sameness. Problems in the modern world are not so much about coming to grips with or addressing differences, but of addressing the desire for sameness and its consequences.

This term 'difference' underpins the enterprise of analysing 'identity' (among many other issues). In the case of identity there are two basic ways difference works to operationalize identity. The first, and most familiar, is to place identity formation in the context of the differences between social groups or classes. Thus, here one's identity depends upon where one falls – or is placed – in a hierarchical social structure, and this is predicated on recognition of that difference relative to the places of others. The second way difference works with respect to identity is to pitch it more directly within the recognition and misrecognition structure of the visual metaphor. Thus, here identity depends upon the difference between the subject and its reflection in the mirror of 'the Other', towards which it metaphorically gazes (recall here, once again, the triadic formulation of conventional ecclesiastical thinking outlined in Chapter 1 – Subject, Object, Other).

The implications of the above analysis, however, would be to displace this emphasis on difference as the key to understanding identity, and to refocus it upon the notion of 'sameness' as outlined there. The problem from the point of view of fundamentalisms is not difference but sameness; how to arrange samenesses. And while these two are closely related – in a sense they are the *recto* and the *verso* of the same relationship – the burden of the argument is to shift attention to the sameness side of the dichotomy, and away from an almost exclusive emphasis on difference and its others (and 'the Other'). Continually re-emphasizing 'difference' and 'the Other' will get us little further in the analysis of fundamentalisms. This leads into a more detailed investigation of the actual nature of fundamentalisms in the image of a 'thick description', as advocated in Chapter 1 of this volume.

Religious fundamentalisms and 'globalization'

For the most part what has been written about Islam – and to a lesser extent Christianity – in relation to globalization, is to ask the question, 'What has been the reaction of these religious movements to the process of globalization?' (Marty and Appleby 1993; Mohammadi 2002; Dunning 2003; Tétreault and Denemark 2004). Thus, this form of analysis seeks to explore how these religions have reacted *to* 'globalization'. The following analysis seek to redress this a little by asking not so much what their reaction has been to this process, but what their conception of it is. It is argued that these religious ideologies are not just the passive recipients of the globalization process, but are active agents in shaping that process and its discourses. Although this chapter cannot fully explore all the complex reciprocal relationships between the religious ideologies and globalization, what it seeks to uncover as a first encounter is the nature of their own 'analyses' and views in respect to their place in the contemporary global system. And this is further limited in that it concentrates upon the fundamentalist position in respect to these religions, while fully recognizing that mainstream Christianity and Islam express a quite different position from those outlined below. But it concentrates upon these fundamentalist variants in the first instance because these are the ones that are most extreme, and probably the ones having the most direct and immediate impact on the current politics of the international system. Near the end, there are also some shorter reflections on Jewish religious fundamentalism and its importance.

Generally, the discussion pays special attention to the way territory operates in the public pronouncements and writings of religious fundamentalists (though at times these conceptions have had to be reconstructed from the fragments offered in the writings and pronouncements of fundamentalist organizations that are not so public – see Thompson 2007). Given that territory is a key term in the debates about globalization (Chapter 1) it is appropriate to concentrate upon this in any examination of how globalization is implicated in fundamentalist religious discourse: it represents the main way such fundamentalisms engage with that debate and insert themselves into its emergent characteristics.

Al-'Awlama (globalization) according to Muslim fundamentalists

In this section I concentrate upon the position as announced by al-Qa'ida.[8] Clearly there are other groups closely associated with Islamic fundamentalism (such as the Taliban in Afghanistan and Pakistan, the Islamic State of Iraq and al-Sham (ISIS) currently very active in the Syrian and Iraqi conflicts, and the affiliate of al-Qa'ida in the Arabian Peninsula (AQAP), mainly active in the Yemen, among several other groups), but for the most part in what follows I take al-Qa'ida as the emblematic case. It conducts its activity very much in the name of Islam (even though it does not necessarily always conform to the generally recognized practice of Islam), and it has the most visible expression in the international arena. The fortunes of al-Qa'ida have, of course, fluctuated since what has often been viewed as its heyday in the early 2000s. Despite the killing of its founder Osama bin Laden in May 2011 the 'organization' has reappeared as a loosely aligned network of affiliated groups with added momentum in the conflicts in the Horn of Africa, the Arabian peninsula proper, Muslim East Asia, the central Middle East and particularly in the Syrian/Iraqi conflicts.

So it continued to be the most active such group with an ostensibly 'global' orientation (though it has fallen out politically with ISIS).

In early April 2005, a few weeks after the Madrid bombings by Islamic extremists, a key ideologist of al-Qa'ida, Lewis 'Atiyyatullah, published an article in the Global Islamic Media internet forum in which he outlined al-Qa'ida's perception of the international situation at that time and into the future. In this 'Atiyyatullah suggested that 'the balance of power will change; the international system built up by the West since the Treaty of Westphalia will collapse; and a new international system will rise under the leadership of a mighty Islamic state'. (This appears under the heading 'Al-Qa'ida: Islamic state will control the world', posted by an Israeli news bureau, available at: http://www.themedialine.org/news/print_news_detail. asp?NewsID_/5420_/, last accessed 2008.)

Lewis 'Atiyyatullah is a pseudonym for a rather mysterious Saudi dissident who, it seems, actually lived in exile in London. The article appeared as a letter to Reuven Paz ('So said Al-Qa'ida: a letter to Reuven Paz'), an independent Israeli scholar heading a think tank called the 'Project for Research of Islamist Movements' – PRISM (http://www.e-prism.org/).

In his letter, 'Atiyyatullah explains that he wrote it to Paz because he was 'one of the first of those who showed interest in Osama bin Laden's old article entitled "The New International Regime" … and you advocated that those in the US and Europe interested in al-Qa'ida must read the article seriously'.

In fact, this article is titled 'The New World Order as written by Usama bin Ladin' and was originally published in November 2002 on 'Atiyyatullah's website (at the time: http://www.yalewis.com/) and subsequently appeared on several other such websites (Paz 2003)[9]. This 'New World Order' article is important since it lays out the change in strategy that al-Qa'ida adopted in the second half of the 1990s, namely to switch from attacking Islamic 'near neighbours' to targeting the US, its allies and the West in general. It contained two key aspects: (1) there is no chance to change the situation of the Islamic world unless the role of the United States is singled out, and (2) the United States could not be defeated by an army or by any traditional military confrontation (or at least not immediately – see below).

Here, then, was the origin of the so-called global jihad. According to bin Laden this jihad would have four stages: the first stage was the then current offensive by jihadists and suicide bombers on the home ground of the enemy (the Arab states). The second stage – and a first priority for the near future – was to defeat Arab governments. This would be achieved by

> [i]mposing upon the American administration direct cooper-
> ation with us. The United States itself will remove the legitimacy
> of the [Arab] cartoon states. The American direct involvement in
> the affairs of the Muslim world, by limiting the power of their rul-
> ers or by encouraging them to behave according to the American
> dictates, is the ideal situation that we have wished for a long time.
> When the direct confrontation between the Americans and us
> comes, the agent Arab and Islamic governments will be of no
> importance.

The third stage, called the stage of isolation, would involve the Islamists isolating the American administration from its own people, on the one hand, and from its allies on the other. The final stage would be direct confrontation with the United States – the defeat of its global power by destroying it and the rest of the West on its own soil. This would shift the centre of gravity back to the Islamic world and create the conditions for a new global Islamic *ummah*.[10]

This 'vision' is important, bin Laden emphasized, because it differ-entiated the al-Qa'ida group from other Islamic movements that have been paralyzed by their twin obsessions with, first, a limited regional perception to their activities (notably the Taliban) and, second, with the purely national-statist dimension to political reconstruction (e.g. the PLO). As argued strongly by Olivier Roy (2004), contemporary Islamist projects – both pietistic and radical – are becoming increas-ingly disconnected from particular territories. These are creating, in their eyes, the conditions for a new global deterritorialized *ummah* (though, perhaps this would be better described as a differently ter-ritorialized or reterritorialized *ummah* – see below).

But there is an issue as to exactly what the political form of a post-Western Islamic *ummah* would take for the likes of al-Qa'ida. In the missive from bin Laden about his 'New World Order', this is left unspecified and generally remains vague. Although in the letter to Paz 'Atiyyatullah speaks of a mighty global Islamic state, this is con-tentious since, in general, bin Laden and the subsequent leaders of al-Qa'ida eschew the explicit idea of a state in the commonly under-stood meaning of that term, because their religious ideology is genu-inely trans-territorial. So perhaps it is worth recalling at this stage Max Weber's classic modernist definition of the nation state as 'the legitimate monopoly over the use of violence within a recognized and bounded territory'.[11] Thus, modern statehood is based upon the coupling together of the principles of territoriality, jurisdictional or administrative capacity, and military monopoly, including the use of violence and the legitimacy to do so. By contrast, the Islamic fundamentalists often speak in terms of a global 'community' or (less often) a global 'nation' rather than a state.

The key stated objective of that jihad is to rid the soil in the Islamic world – and particularly the 'Holy Places' – of foreign control and influence. But in addition to this primary objective there is the waging of the genuinely global jihad against the infidels, and their eventual outright defeat. The post-1990s period is typified by an uneasy oscillation between these two objectives, possibly deliberately fostered by al-Qa'ida in its efforts to keep the West unsettled and the Middle East focused on its main grievance.

But what of the political form that the post-Western global system would take from the point of view of this Muslim fundamentalist position? Clearly, there is at least a gesture towards the Caliphate – and the Ottoman Empire remains something of a model (see Mattera 2005 for background to the geopolitical history of Islamic expansion and retreat, and also Ruthven and Nanji 2004). But both the Islamic Caliphate and the Ottoman Empire were overtly political institutions rather than religious ones. And hereby hangs the issue. As stressed by those most astute of the 'political Islam' commentators, Roy (1994, 2004) and Kepel (2004a, 2004b), this division between the political aspects of radical Islam and its religious expression creates a tension that is not easily resolved, if indeed it is resolvable at all. Broadly, however, they both argue that this 'resolves' itself in a political formation, to some extent at the expense of religious purity, even for extreme fundamentalism.

In connection with this, Paz suggests that it indicates the beginning of a new general Islamist trend and doctrine, that of 'The non-territorial Islamic State' – a kind of *supra trans-state* perhaps: 'In this framework of doctrine, Muslim communities in the West should be perceived as a kind of Islamic State without territorial dimensions and the ideal and religious mission of Islam to establish the one Islamic state and rule' (Paz 2001: 1). The origins of this doctrine were developed by Islamic scholars, again in the UK. It puts the emphasis on the socio-cultural, economic and political levels of the consolidation of Muslim communities – particularly those in the West – but also on uniting them with those in the Middle East, Africa and Asia. In theory this also gives freedom to the principle of Islamic pluralism and the activity of a variety of organizations, groups and institutions, from all kind of trends of modern Islamic thought. The democratic and liberal environment of Western countries mostly influenced this pluralism, but it also served to carry the fundamentalist message from the Islamic homelands to this newly emergent *ummah*.

In part this would account for Kepel's belief that the struggle for Muslim minds may hinge most of all on European Muslims. In France, Britain and Germany, large Muslim populations are living in secular, democratic societies. All the tensions and contradictions of the larger Muslim world are compressed into the lives of these European Muslims, but they are free to let the struggle play out in open debate. Thus, it is in Europe that Islam may finally find its accommodation with modern life. And this would emphasize a conservative Islamic *dawah* (preaching and propaganda), as against the radical extremist jihad.

But the globalization of the reaction to this threat has also led to the doctrine of a global jihad. Clearly, the al-Qa'ida movement is an attempt to capitalize on these developments by presenting itself as the vanguard in the fight for Muslim self-esteem. To some extent it does this by encouraging what Paz calls 'Social Terrorism': terrorism that is primarily motivated by social elements, such as the hatred of foreigners, growing unemployment, poor economic circumstances, difficulties in coping with Western modernization, the change and dismantling of traditional values and of family ties, etc. This, of course, is different to 'Religious Terrorism', which would seem to be its main motivation, but al-Qa'ida has often been able to marry these two forms of terrorism neatly together, particularly in Europe (Paz 2002). As Roy (2004) has shown, their main points of contact are fostered within a 'virtual community' based upon the Internet, which is devoid of local place. Indeed, Khatib (2003) describes the Internet as a 'portable homeland' for fundamentalists – a 'space' where they can strengthen their global ties and not just communicate with each other, but also engage with the wider world at large (for her it is described as a 'glocal force of citizenship' – recall the reference to 'glocalization' in Chapter 2, of which this would be an example). Alternatively, it is increasingly in a temporary local place, such as a prison, that militants meet and are recruited. In addition, they are often found moving regularly between their 'homes' in Western countries, and training and spiritual camps and places in the traditional Muslim heartlands. And what is true of the militants is also to some extent true of their spiritual leaders, the radical imams. They act as a kind of roving internationally itinerant 'spiritual Club Class', preaching in and moving between friendly mosques, often from one country to another.

In his discussion of 'globalized Islam' Roy (2004) identifies two types of globalization processes. On the one hand, there is the migration of Muslims from their countries of origin to the West; and then there is the process – the one mainly discussed so far here – of a jihadist movement of expulsion and conquest. Roy suggests both of these processes are undermining the idea of community at the same time as they celebrate it. Both are devoid of a real sense of a cultural community of belonging. Their only common link is to a religious community of faith and struggle. Thus, from his perspective, there is little point in trying to reactivate the idea of an embedded community at the local level, into which the disaffected young potential Islamic activists could be reconnected and re-embedded (broadly, the conception behind a liberal strategy of 'multiculturalism').[12] This does not exist from the militants' point of view. Rather, their perspective is one of a radicalized, essentially itinerant and deterritorialized, 'warrior politics' aimed at establishing a religious *ummah* on a global scale. Their 'new frontier' is a fluid one: first, the reconquest of the 'taken' Islamic lands, then the push to extend Islamic rule and *sharia* law to the rest. They face an open, ever-moving frontier of struggle and conquest; their 'politics' is deterritorialized and abundantly unconstrained. Small roving bands of militants are the iconic (if not necessarily the actual) organizational form, loosely linked by a global network. The traditional nation state is redundant to this conception – hence the end of the Westphalian system as announced by 'Atiyyatullah.

But is this *ummah* little more than an imaginary community? Roy (2004) strongly suggests that it is not. His point is that the current movement of fundamentalists is not based on any actual community or territory; their only resort is to an imagined *ummah*, which is everywhere and nowhere at the same time. But perhaps it is also more than this. It may be a fanciful dream but there is a real dynamic of conquest, conversion and (new) territory-building in the ideology of fundamentalist Islam. It is not quite the extraterritorial movement it is often made out to be. The operatives of al-Qa'ida, for instance, do genuinely want (though perhaps also ambivalently) to construct an 'Islamic (super) State' in the image of the Caliphate despite the deterritorialized nature of their immediate struggle. And this is a sentiment shared by other Islamic fundamentalist groups.[13]

In her analysis of the nature of space, geographical theorist Doreen Massey calls for a multiplicity of conceptions of 'globalization' and the different spatial imaginations and relationships they construct (Massey 2005: Chapter 8). I would suggest that the jihadist conception just outlined at least partially meets that request. But at the same time it is perhaps surprisingly similar to quite conventional conceptions of what globalization means and implies, particularly those that emerge from a culturalist reading of globalization. Also, there is a more general dismissal of the continued pertinence of the nation state from wider political economy and cosmopolitan positions on globalization. In this sense, then, the Islamic fundamentalist ideology outlined here has much in common with a wider anti-globalization movement in the West, something stressed by Roy (2004) in particular. It shows that Islamic fundamentalism is a thoroughly 'modern' movement – one emerging from, and directly engaging with, Western modernization – despite its own disavowal of this and a continual emphasis on its Muslim historical roots and the restoration of past glories.[14]

There is also a similarity in spatial imagination over the question of 'difference'. As suggested earlier, fundamentalists work against the disavowal of sameness and the displacement of difference on to others. They represent a retreat, or a withdrawal, from difference in the name of sameness. They want us to all be the same – the same as them – and many of them are prepared to die to achieve this.[15] Indeed, as has been often stressed, socially, the suicide bombers of al-Qa'ida have been rather like 'us': many from the West, educated, urban, linguistically polyglot, not particularly 'religious' in the actual practice of their day-to-day lives, originally from caring and largely intact families, they inhabit a thoroughly ordinary and unremarkable world (Sageman 2004). And, in a somewhat different register, this disavowal of difference is a view shared by neoliberal economic fundamentalists in their view of globalization: there should be no spatial obstacles to the operation of the market – the same undifferentiated conditions of competition should be faced by all.

Of course, there are other Islamic conceptions of globalization in contrast to the extreme one presented here (see Kuru 2005 for responses in the case of the Turkish example). Indeed, there are very different ones even within the radical Muslim world. Take the cases of Hamas and Hezbollah (the 'Party of God'). Despite their differences, these two movements share a common commitment to an essentially 'national struggle': they are fighting for a Palestinian national state above all else. Thus, despite the often extreme nature of their operational practices, these two movements remain part of a rather older tradition of 'national liberation struggles', something they even share with the mainstream PLO. The PLO is not a fundamentalist, but rather a secularist organization, and many of its leaders have been Christians.[16] These organizations also hark back to the Arab nationalist movement, which also had many Christian leaders. What is more, it could be argued that the current struggles in Afghanistan, Iraq and Syria owe as much, if not more, to a nationalist agenda than to the global jihad, though here things remain confusingly complicated. But this is the main general point made by Kepel (2004a, 2004b), Roy (2004) and Tibi (2002): that radical Islam cannot avoid eventually taking a political path or form.[17]

This also accounts for al-Qa'ida's at-best ambivalent attitude towards the Palestinian cause. Of course, bin Laden and his followers always included a concern for this in their public pronouncements, but its overt nationalism does not altogether suit their purpose. The PLO, on the other hand, takes a view on globalization that would continue to stress strongly the importance and role of the nation state – in distinction to the global jihadists, political economists and cosmopolitans alike. The PLO has a very clear idea of the importance of a specific territory with boundaries around it, even if it may condemn other alleged and real pernicious aspects of globalization. And this might also enable us to rethink a response to the global jihadism. One of the key motifs of the conventional reaction is to worry about the 'identity' issues associated with disaffected Muslim youth, jihadists, fundamentalists and their like. In principle, identity can be attached to a number of aspects of individual or cultural features: race, class, gender, sexual orientation, ethnicity, colour, religion, nationality, language, etc. Thus there exists a 'menu' of possibilities to which identity could be attached – individually or collectively – to one or other of these dimensions or to a combination of them. In a perceptive account, Amin Maalouf (2000) suggests that primary personal identity is dependent upon that feature or dimension of social existence that is considered to be under the fiercest threat or attack. Clearly, for Muslim youth – those considered most vulnerable to the attractions of fundamentalism – it is religion that has captured their primary identification.[18] What should be the response to this? Maalouf suggests that only 'universal values' of humanity and tolerance can hope to provide an alternative in a globalized world. This, then, mirrors the calls of many others who see the need for a response like this at the 'global level', to what is, in effect, a truly global threat (to 'us'), one that would stress universal and enlightened values. But is this possible, feasible or realistic?

An alternative – much despised by the globalists of almost whichever kind – is to re-emphasize the need for a reterritorialization of international activity, to re-emphasize the advantages of the national state as the primary site for identification and focus of loyalty, to stress the nature of civil citizenship and civic virtue in this context, to focus on the law as a mechanism for dealing with religious strife, and so on.[19] From a globalist point of view, of course, this particular response is pointless: it speaks to a Westphalian world that has now passed. But has it? Clearly, the analysis above suggests the opposite, something that 'political Islam' has also (often only implicitly) stressed. A programme of reterritorializing the international in various ways and to various degrees, in the face of supposed 'globalization', is not beyond conception or feasibility, as other chapters in this book demonstrate.

Finally, what about the specific case of the global jihad? Clearly this has little hope of being successful. Not only does it come up against the obstacles of politics and 'nationalism' within the Muslim world, or the deep unattractiveness of a 'mighty Islamic state' for the rest of those in the West, it also ignores the real changing actuality of global power. The new big powers in the global system are China and India (who between them have a population of 2.3 billion). These new powers will soon be followed by the likes of Russia, Brazil and east Asian nations more generally. The idea that these countries are going to bow down before the followers of global jihad, and roll over in front of them, is almost as unworldly as thinking that al-Qa'ida could actually defeat the US militarily on a global scale. But that does not diminish the threat that fundamentalisms pose, particularly as this has now invaded the US itself in the form of a newly invigorated Christian fundamentalism, a phenomenon that is examined in the next subsection (in addition to its commitment to a market fundamentalism, which we pursue in the following chapters).

Christian fundamentalism, globalization and its consequences

The background context to this discussion of the Christian fundamentalist engagement with 'globalization' is the rather unexpected rapprochement between Zionism and Christianity currently observed in the international system.[20] From the point of view of religious doctrine it might be thought that Christianity and Judaism were incompatible (the Jews are traditionally argued to have been responsible for the death of Christ within the Christian tradition). But under the auspices of the 'born-again' movement, with its fundamentalist reinterpretation of the Christian message, there is opened up the possibility of a reconciliation between these two religious traditions. And this reconciliation is most acutely posed by the newly invigorated 'Christian Zionist' movement in the US.

In fact, 'Christian Zionism' is just that: a reconciliation between Christianity and Zionism – rather than between Christianity and

Judaism – though it does strongly implicate the religious aspect to Zionism and its particular political project. But, strictly speaking, Zionism is a secular political project. That political project is, of course, the establishment and securing of the State of Israel in the land of Palestine, and Christian Zionism in the US strongly endorses this project, even with its Jewish religious overtones and its sometimes extremist Judaic organizational thrust. Additionally, there is the complicated relationship between Zionism and ultra-Orthodox Judaism discussed below, but this is left aside for the moment.

However, the 'reconciliation' between Zionism and Christianity is also somewhat ambivalent since the final 'final solution' is promised in the Old Testament tradition as Armageddon approaches: Jewish assimilation or its genuine annihilation. In the meantime, political pragmatism prevails.[21] But, for obvious reasons, it remains a rather uneasy pragmatism, as indicated in a moment.

The main doctrinal basis for the Christian–Zionist reconciliation is what is known as 'dispensational theology', and without enquiring into the nuances of this doctrinal position the new 'global play' of its implications will remain obscure.[22] Dispensational theology is that system of theology that attempts to develop the Bible's philosophy of history on the basis of the sovereign rule of God. This philosophy is particularly concerned with the ultimate purpose or goal of history, towards the fulfilment of which all history moves. It presents the whole of Scripture as being covered by several (seven in all) dispensations of God's rule. The 'dispensations' concern the divine administration or conduct of the world. The word 'dispensation' has its etymological roots in the Greek terms for household administration and the proper dispensing of tasks through the operation of stewardship (i.e. a responsible office or ministry entrusted with care by a higher authority). Thus these dispensations are the particular and distinct ways that God administers his rule over the world. But failure is built into these dispensations because mankind continually refuses to obey the dictates of the dispensations, thereby requiring divine judgement. Dispensational theology is thus ideologically millenarian, pessimistic and cataclysmic.

The failure of large numbers of people to follow the dispensations demonstrates that the ultimate cause of man's undoing and rebellion throughout history is not his external environment and circumstances, but his own inward, sinful nature, which rejects the rule of God and asserts self-rule.[23] Thus, Christian fundamentalism and its Islamic counterpart are thoroughly 'individualistic' in their doctrines.

They both involve practices of individual conversion and redemption. They are not 'social' movements – see below.

Mankind's failure in conjunction with all seven of the dispensations will bring God's vengeance after the final one – Armageddon. Those people who rebel outwardly during Christ's reign will be executed. In addition, God will crush the huge revolt that will take place immediately after the seventh dispensation by casting Satan (the Antichrist) into the lake of fire for everlasting torment. God will finally glorify himself by crushing Satan and his kingdom, restoring his own Kingdom and rule to the earth through Jesus Christ, and thereby reversing the tragic consequences of man's rebellion. A controversial aspect of dispensational theology within the born-again tradition is that it maintains a strict differentiation between the Church and Israel. The dispensationalists believe that throughout the ages God is pursuing two distinct purposes: one related to the earth with earthly people and earthly objectives involved, which is Judaism; while the other is related to heaven with heavenly people and heavenly objectives involved, which is Christianity. In an apparent attempt to keep law and grace distinctly separated, dispensational theology has divided the nation of Israel from any connection with the Church of Jesus Christ. The physical race of Jewish people is regarded as God's 'earthly people' while Christians are regarded as God's 'heavenly people'. Dispensational theology indicates that separate promises are given to Jewish people and to Christians, and differing destinies await them. In particular, it seems, the earthly people (the Jews) are likely to experience Armageddon somewhat more severely than are their heavenly counterparts (the Christians). In particular, those 'saved Christians' who follow the fundamentalist dispensational theological line will be the overall beneficiaries, since they will be exempt from the punishments and tribulation associated with Armageddon. The 'saved' will ascend to heaven (through the 'Rapture') – while the battle goes on at ground level – and stay there until Jesus finally returns triumphant.

What this all amounts to is the belief that God has given a series of dispensations to the Jewish people to prepare the way for the Second Coming (though they will suffer, in particular, in both the run-up to, and after, this Second Coming). In particular it is necessary for the Jews first to return to Palestine and then to establish a Jewish-Israeli state there to fulfil the biblical prophecy and hasten the Second Coming (since Jesus will of necessity appear through Israel). And this is the basis for the reconciliation of Christianity and Zionism, since it is Zionism that has brought the modern

Israeli state into existence. But any build-up of armies on its borders ready to attack it is seen as a sign that the final battle is imminent. The Antichrist will appear and the final climactic Battle of Armageddon commence.[24] In the meantime, the Christian Zionists are absolutely opposed to the creation of a Palestinian state – in favour of the unity of Jerusalem under direct Israeli control – and vehemently hostile towards Muslims, who they see as worshipping a false God.

However, as just indicated, there is a rather profound ambiguity operating here, since the object of all of this is to see Jesus return as soon as possible so as to put his heavenly people out of their misery. But the consequence of bolstering the State of Israel and supporting the Jewish people against their enemies would seem to be to put off this final judgement. As far as I can make out, this ambiguity has not been fully resolved within dispensationalist teaching.

Before we proceed to assess the importance of this 'turn towards fundamentalisms' among the Islamic and Christian traditions, there follows a section on Jewish religious fundamentalism, which, while not unimportant, is less significant in its consequences for the future of the international system. What it demonstrates, however, is why the reconciliation with Christianity is so ambiguous.

Jewish religious fundamentalism[25]

Judaic religious extremist fundamentalism, rather like its Christian and Islamic counterparts, is a highly complex formation. First there are the ultra-Orthodox Jews in Israel itself. These could amount to as much as 12 per cent of the population. At its extreme, this ultra-Orthodoxy consists of groups of anti-Zionist fundamentalists who reject Israel and view it as a heretical entity. They want nothing to do with the state and live in enclaves where they shut out the secular modern world as much as possible. But among the ultra-Orthodox can also be included some who accept the State of Israel, although not its messianic pretensions, and work within many of its institutions. Their primary mission is to rebuild the seats of rabbinic learning that the Nazis extinguished, and they concentrate on such things as securing state aid for their school system or exemption from army service for their Talmudic students (as of 2014 all Orthodox Jews were exempt from military service, though there were moves afoot to change this). They have had ministers in various Israeli governments. Such compromises are anathema to the ultra-Orthodox – who regard themselves as the sacred remnant – while others have supped with the devil. These sects do not recognize the State of Israel. They consider it blasphemous to create a Jewish state in the Holy Land before the coming of the Messiah.

The traditional role of these groups, however, has been 'isolationist'. They have sought to isolate themselves from an engagement with the outside world (especially international matters), and live quite 'contemplative lives'. They see the Zionist movement as presumptuously trying to pre-empt the hand of providence by wanting to cast off 'the yoke of exile' before the divinely appointed time of redemption. In particular, the rabbis cite a Talmudic passage referring to 'three oaths' governing the Children of Israel in exile. The Jews had undertaken not to return to the land of Israel en masse, or to 'rebel against the nations' who hosted them, while the nations had agreed not to oppress the Jews too severely in return.

Then there are a significant number of religious Zionists who view Jewish rule over the entire territory of biblical Israel (the *Eretz Yisrael Ha-Shleyma*) in apocalyptic terms. They depart from the essentially quietist and passive posture of traditional Jewish messianism. These groups are often referred to as 'Orthodox Zionists'. They have been represented historically by a number of political parties or coalitions, and have been the driving force behind many of the extraparliamentary social, political and Jewish terrorist movements that have characterized Israeli society since the June 1967 war (http://www.countrystudies.us/israel, last accessed 2008). Most Orthodox Zionists have been 'ultra-hawkish' and irredentist in orientation. But among the religious Zionist zealots have been small, explicit terrorist groups such as Kach ('thus') and Kahane Chai ('Kahane lives') (http://www.cfrterrorism.org/groups/kkc.html/). These have operated since the 1980s to attack Arab and Muslim holy sites in an attempt to expel the Palestinians and extend Israeli settlement control over the entire West Bank.

The second element to Jewish fundamentalism is the American connection. Many of the domestic groups and movements discussed above have their counterparts among the US Jewish community. Of particular significance here are the 'True Torah Jews', who live to promulgate the teaching of the Torah (the sacred book of Jewish law). They want to inform the American public, and politicians in particular, that all Jews do not support the ideology of the Zionist State of 'Israel', which in their eyes is diametrically opposite to the teachings of traditional Judaism. Their website opens with the following statement, which neatly summarizes the reasons for opposition to Zionism prevalent among these groups:

> Torah-true Jewry has steadfastly opposed the Zionist ideology. This struggle is rooted in two convictions:
>
> (1) Zionism, by advocating a political and military end to the Jewish exile, denies the very essence of our Diaspora existence. We are in exile by Divine Decree and may emerge from exile solely via Divine Redemption. All human efforts to alter a metaphysical reality are doomed to end in failure and bloodshed. History has clearly borne out this teaching.
>
> (2) Zionism has not only denied our fundamental belief in Heavenly Redemption it has also created a pseudo-Judaism which views the essence of our identity to be a secular nationalism. Accordingly, Zionism and the Israeli state have consistently endeavoured, via persuasion and coercion, to replace a Divine and Torah centred understanding of our people-hood with an armed materialism.
>
> ('True Torah Jews against Zionism – Our Mission', http://www.jewsagainstzionism.com/, last accessed 2008)

What this quote demonstrates is that ultra-Orthodox Jewry also has an implicit vision of 'globalization' written into its basic precepts. The Jews live a divine existence by being in exile. Their diasporic existence confirms this. Thus the Jewish people are already trans-territorial. But they must rely upon the 'hospitality of the nations' (as mentioned above) not to oppress them, rather than return en masse to Israel. This, then, looks suspiciously like a form of 'religious cosmopolitanism' reliant upon a kind of covenant to ensure compliance. However, like all covenants of this kind – and forms of trans-territoriality – it is open to abuse, something the Jewish people have experienced at first hand and on a terrifyingly large scale.

A second US connection to Jewish ultra-Orthodoxy is represented by the Chabad-Lubavitch sect, which, among other things, is aggressively outward-looking and evangelical. This practice goes against the traditional ultra-Orthodox sentiment of isolation and quietism in the hope of an eventual mystical final redemption. The Chabad-Lubavitch are accused of extremist fundamentalism as a result. One of the important features of this sect is that it has had its greatest success in the US, which itself has a long tradition of fundamentalist evangelicalism among Christian communities. The national-cultural cross-over involved here is probably not unconnected to the modern Chabad-Lubavitch history as a US phenomenon. And this mutation is further illustrated by the proselytizing 'Jews for Jesus' movement in the US.

Perhaps all this would be unimportant were it not for the political impact the rise of Jewish ultra-Orthodoxy is having in Israel. This is mainly 'domestic' in consequence, however – to do with who controls which political districts and funds, who can be a citizen, the kind of law that should rule everyday practices, etc. For secular Jews in particular, the escalating power of ultra-Orthodox values over those of modern Orthodoxy – and thereby on the totality of Jewish life – is unsettling. The far right in Israel has effected a quantification of piety that steadily ups the religious ante for all Jews. Thus, any observer of the Jewish culture can attest to ever-more products at Passover with special certification, ever higher *mehitzas* separating men and women in the synagogue, the growing demand of candidates for conversion to observe every single commandment of Judaism, religious authority measured by years of study rather than quality of thought, the infallibility of policy decisions rendered by a council of Torah sages (the twentieth-century innovation of *daas Torah*) and the triumph of *glatt* kosher (an animal with no adhesions on the lung) in America since the Second World War. As yet, though, any effect on the international system of a purely Jewish religious ultra-Orthodox revival has still to emerge, which is obviously not the same as saying that the effects of Zionism on the international arena have not yet been felt.[26]

Why is all this important?

The reason why Christian Zionism is of current interest – and positively reeks of political pragmatism – is because of its connection to the legacy of the American presidency of George W. Bush. There is good evidence that Christian Zionism and the neoconservatism of the Bush administration were closely linked.[27] The neoconservatives – of whom Dick Cheney (the US Vice President, 2001–9), Donald Rumsfeld and Paul Wolfowitz (the US Defense Secretary, 2001–6, and his deputy respectively, 2001–5) are probably the best known, but which included such influential commentators as William Kristol, Robert Kagan, Richard Perle and John Bolton[28] – took the US into its various ventures in the Middle East on a basically unilateralist, interventionary and militaristic ideology. And although this neoconservative faction may have diminished in significance since the advent of the Obama presidency in 2009, its influence in the Republican Party remains, and it still provides a persistently shrill voice of consultancy and commentary on international affairs in the US.

But how seriously should we take the Christian-Zionist character of the neoconservative adventure? Clearly their unconditional support for Israel is real, the influence of fundamentalist Christianity on their approach well documented, and the fact that they believe what they say – and in the literal interpretation of the Bible's message that is expressed by the fundamentalists – should not be underestimated. While one might have some reservations about the direct relationship between religious ideology and political strategy, this does not mean that they are unconnected. The nature of these reservations is picked up in a moment.

The Christian evangelical movement is the fastest growing sector of the American Christian churches. In 2004 the number of their followers was estimated at 75 million (26 per cent of the population, see: http:// www.pewforum.org/publications/surveys/green.pdf/, last accessed 2008). Of course, not all of these are Christian Zionists – in the Pew survey just referred to, only half described themselves as 'traditional evangelical', which is the nearest equivalent. In a previous Pew survey, 60 per cent said they believed in the Battle of Armageddon. They are formidably efficient in terms of activism in the service of Israel, and equally important electorally.

However, the relationship between this Christian Right movement and the political programme of the Bush presidency is a fiendishly complicated, controversial and difficult one. Do we really find the following:

> a Christian President of a secular Republic using the apocalyptic language of a crusade, sacred charge, universal good and axis of evil, to prosecute a preemptive military campaign without territorial limit against a predominantly Islamic enemy in defence of Enlightenment notions of freedom.
>
> (Northcott 2004: 80)

Perhaps not quite. As one commentator has argued:

> Ironically for a man who once famously named Jesus as his favourite political philosopher during a campaign debate, it is remarkably difficult to pinpoint a single instance wherein Christian teaching has won out over partisan politics in the Bush White House. Though Bush easily weaves Christian language and themes into his political communication, empty religious jargon is no substitute for a bedrock faith ... George W. Bush is neither born again nor evangelical ... the president has been careful never to

use either term to describe his faith. Unlike millions of evangelicals, Bush did not have a single born-again experience; instead, he slowly came to Christianity over the course of several years … And there is virtually no evidence that Bush places any emphasis on evangelizing – or spreading the gospel – in either his personal or professional life. Contrast this to Carter, who notoriously told every foreign dignitary he encountered about the good news of Jesus Christ.

(McGarvey 2004)

But this is highly controversial, as some have argued that Bush did have a born-again experience (apparently, in a pizza parlour during his youth) and that he remained a practising evangelist during his presidency (Denton 2005: 13–14).

What is less controversial, however, is that the influence of the neoconservative Project for the New American Century (PNAC) on US political policy – particularly military and defence policy – is clear, and this strongly endorsed the Christian Zionist message, even if it would be pragmatically adapted or applied as circumstances change or permit. The PNAC was established in 1997. Its major 'founding document' on defence policy – *Rebuilding America's Defences: Strategy, Forces and Resources for a New Century* – was issued in 2000 (http://www.newamericancentury.org/RebuildingAmericas Defenses.pdf, last accessed 2008). This suggested that the 'Core Mission' of the US in the international arena was to 'fight and decisively win multiple, simultaneous major theatre wars' and 'perform "constabulary" duties associated with shaping the security environment in critical regions'. This analysis is argued to have heavily influenced the Bush administration's 2002 National Security Strategy of the United States of America (http://www.whitehouse.gov/nsc/ nss.pdf, last accessed 2008), which in many places matched the PNAC document word for word (see William Rivers Pitt, 'The Project for a New American Century', http://www.informationclearinghouse.info/article1665.htm, last accessed 2008). Here the point is to establish that Christian Zionism has provided *one* of the main intellectual foundations for the PNAC and the neoconservative turn in the US, but not the only one. Its 'theological' character has been supplemented by other conservative intellectual currents, particularly that of the 'realist' Straussian trend (named after the political philosopher Leo Strauss (1899–1973): see http://www.opendemocracy.net/faith-iraqwarphiloshophy/ article-1542.jsp, last accessed 2008).[29] In addition, these intellectual trends do not translate directly into clear political policies or military strategy. That change in strategy, however, suited the Christian Zionist position, confirming the support for Israel at almost any cost, and strongly advancing the Christian message at a global level (among other messages, of course, those of democracy and freedom come immediately to mind in particular). Thus, the advantage for the Christian fundamentalist Right in the US is that they already had a formidable fighting force and a global reach through which to advance their purpose. By contrast, Islamic fundamentalism is in a totally different situation, which, in part at least, must account for its different tactics and strategy. And of course, this general change in strategy by the US – inaugurated by the Bush administrations – led many commentators to suggest that it amounted to a radical attempt by the US to establish a new global empire under its imperial rule (e.g. Northcott 2004, among many others). As suggested in Chapter 1, the idea of a new imperial age under US dominance became a very popular academic motif from the mid-1990s – though for the reasons outlined there, such a project was dismissed as a sensible description of contemporary US 'global' strategy.

Conclusions

What are the implications of, first, the re-emergence of 'religions' as an important element in international relations – particularly in the form of their fundamentalist variants – and second, the location of this 'fundamentalist turn', in the context of 'sameness and difference' as a way of understanding fundamentalisms? In the previous chapter the suppression and reconciliation of religious-based strife was established as a key mechanism for the emergence of a nation-based international system that in the long run provided at least a modicum of security. This is now seen to be under threat from precisely those newly vibrant forces outside the control of a national state context. The 'globalization' of social relationships includes the transterritoriality of religious-based movements, but how do they fit into a notion of cultural?

One implication of the emphasis on sameness is that it helps clarify why fundamentalisms are not 'cultural movements'. They do not care much, or indeed at all, about practices of different cultures. They are deeply 'deculturalized' (this is contrary to Turner 2002, for instance). They are idealized religious movements that transcend cultures in their single-minded devotion to the word of God. The Taliban, for instance, banned Afghan music, dancing, local festivals; they destroyed the Bamiyan Buddhist effigies (since Islam does not allow any representation of Allah or any other God). They are also indifferent to any particular cuisine; as long as it serves halal meat.

Particular territories do not matter, nor particular cultural, ethnic or linguistic groups. As long as individuals commit themselves absolutely to the word of God, anyone can be a member, from anywhere, and from any community. They demonstrate a genuine radical universalism in this respect. They treat everyone as, in principle, 'the same'. The ultimate cause of man's failure and rebellion throughout history is not his external environment and circumstances but his own inward, sinful nature, which rejects the rule of God and asserts self-rule. Thus, Christian fundamentalism and its Islamic counterpart are thoroughly 'individualistic' in their doctrines. They both involve practices of individual conversion and redemption. They are not 'social' movements as usually understood.

A second point to note is the way the analysis of sameness as the basis for an individualized commitment to fundamentalism outlined above could be generalized to take account of the way fundamentalisms, as a collective endeavour, can be analysed. Take, for a moment, the question of national borders. The strong globalization thesis argues that these are no longer pertinent to the international system, since they have been permeated and undermined by truly global economic and political forces. In fact, this is exactly what fundamentalisms argue as well. Borders are something we share, but at the same time they divide us. So let us get rid of borders! As we will see in subsequent chapters, market fundamentalists argue this strongly; they view national borders as a major constraint to trade and other spatial economic interactions, and argue that they should be eliminated in the name of sameness. All economic agents should face exactly the same conditions of competition. There should be no spatial obstacles to the operation of the market. A 'level playing field' (flat and characterized by sameness/smoothness) is the ideal image. The complete international harmonization of trading arrangements is called for. Even for conventional economics, the existence of national borders is a nuisance, since this impedes the extension of the market and the international division of labour.

But this antagonism towards national borders is also a feature of religious fundamentalisms. Militant Islam is an essentially trans-territorial movement. It is devoid of a real sense of a cultural community of belonging. Its only common link is to a religious one of faith and struggle. Thus it undermines the idea of community at the same time as it celebrates it. Its perspective is one of a radicalized itinerant and deterritorialized 'warrior politics' aimed at establishing a religious *ummah* on a global scale. The current movement of fundamentalists is not based on any actual community or territory; their only resort is to an imagined *ummah* that is everywhere and nowhere at the same time (Roy 2004).

Their 'new frontier' is a fluid one: first the reconquest of the 'taken' Islamic lands, then the push to extend Islamic rule and *sharia* law to the rest. From their point of view they face an open, ever-moving frontier of struggle and conquest; their 'politics' is deterritorialized and abundantly unconstrained. Small, roving bands of militants are the iconic (if not necessarily the actual) organizational form, loosely linked by a global network. The traditional nation state is redundant in this conception; hence the end of the Westphalian system, as announced by so many of al-Qa'ida's ideologues (discussed above). Similarly with Christian fundamentalism, as promoted by dispensational theology. For them, when the 'Second Coming' happens, and after Armageddon, God will cast his rule over the entire earth. The world will have a true theocratic government in which the rule of God will be administered worldwide through his representative, Jesus Christ. This is the particular Christian fundamentalist conception of 'globalization'. Again, we have the idea of an extraterritorial global 'politico-confessional community' driven exclusively by religious commitment. Both of these fundamentalisms are predicated on an ideology of sameness, which provides the required unifying condition for the exercise of their respective competing ('different') visions of the good life.

In previous chapters it was suggested that the international system might be profitably explored as an emergent 'durable disorder'. In the light of the analysis of both Muslim and Christian fundamentalisms, how does this 'durable disorder' shape up as an imaginary for the global system? Such that one can realistically imagine an international order run along religious fundamentalist lines (or any other fundamentalist lines for that matter), this would produce more of a *non-durable disorder* than a durable one. Presumably there would be constant clashes between them. The (re-)establishment of social peace would be needed anew. But peace is an undertaking; it must be fabricated and constructed between the parties (see Thompson 2004, 2007; and Chapter 2). And the gods would need to be taken into the peacemaking chamber. It is difficult to see them being 'left outside', as it were. Any such renewed peacemaking endeavour would likely take a long time, and to some extent the longer the better because it means all parties would need to learn to live in a different world. But Muslim fundamentalism and Christian fundamentalism are clearly both hopelessly unrealistic and politically naive in any modern sense of the term. However, that does not prevent them offering a simple and attractive vision for many millions of religious zealots. In a period when religious ideologies and movements are once again – perhaps rather unexpectedly – emerging as powerful forces challenging the continued possibility of liberal domestic systems and international orders, to ignore the characteristics of the most extreme versions of these religious ideologies is to ignore a genuine and ubiquitous challenge, if not a direct threat. Such an attitude of dismissal or simple condemnation could prove perilous for the future. In the meantime, a programme of reterritorializing the international in various ways and to various degrees – in the face of supposed 'globalization' – is not beyond conception or feasibility, and it has distinct advantages over either an idealistic global cosmopolitanism, on the one hand (whether secular or religious), or a tendency towards interventionary repression on the other. These are both equally dangerous responses to the present international predicament. Forging this alternative agenda forms the basis for the chapters that follow.

Notes

1 It is perhaps surprising that the little book by Freud has not been more fully recognized as offering a contribution to the understanding of the modern predicament associated with fundamentalisms, particularly as its title more than hints at an engagement with the 'clash of civilizations' debate so prevalent in contemporary discussion of religious fundamentalism and international conflict (e.g. Huntington 1996, and Chapter 1 above).

2 Narcissism is the self-regard for the self. So the self itself is always and already differentiated. This thus renders problematic any simple relational structure involving 'the Self and the Other'.

3 Without wishing to appear over-simple, in psychoanalysis this fascination with small differences arises because of the primacy of touch in the organization of desire. Touch is the primary sensation. The visual is also predicated on touch. Thus the desire to look – voyeurism – is driven by a desire to touch the object of the look. And touch has two obvious components: the smooth and the rough. The smooth (sameness) is interrupted by the rough (difference), which accounts for the fascination with (small) protrusions and crevices in the bodily make-up. The smoothness of surfaces so delightful to the touch is interrupted by the roughness of differences. This sets up a whole 'economy of desires' that is not limited to exploring the human body, though it is clearly predicated upon it. Just think of the 'body politic' in this respect, linked to which is the discussion in the main text about 'fundamentalists' desires'.

4 On a personal note, in the methodological discussion in Chapter 1 I described myself as a critical, non-humanistic, pragmatic sceptic. In the context of the discussion here I might add the term 'fundamentalist'. Or (given the issues of reluctance just mentioned in the main text) to try *not* to be this. I try to escape the intellectual tyranny of the numbers 1–5 – and to live the number 7 – at the same time as I find it difficult to avoid such a fate. This is because of some important points that follow in the main text as well as the general discussion about 'being/not being the number 7' conducted in Chapter 1.

5 'Submission' is also a key aspect of religious fundamentalism. God exists because we serve him. If he did not exist we would not serve him. So, the fact that we do serve him confirms his existence.

6 As should be clear, Chapter 2 discusses toleration in the context of the international sphere, in a somewhat different way to that just mentioned in the main text.

7 And one could add many more of these 'D' words that dominate intellectual discussion: deconstruction, dissonance, dissolution, decoupling ...

8 There are of course several variants of 'Muslim fundamentalism'. These range from what Roy (2004) has called Islamists – those concerned directly with politics and who are sometimes designated the adherents to 'political Islam' – to the 'neofundamentalists' who eschew politics in the name of a devout adherence only to the word of Allah – through to the violent, often nihilistic, terrorist activity of al-Qa'ida or Islamic State (ISIS) and its like. In my view these are not quite as separate as Roy would like to make them out to be, certainly not at the discursive level in respect to their views about globalization.

9 A slightly updated version of this declaration was published in March 2005 in the newspaper *Al-Quds Al-Arabi*, authored by another al-Qa'ida operative Saif al-Adel (interim commander immediately after bin Laden's death, replaced by Ayman al-Zawahiri as permanent commander in June 2011). This was entitled 'Al Qaeda's strategy to the year 2020'. Its message does not differ significantly from the earlier version discussed in the main text.

10 A number of respected commentators on Islamic fundamentalism, and on al-Qa'ida in particular, have argued that the organization has no proper 'strategy' (e.g. Roy 2004: 55, 294; Devji 2005). These commentators argue that al-Qa'ida is fundamentally messianic and reactive, or aesthetic and metaphysical in orientation. The discussion here indicates that this is not altogether the case, but what the al-Qa'ida movement seems to lack is a seriously strategic view of the real balance of forces it faces, with whom it might strike alliances, how to advance its territorial claims, what compromises it might have to make, etc. With respect to Muslim fundamentalism more widely, however, this may have changed subsequently in that it is pragmatically viewing the Western anti-globalization movement as a potential ally (Roy 2004: 332–3). This might be further reinforced by al-Zawahiri's call for a common coalition against the tools of the West that are being used to fight Islam. These include a litany of institutions and organizations, many (though not all) of which are also condemned by the anti-globalization movement:

> (1) The United Nations, (2) The friendly rulers of the Muslim peoples, (3) The multinational corporations, (4) The international communications and data exchange systems, (5) The international news agencies and satellite media channels, (6) The international relief agencies, which are being used as a cover for espionage, proselytizing, coup planning, and the transfer of weapons.
>
> ('Knights under the Prophet's Banner, Part 11', available at: http://www.liberalsagainstterrorism.com/wiki/index.php/Knights-Under-the-Prophet's-Banner#Title:-Al-Sharq-Al-Awsat-Publishes-Extracts-from-Al-Jihad-Leader-Al-Zawahiri.27s-New-Book/, last accessed 2008)

11 Max Weber (1978: 904–5). Here Weber adds: 'However, the monopolization of legitimate violence by the political-territorial association and its rational consociations into an institutional order is nothing primordial, but a product of evolution.' This clearly differentiates Weber from the celebration of the nation state to be found in the work of Leo Strauss and contemporary American neoconservatives. Strauss believed the political state to be 'rooted both in human nature and humanity's place in nature' (from 'Correspondence concerning modernity' (1946), in *Independent Journal of Philosophy*, 1983, 4: 107–8). The neoconservative connection to fundamentalism is taken up later in the main text.

12 Both Kepel and Roy are hostile towards multiculturalism. Kepel has argued that it allows 'local strongmen' to dominate, and reinforces a narrow world view that disenfranchises the young. Roy says Islam should be treated simply as a religion like any other, and not linked directly to ethnic or cultural minority groups. Of course, these reactions may have a lot to do with the way France has tried to deal with immigration and Islamic activity (Kepel and Roy are both French). The riots throughout France in November 2005, for instance, focused attention on these attitudes and could perhaps lead to a positive reassessment of the virtues of multiculturalism.

13 For instance, in the UK, the Islamic group Hizb ut-Tahrir argues for this explicitly as its main political objective:

> [Our] aim is to resume the Islamic way of life and to convey the Islamic da'wah to the world. This objective means bringing the Muslims back to living an Islamic way of life in Dar al-Islam and in an Islamic society such that all of life's affairs in society are administered according to the Shari'ah rules, and the viewpoint in it is the halal and the haram under the shade of the Islamic State, which is the Khilafah State. That state is the one in which Muslims appoint a Khaleefah and give him the bay'ah to listen and obey on condition that he rules according to the Book of Allah (*swt*) and the *Sunnah* of the Messenger of Allah (*saw*) and on condition that he conveys Islam as a message to the world through da'wah and jihad.
>
> (http://www.hizb ut-tahrir.org/english/english.html/,
> last accessed 2008)

14 Hizb ut-Tahrir, for instance, discusses 'globalization' in quite conventional terms. It is seen as one of five dangerous concepts (the others are terrorism, interfaith dialogue, compromise and fundamentalism) deployed to mislead the true faithful (*Dangerous Concepts to Attack and Consolidate the Western Culture*, Al-Khilafah Publications, London, 1997). But the discussion of it is surprisingly similar to most critical and leftist analyses made by the anti-globalization movement (that it is led by multinational companies, driven by global financial flows and the communication industries, a disguise for American imperialism, etc.), and it is compared to the missionary invasion of the nineteenth century (though this time it is more dangerous to Islam because it is not carried out under the cover of religion).

15 This is the site of the more general theoretical issue discussed in the earlier part of this chapter: the relationship between difference and sameness. In the case of national borders (something shared) these establish a

difference and are thus an obstacle to sameness, hence their unimportance from the point of view of the *ummah*. And also, indeed, for conventional neoliberal economics, national borders are an obstacle to competition, and hence restrictions they place upon the market mechanism should be eliminated so as to create a 'level playing field' The implications of this are pursued in the following chapters.

16 For instance, one of the constituent elements of the PLO, the Popular Front for the Liberation of Palestine (PFLP), was founded by the Christian, George Habash.

17 Strictly speaking, however, from the fundamentalist position, engaging with political activity is akin to collaboration with the enemy, which will result in punishment in the hereafter. If, for instance, a vote is cast in a *kufr* election, this commits the mortal sin of *shirk* – which is to associate other gods or rulers with Allah. Only God can be so endorsed (Sayyid Qutb, 'A Muslim has no nationality except his belief', *Milestones*, 1964). *Kufr* is disbelief; *kuffar* are unbelievers or infidels. 'It is a fact of life that we must, to some extent, keep close company with the kuffar. This is almost unavoidable given that we work, study, and unfortunately play with them', Amir Abdullah wrote in an article entitled 'Preserving the Islamic identity in the West: threats and solutions', published in the magazine *Nida'ul Islam*, in the spring of 1997.

> The likeness of Islam and *kuffar* is like that of fresh clear spring water and water brought up from the bottom of a suburban sewer. If even a drop of the filthy water enters the clear water, the clarity diminishes. Likewise it takes only a drop of the filth of disbelief to contaminate Islam in the West.

18 For instance, Mohammad Sidique Khan, the presumed ring leader of the 7 July 2005 bombing in London, was a devout Deobandi Muslim. The Deobandi are a large Sunni revivalist sect with their world headquarters, outside their northern Indian base, located in Dewsbury, Yorkshire. They preach a puritanical and literalist form of Islam, including segregation of the sexes and abstention from any form of participation in politics. The basic rationale for these beliefs is that legislative authority belongs only to God; thus, for men to sanction their own governance even in the smallest way would be anti-Islamic. So the Deobandi interpretation holds that a Muslim's first loyalty is to his religion and only then to the country of which he or she is a citizen or a resident. Their preferred method of interacting with the rest of society is through propagation, and they are segregationist in attitude. In addition, the Deobandi sect stresses that Muslims recognize only the religious frontiers of their *ummah*, and not national frontiers. Finally, it preaches that the Deobandi have a sacred right and obligation to go to any country to wage jihad to protect the Muslims of that country (http://www.globalsecurity.org/military/intro/islam-deobandi.htm_/, last accessed 2008). See also Masood (2005: 42–7) and Lawrence (2005: 95). According to reports after the bombing, Khan's family and friends had no idea that he was involved in suicidal religious activity (http://www.thetimes.co.uk/tto/faith/article2098587.ece, accessed 8 October 2014). This sect is not unique or unusual among Muslim migrants.

19 On the questions of whether Muslims can be loyal citizens to European governments, the influential radical Islamist Tariq Ramadan has argued that, when Muslim immigrants sign a work contract or accept a visa, they also recognize 'the binding character of the constitution or the laws of the country they enter into and then live in'. Unless a government specifically contradicts Islamic ways, Muslims are obliged to be loyal citizens and to influence the polity in constructive ways. 'We have to make it clear that this is not the reality. They have to accept that Islam is part of Europe. We are European citizens with a Muslim background' (Report on interview in Brussels with Tariq Ramadan, Iranian News Agency, http://www.payvand. com/news/02/sep/1077.html/, last accessed 2008)).

20 Of course, this is not simply a modern reconciliation: there is a long history of radical Christian support for Zionism, going back to as early as the seventeenth century, and to the Earl of Shaftsbury's support for the establishment of a Jewish state in Palestine in 1839 and the Balfour Declaration in 1917 (Wagner 2003; Northcott 2004: Chapter 2).

21 This pragmatism is clearly indicated by Binyamin Netanyahu (the current Prime Minister of Israel in 2014 when this chapter was being prepared) in response to a question from the academic Jacqueline Rose:

> I once asked Binyamin Netanyahu why he accepted the support of the Christian fundamentalists, since they believe that at Armageddon all the Jews will be destroyed or converted? He said that he tells them that he welcomes their support and that when they get to Armageddon, they can argue about it then.
>
> ('Nation as trauma, Zionism as question: Jacqueline Rose interviewed', available at: http://www.opendemocracy.net/conflict-debate_97/zionism_2766.jsp/, last accessed 2008)

22 This discussion relies heavily on the exposition by Renald E. Showers, 'An introduction to dispensational theology', available at: http://www.ankerberg.com/articles.html/, last accessed 2008.

23 Here, also, is signalled another difference between Muslim and Christian fundamentalisms. For the Christian variety there is a history, if an entirely teleological one. This is not the case for radical Islam, however, since its religion is an expression of a universal truth only – the necessity to wage a permanent and endless jihad that is blind to different cultures.

24 President Ronald Reagan expressed belief in the Battle of Armageddon in 1971 after Gaddafi's coup in Libya:

> That's a sign that the day of Armageddon isn't far off. Everything is falling into place. It can't be long now ... fire and brimstone will rain upon the enemies of God's people. That means that they'll be destroyed by nuclear weapons.
>
> (quoted in Northcott 2004: 66)

And again in 1984: 'You know, I turn back to your ancient prophets in the Old Testament and the signs foretelling Armageddon, and I find myself wondering if we're the generation that is going to see that come about' (in a conversation with Tom Dine, Director of the American-Israel Public Affairs Committee, available at: http://www.rotten.com/library/bio/presidents/ronald-reagan//, last accessed 2008).

25 For the details of all the groups and positions discussed here, see Thompson 2007.
26 Of course, for Islamic fundamentalists, Jewish ultra-Orthodoxy and fundamentalism are far from simply 'domestic' in significance. They have a resonance far beyond the borders of Israel.
27 Paul Rogers, *Endless War: The Global War on Terror and The New Bush Administration*, Oxford Research Group, Briefing Papers, March 2005: 5–6; and 'A heavenly match: Bush and the Christian Zionists', Donald Wagner Daily Star, 10 December 2003 (http://www.informationclearinghouse. info/article4960.htm).
28 These commentators are closely associated with the neoconservative 'New American Century' project (http://www.newamericancentury.org//, last accessed 2008). John Bolton was made the US Ambassador to the UN in 2005. Kagan's best-known books are *Warrior Politics: Why Leadership Requires a Pagan Ethos* (2001), and *Paradise and Power: America and Europe in the New World Order* (2003), in which he argues (p. 3):

> Europe is moving beyond power into a self-contained world of laws and rules and transnational negotiation and cooperation … Meanwhile, the United States remains mired in history, exercising power in an anarchic Hobbesian world where international laws and rules are unreliable, and where true security and the defence and promotion of a liberal order still depend on the possession and use of military might.

In Perle's book – *An End to Evil: How to Win the War on Terror* (2004) – he writes (p. 279):

> A world at peace; a world governed by law; a world in which all people are free to find their own destinies. That dream has not yet come true, it will not come true soon, but if it ever does come true, it will be brought into being by American armed might.

These are characteristic quotes from the neoconservative tradition. Whether they were closely echoed by the likes of Cheney and Rumsfeld remains controversial, of course, since – as suggested in the main text – political opportunism and pragmatism inevitably intervene in the actual practice of politics. But the weight of opinion is that there was at least some influential pressure that emanated from neoconservatism impacting on actual policy.
29 In fact, in the 1920s Strauss was an explicit Zionist (Zank (ed.) 2002). Indeed, he struggled with political Zionism and Judaic religiosity for some time before committing himself to a more philosophical politics of ultra-conservatism and 'noble lies', but he never quite fully renounced the importance of religion for moral purposes. Thus there is a certain continuity between Christian Zionism and the neoconservatives, via Strauss.

4 Globalization, finance and the 'crisis'

A critical assessment

Introduction

This chapter signals a move away from broadly geopolitical matters concerning globalization to concentrate upon more specific socio-economic issues associated with international financial and economic relationships, particularly in a post-crisis world. But this and the following three chapters do not offer yet another full account of the 'financial crisis and its aftermath'. Rather they approach this through an examination of whether such a crisis should, in the first instance, be viewed as a 'global' one, and then to assess the political response to this in terms of reform of (in particular) the financial system, governance initiatives, economic policy consequences, etc.

Measuring the extent of globalization as a general phenomenon is multifaceted and complicated (OECD 2013, Vujakovic n.d.). One of the most widely referred to indicators is shown in Figure 4.1. This comprises an index compiled by the Swiss Institute of Technology, which breaks globalization down into several separate dimensions – social, political and economic – as well as showing an overall aggregated measure. These dimensions are themselves the result of aggregating several separate variables; weighting them and rendering the results into a composite index (see KOF 2013: Appendix, 'Variables and weights'). As is evident, using these measures there can be seen a steady rise in the extent of globalization from 1980 until the economic crisis of 2007–8 – at which point growth slowed and slightly reversed (we return to this slowdown/reversal later).

A similar picture emerges from Figure 4.2, Figure 4.3 and Figure 4.4, which deal with three of the main elements of economic globalization: trade, investment (in this case, FDI) and a measure of financial transactions. Trade openness is represented by the ratio of international trade to global GDP, while FDI is shown in both flow and stock terms,

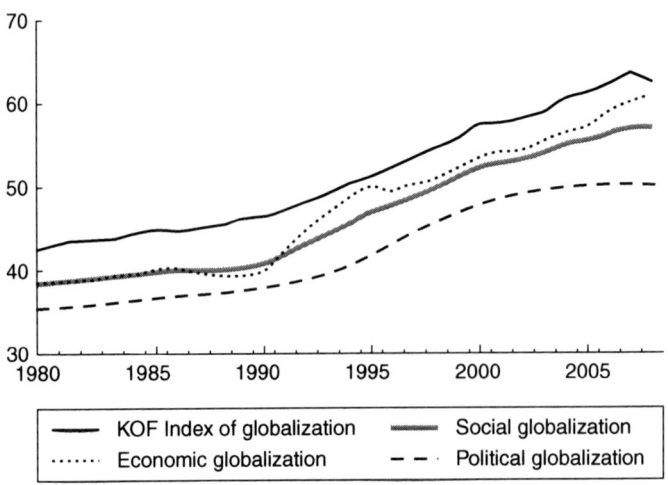

Figure 4.1. KOF Index of Globalization worldwide
Source: KOF 2013.

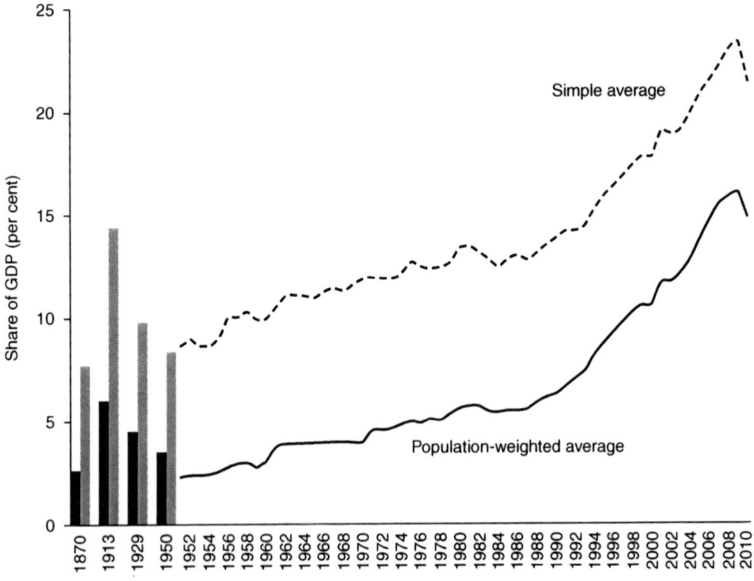

Figure 4.2. Trade openness
Source: Subramanian and Kessler 2013: Figure 2.5, p. 11.
Notes:
a openness is measured in terms of exports to GDP ratio.
b Small countries (those with fewer than one million inhabitants) and oil exporters
are excluded.

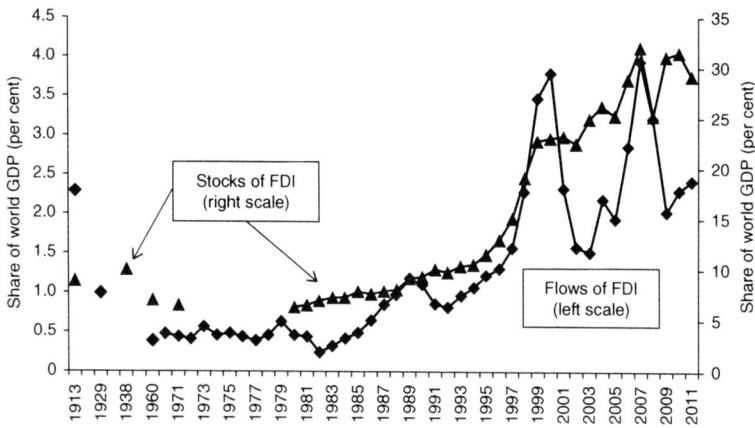

Figure 4.3. FDI flows and stocks
Source: Subramanian and Kessler 2013: Figure 2.2, p. 7.

also relative to global GDP. FDI flows have tended to fluctuate erratic-ally, while accumulated stocks show a more stable trend and indicate to the economic slowdown in 2007–8, which we come back to in a moment.

A different measure of globalization is provided in Figure 4.4, where it is purely the results of financial transactions (as represented by aggregating national balance sheet assets and liabilities) that are concentrated upon. This shows the remarkable expansion in cross-border financial positions for the advanced economy group, which rose from 68.4 per cent of GDP in 1980 to a peak of 438.2 per cent in 2007. And although starting from a much lower base point, the emerging economy group of countries also experienced an increase in this ratio: it more than doubled from 34.9 per cent in 1980 to 73.3 per cent in 2007. This is far below the level of cross-border positions recorded by the advanced economy group. In addition, the ratio was quite flat between 1999 and 2007, so that the emerging economy group did not participate to the same extent in the international financial boom in the mid-2000s (Lane 2012: 1).

At first glance all these indicators would seem to demonstrate a fairly obvious unproblematic and continuous growth in economic 'globalization' since the 1980s, at least until the crisis of the late 2000s. But the contribution of this chapter is to examine and trouble sev-eral crucial aspects of these trends. The argument is that these are

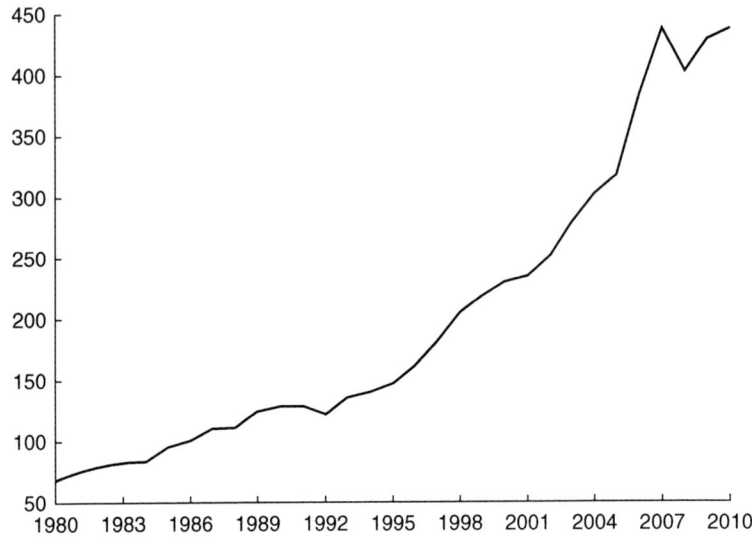

Figure 4.4. Ratio of foreign assets and liabilities to GDP for advanced group
of countries

Source: Lane 2012: Figure 1.

Note: Advanced 'countries' are Europe, the US and Japan.

highly problematic, and critical attention needs to be brought to bear
in respect to them. The chapter goes on to analyse why the existing
explanatory frameworks for the 2007–8 crisis were at best partial, and
at worst wildly inadequate. This critical approach is then extended in
the following chapters, which take up the form of analysis suggested
by this preliminary specification to deal with the analysis of international financial relationships more generally.

Financial globalization?

The context for this investigation is a simple analytical distinction drawn between an *inter-nationalized economic structure* (note the
hyphen – not an 'international' one) and a *globalized economic structure*. An inter-nationalized economy is an economy composed of a
series of individual national economies that interact between themselves mainly via activities such as trade interdependency, investment
integration and migration flowing across borders. The most significant feature of this – though not the only one – would still be these

separated national economies that interact between themselves to form the inter-nationalized economy.

On the other hand a globalized economy would be an economy that existed as a single economic entity in its own right, somewhat beyond the interacting individual national economies. This economy would be driven by market forces and competition between 'footloose' economic agents (companies, banks, financial institutions, individuals) that are not clearly tethered to any single national economy but which take the global arena as their sphere of operations: producing, sourcing, marketing etc., and moving their operations across the globe according to the competitive advantages and profitable opportunities that present themselves anywhere.

The logic of these two types of economic mechanism is conceptual. They are 'ideal types' that do not exist as such in practice or on the ground. They provide an abstract image of two different possible types of economy. A difficulty is that traditional discussions of the 'international economy' or 'global economy' do not draw this crucial distinction between the two forms of economic mechanism just outlined – they tend to use these terms interchangeably. But the distinction is important for the analysis that follows. It provides a reference point from which we can examine the actual complexity of the real economic flows and relationships that make up the international economy.

So, to start with, do we have a genuinely 'global' financial system? One of the many definitions of financial globalization is integration of the domestic financial system of a country with the global financial markets and institutions. The enabling framework of financial globalization essentially includes liberalization and deregulation of the domestic financial sector as well as liberalization of the capital account. Strictly speaking, financial globalization would involve a set of financial markets, exchanges and institutions that trade in financial instruments and channel global savings (wherever they are generated) to investment wherever the risk-adjusted rate of return is the greatest. In this way, financial institutions and markets intermediate between agents irrespective of their location or that of the institution or market. Such a liberalization of trade in financial assets would make countries irrelevant; asset prices, portfolios and firm financial policies would no longer be in any way country-dependent or necessarily tethered to domestic financial markets (Stulz 2005). But the reality is that these conditions are not met by the current international financial system, and are unlikely to be so for the foreseeable future (Hirst *et al.* 2009: Chapter 6). The rest of this section provides evidence for this and suggests that there is no truly 'globalized' financial system, despite recent events that seem to have confirmed that the crisis took a quintessentially global form. The apparent paradox of there being no truly global financial system at the same time as there seems to have been a global crisis and slowdown, will be addressed in a later section.

Subsequently the chapter develops an alternative assessment and explores some of its consequences. This is important because unless the key characteristics of the international financial system are fully recognized it is difficult to suggest sensible measures that might be employed to address its shortcomings and deal with its failings.

A key element in this assessment relates to the way conventional economics goes about analysing the international economic system and globalization. Although there are many alternative specifications and nuances, the basic approach continues to be one that models global economic welfare in a perfectly competitive world (though there are models of the kind considered in a moment that work with oligopoly). As the above outline of financial globalization indicates, many presumptions that are controversial and unrealistic would need to be built into such a modelling environment. Nevertheless, such a modelling framework continues to drive the conventional understanding of the financial system as it operates in an international context. One of the specific approaches is to develop a computable general equilibrium model (or C-GEM), the characteristics of which can be used to illustrate many of the difficulties and misunderstandings associated with globalization as it is conventionally understood.[1] Although such C-GEMs are too mathematically sophisticated and complex to be fully considered here, at their heart is an expression such as the one shown in square brackets in equation (1), which can be used to illustrate the basic approach (though this is not meant to be systematic).

$$\Delta W_G = \bullet\bullet\bullet\bullet\bullet\bullet\left[P_X^i - P_W^{i(c)}\right]\bullet\bullet\bullet\bullet\bullet\bullet\left[P_N^n - P_W^{n(c)}\right] \tag{1}$$

Suppose we were interested in assessing the consequences for 'global welfare' (W_G) of the development of a truly barrierless global economy – i.e. full global liberalization. This would involve comparing and then aggregating all the differences in actual variable prices of goods and services operating in different markets and countries, with those single prices prevailing in such a barrierless, perfectly competitive world. For any particular price (P) of a good or service 'i' in country X, (P_X^i), the comparison is with the single price that would prevail for that good or service under conditions of perfect equilibrium at the world level ($P^{i(c)}{}_W$). These comparisons would be made for every good and service in each country ($P^n{}_N - P^{n(c)}{}_W$), and the differences aggregated to compute the change in global welfare (ΔW_G) consequent upon the 'introduction' of a truly barrierless global market (a complete deterritorialization of the market system). In very simple terms this is what a C-GEM does, and it provides the basic justification for considering the beneficial welfare effects of liberalization and globalization, one where there are no impediments to trade or financial flows. National borders would cease to exist as obstacles to trade and investment.

But herein lies the issue. In contrast to the formation and use of C-GEMs, the actual empirics of modelling international trade and investment flows usually involves the operationalization of a gravity model, as specified in general terms by the second equation, given below. Again, this is used for illustrative purposes only.[2] What it shows are all the elements that keep the two main variables in equation (1) apart, so to speak (i.e. $P^i{}_x - P^{i(c)}{}_w$): what goes on in between these two variables and accounts for their differences.

$$Iij = a + b\left(\frac{GDPi}{Pi}\right) + c\left(\frac{GDPj}{Pj}\right) - d\left(Dij\right) + e\left(BDRij\right) + f(LANij)$$
$$+ g\left(COLij\right) + h\left(BLOCij\right) + k\left(LAWij\right) + l\left(CURij\right) + u \qquad (2)$$

The first line of equation (2) gives the basic gravity model variables. In this case, investment flows (such as foreign direct investment (FDI)) between countries i and j (I_{ij}) – but this could alternatively be trade flows – are a positive function of the per capita income of the two countries and a negative function of the distance between them. But that is not the end of the matter because a series of control variables are added to account for institutional, cultural and geographic differences between countries, which can also (partially) account for the amount of investment (or trade) flows between them. Only the most common and important of these are used in this illustrative exercise. The subsequent variables indicate whether the two countries share a common border (BDR), whether they share a common language (LAN) and whether there is some colonial history between them (COL). This is followed by added dummy variables to indicate whether the countries belong to a common trading bloc (BLOC), whether there is a common legal framework (LAW – so that contracts can be confidently enforced) and finally whether the two countries share a common currency (CUR). All these have been shown to significantly contribute to investment (and trade) flows between countries (Hirst *et al.* 2009). Other variables could be added and some subtracted as suits the analytical purpose or issue being confronted.[3]

The point about this discussion is that the cultural, institutional and geographical variables shown in equation (2) cannot just be wished away via a process of 'liberalization'. The barriers they produce to international economic interactions (trade and financial) are real. They constitute part of the 'structure' of the system, and inhibit the full realization of 'global' welfare benefits. Indeed, the continued existence of countries with borders, territories and jurisdictions implies modelling the international system in a different manner, one that does not presume that a single global market could somehow be conjured into existence: differences between the P^i_xs will always remain pertinent, even in the context of financial markets.[4]

Global or supranational regional?

One of the problems with existing dominant approaches towards the analysis of globalization and the international financial system is indicated by the data plotted in Figure 4.1, Figure 4.2, Figure 4.3 and Figure 4.4. While these show typical measures of globalization, they are highly aggregated. A question to ask of this data is exactly *where* all this activity is taking place? Taking the ratio of foreign assets and liabilities to GDP as shown in Figure 4.4 above, Figure 4.5 disaggregates this into three country sets: the Euro area, the US and Japan (where intra-area cross-border positions are included in the calculated ratio for the Euro area). Within the advanced economy group, this underlines the fact that the level of cross-border financial integration within Europe far exceeds the levels observed for other high-income countries.

But this preliminary disaggregation does not go nearly far enough. Clearly, the international financial system is very unevenly configured. And this is demonstrated by the pattern of financial flows shown in Figure 4.6 (a and b). This breaks up total 'global' financial flows into the patterns of flows between geographical areas for 1999 and 2009 respectively (expressed as a percentage of world GDP), and shows the size of domestic financial assets in each area (proportionate to circle sizes). What are we to make of this data?

Clearly between 1999 and 2009 there was a growth in the complexity of financial integration. But there is also a certain continuity. As might be expected, it is the US and greater Europe (Western Europe, the UK, Russia and Eastern Europe) that dominate in terms of both flows and the size of domestic financial assets. And this pattern did not

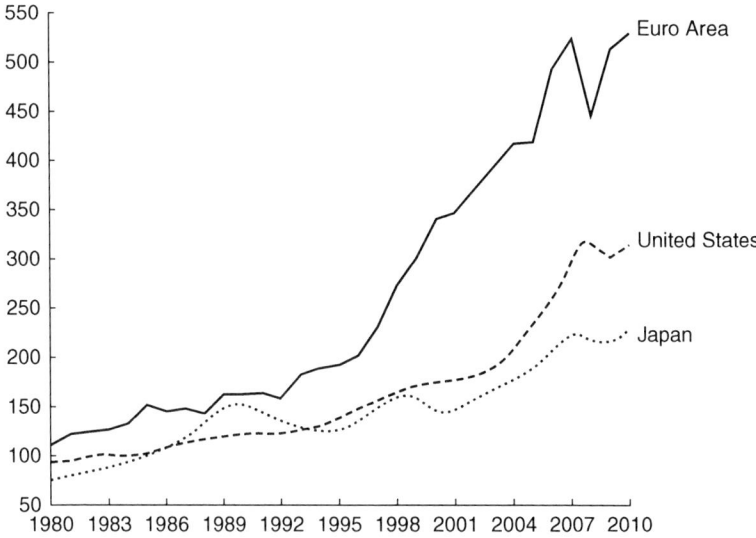

Figure 4.5. Ratio of foreign assets and liabilities to GDP for the Euro area, the
US and Japan

Source: Lane 2012: Figure 3.

change much between 1999 and 2009. Even in 2009 – on the downside of the crisis – these two areas alone accounted for over 70 per cent
of global domestic assets and global flows. This is why the financial crisis could legitimately be described as a North Atlantic crisis and not a
global one (e.g. Gowan 2009; Nesvetailova and Palan 2008). And this
description is reinforced by the data included in Figure 4.7, which
shows where financial write-downs of the banking sector happened
over the early crisis period. These were almost entirely accounted for
by the Americas and Europe.

And this is reinforced by the close integration of banking exposure demonstrated by Figure 4.8. In terms of the size of interbank
claims on other banking systems, global interbank exposures are very
large for banks in most-advanced economies, particularly those in the
core Euro area countries. Intra-European claims, and those between
Europe and the US, still represent the key linkages.

Thus, to all intents and purposes, the financial crisis was not a truly
global one. It was more of an inter-national one centred on the North
Atlantic economies, with just a very few exceptions. And the reasons
are clear from the analysis of what a truly global financial system would
look like, and the data shown in Figure 4.7. If the financial system

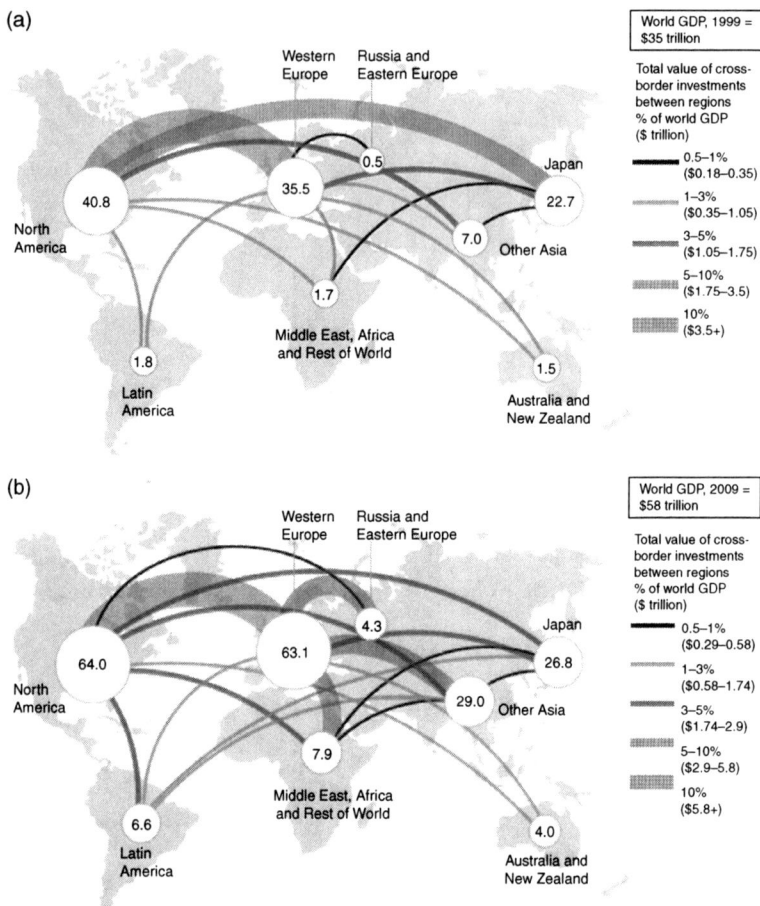

Figure 4.6. (a/b) International financial flows between geographical areas (1999 and 2009)

Source: McKinsey Global Institute 2011: Exhibits 20a and 20b, pp. 32, 34.

Note: Includes total value of cross-border investments in equity and debt securities, lending and deposits, and foreign direct investment.

were truly global then losses of this magnitude would have had a devastating impact 'globally' on commercial banks in many other countries – but this did not happen.[5] The analytical distinction mentioned above between an inter-national economic structure and a global economic structure becomes important at this point, as it enables us to demarcate more clearly the exact nature of the international financial

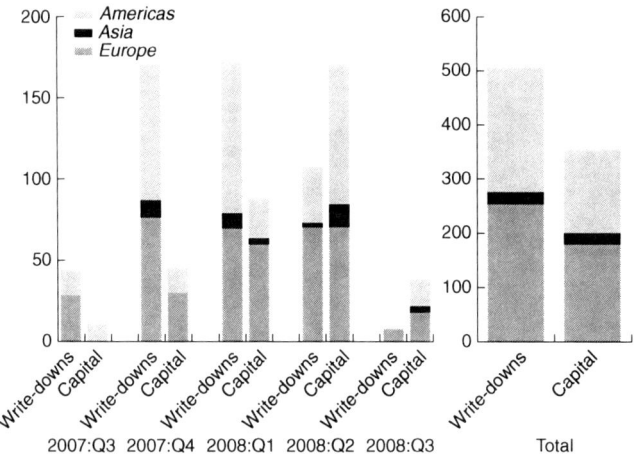

Figure 4.7. Bank write-downs during the crisis
Source: IMF 2008: Figure 1.3, p. 23.

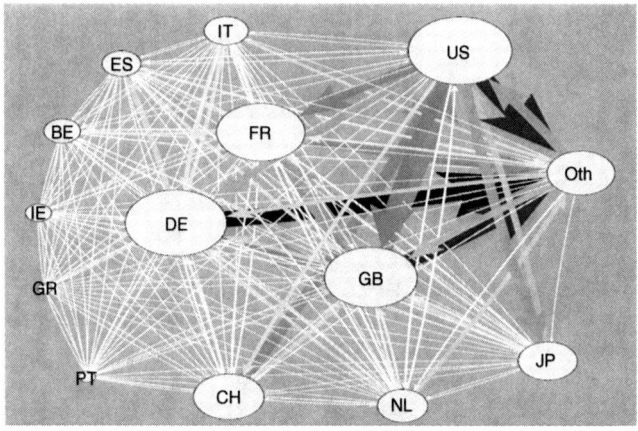

BE = Belgium; CH = Switzerland; DE = Germany; ES = Spain; FR = France; GB = United Kingdom; GR = Greece; IE = Ireland; IT = Italy; JP = Japan; NL = Netherlands; PT = Portugal; US = United States; Oth = Other countries.

Figure 4.8. Linkages between banking nationalities (2010)
Source: BIS 2011: Graph 19, p. 26.
Notes:
a Data are as at end December 2010.
b The size of each circle is proportional to each bank nationality's share of total inter-bank claims on all other banking systems.
c It is based on consolidated data, so exposures through subsidiaries are included in those of the home office.
d The thickness of the arrows from bank nationality A to bank nationality B is proportional to the size of the inter-bank claims between those two bank nationalities.
e Data for Belgian and German banks are on an immediate-borrower basis rather than an ultimate-risk basis.

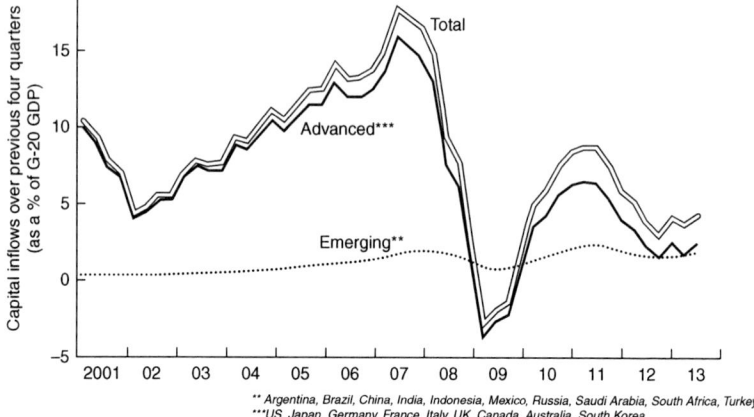

Figure 4.9. The retreat of financial globalization?

Source: Ralph Atkins and Keith Fray, 'Capital flows: powered down', *Financial Times*, 7 January 2014, p. 9.

Note: Compared to the size of the world economy, flows are heading back to levels of a decade ago.

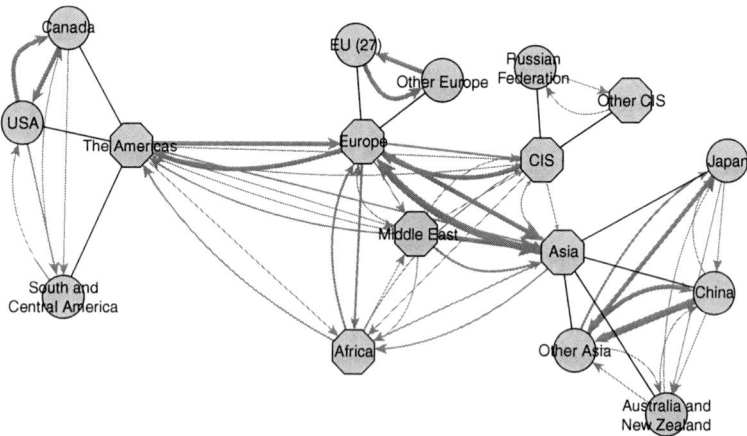

Figure 4.10. Global network of manufacturing trade (2010)

Source: Calculated from *World Trade Organization International Trade Statistics 2011*: Table II. 29, p. 81.

Note: The size of the connecting lines corresponds to the size of the trade between countries, scaled as a continuous series from maximum to minimum trade values.

Trade in manufacturing: USA, EU (27) and China, 2010
(% distribution based on origin areas total manufacturing exports)

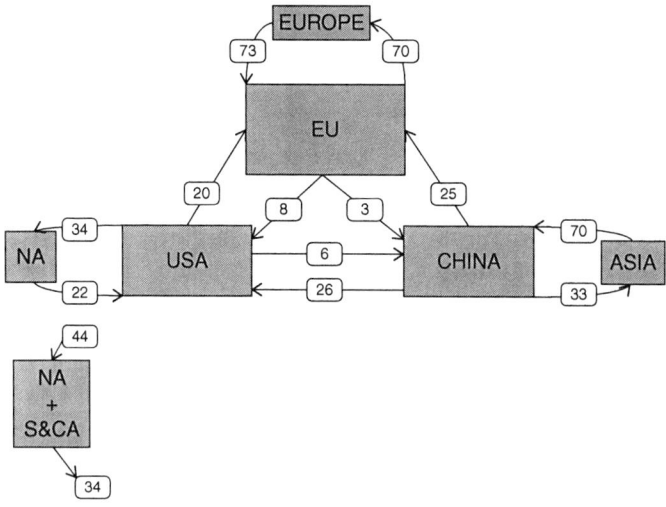

Figure 4.11. Simplified network of global manufacturing trade (2010)
Source: as for Figure 4.10.

system. Of course no empirical data is entirely definitive – there will always be disputes over adequacy and interpretation – but this data and its trends do provide a reasonable basis to remain sceptical about the conventional wisdom in respect to the crisis.

And in the post-crisis period we also observe a possible retreat of financial globalization, as indicated by Figure 4.9. On a whole series of measures there is a slowdown or reversal of international economic integration and interdependency. While 'austerity rules', a different sentiment about globalization might emerge that will see its reputation tarnished and its revival halted.

Finally, the highly uneven nature of the international financial system is mirrored in respect to trade relationships. It is worth drawing attention to the parallel concentrated nature of trade relations that are sketched in Figure 4.10 and Figure 4.11.

The vast bulk of international manufacturing trade is carried out between the three geographical areas shown – the USA, Europe and China. Along with their 'near neighbours', these constitute a triadic trading regime that centres on three continental-sized economy groupings, and which to a large extent mirrors that shown for capital flows in Figure 4.6.

To all intents and purposes, therefore, we observe more of a supranational regionalized economy (based on an 'inter-national' economic structure) than a classic global one (a 'globalized' economic structure). (For a more detailed demonstration of this triadic inter-national economic structure, see Hirst *et al.* 2009: Chapter 6; Thompson and Kaspersen 2012.)

Contagion between markets and economies

So in the context of the 2007–8 economic crisis and its aftermath, how do we account for the fact that although the financial crisis may have been centred on just a few countries stretching across the North Atlantic, it has escalated into a seemingly more global economic crisis involving many more countries and regions? Here we need to recognize the importance of contagion between different markets and national economies. But a preliminary difficulty is that contagion could be a feature of either of the two ideal-types of economy outlined earlier – its existence does not act as a discriminator between them. There was large-scale contagion during the crisis, and there is little doubt that the international economy has experienced a deepening recession. But contagion – the degree of volatility between different markets and between markets in different countries – has been a feature of all financial crises ever since the Tulip speculative bubble of 1637.[6] There is nothing particularly novel about this, so it is not just a feature of a globalized economic structure as defined above. However, measuring the extent of contagion during financial crises is complex and controversial (Allen and Gale 2000; Dungey 2008a). There are several approaches. All estimate correlation coefficients between different markets in different countries. But correlation coefficients do not necessarily say anything about causation, so further analysis is needed to isolate the transmission shock associated with an international disturbance from that associated with a purely domestic disturbance (to establish the degree of 'international contagion' only). But this could be caused by there being 'underlying' macroeconomic variances between countries, or trade disturbances, or simply because of 'news shocks' (see Fernández-Izquierdo and Lafuente 2004; Serwa and Böhl 2005; Nikkinen *et al.* 2006 for representative examples of these approaches). So contagion – the transmission of shocks – should not be confused with interdependency – the existence of high correlations (Eichengreen *et al.* 1997).

In the context of the financial crisis, preliminary evidence shows that there does not seem to have been a growth in the capacity of contagion to translate such volatility between markets and countries between the periods 2000–7 and 2007–8 (Dungey 2008b). The volatility was the same in each period, it is just that the initial shock was bigger for the 2007–8 period, hence the greater magnitude of the impact. So this does not mean that 'globalized' interdependency at the international level had increased, only that the initial shock was greater.

But how did such contagion happen? One might look towards 'financial networks' to address this question (Babus 2007; Pistor 2008; Allen and Babus 2009; Haldane 2009; Gai and Kapadia 2010 – and Figure 4.8 above). Financial networks are building up 'connections' that increase the vulnerability to systemic shocks, although they could also reduce susceptibility to these if they were to spread the risks and dissipate the initial shock (as expected by conventional opinion about risk management – and as echoed by the natural disasters literature considered in a moment). However, Brunnermeier (2009) has shown that network effects of so-called risk-sharing have not worked in a networked financial system; rather, they can exacerbate it.[7] Thus one needs to map these networks and assess the vulnerabilities within them. This is taken up below. But contagion as such is quite compatible with either an inter-nationalized economic structure or a globalized one as defined earlier; it is not necessarily associated just with 'globalization'.

The impossible conditions for a genuine global financial system

The bottom line in respect to this consideration of the extent of financial integration and globalization is to stress the structural limits to this process once again. As long as there remain different currencies tied to different domestic financial systems – that is, no single global currency, no proper global Central Bank to act as lender of last resort for this single currency, and only a few countries that can borrow on the international markets in their own currency to finance their economic activity while the vast majority of other countries must borrow in someone else's currency – there is a necessary structural disjuncture between domestic and international financial systems that cannot be bridged (Arestis and Basu 2003; Arestis *et al.* 2005). This is the structural basis of all the uncertainties and risks in the international financial system, and these conditions will hardly disappear in the foreseeable future. These structural constraints inhibit the formation of a genuinely global financial system, leaving a much more differentiated system of national domestic, international financial and supranational regional relationships and interactions that need to be viewed in their specificity and singularity rather than as a single coherent 'global system'.

This serves to raise a very important point about the future of financial globalization and the consequences for the renewed global regulatory standard-setting debate, particularly in the case of financial
globalization. The consequence of the remarks above is to suggest
that full financial globalization is impossible without such a single global currency, and given that such a single currency is most unlikely
(indeed, for the foreseeable future politically impossible), then there
will be no full 'global' financial internationalization. This looks like
an impossible dream.

Of course there are many calls for a single global currency, mainly
by American economists who see this as a way of further bolstering
the international position of the US dollar (e.g. Rogoff 2001; Cooper
2006; see also Tobin 1998). And it is also important to recognize that
the call for a single global currency is not a new phenomenon. In the
previous period of globalization during the second half of the nineteenth century there were feverish discussions about the possibility
of inaugurating a single 'global' currency, originally based upon the
Latin Monetary Union of 1865 (Einaudi 2001). There were confer-
ences in the 1860s: in Berlin in 1863, though the debate began in
earnest as Napoleon III called an international monetary conference
in 1867. But the vision of the 1860s was never realized (Bordo and
James 2006) as the proposals foundered upon incompatible political
differences as to exchange rate conversion procedures and administrative means to 'manage' monetary policy and banking activity. The lesson of this episode should not be lost on the current debate, however.
It demonstrates that money involves matters of sovereignty; indeed
political issues are at the core of both the creation and the operation
of money (Knapp 1924; Keynes 1930; Goodhart 1998; Ingham 2004,
2006). Without getting into a long historical analysis, the definition of
money, the creation of money and the operation of money require a
political authority to issue it and provide for its credibility.[8] The implication is that there is a need for a 'big government' with a 'strong
Central Bank', and clear 'lender of last resort' facilities, to manage
the financial cycle by constraining the boom and softening the slump.
This is as necessary in an international setting as in a national one.
Without all of these conditions, money and finance will not operate
'efficiently', let alone optimally.

Under these circumstances the introduction of new global banking
and creditworthiness standards may be desirable – even necessary –
but they are also impossible under a regime of financial liberalization
and floating exchange rates. While there are different currencies, not
all of which are used as either international transaction currencies or

as the standard of prices and asset values, uncertainty rules in financial markets, which necessitates the introduction of various creditworthiness standards to try to govern this. However, these standards are inherently unstable given the need for the less-developed and emergent market countries (the vast bulk in fact) to earn foreign currency and finance their commercial activity through the issue of assets not denominated in their own currencies. As we have seen above, this opens up a necessary structural 'rupture' or 'separation', (1) between the 'domestic' and the 'international' financial systems of countries, and (2) between those able to finance their activity in their own currency, and those who cannot.

Such an inherent instability means that there are great pressures to opt for some kind of regional response. This provides for the big government, strong Central Bank and lender of last resort facilities so necessary for some form of financial stability. The European Union (EU) is the current 'home' for such a response, and not just in the case of monetary developments. This is not the place to discuss the enormous range of standard-setting initiatives being promulgated from within the EU. These not only affect intra-EU economic and other activities, but are having important effects on the wider international standard-setting environment. In many respects the EU is the main active player in developing 'international' standards, as the US remains reluctant to initiate or participate in any standard-setting processes that do not meet its own narrow interests and advantage, and while East Asia is still in the early days of forging common rules and norms (Ishaq and Atiq Ur Rehman 2013). However, as has been argued above, at various levels more and more financial standard-setting looks to be becoming 'sub-global' in character, even as current trends are not unambiguous (Thompson 2005, 2012).

A final point to make in this section is that the 'global' character of the crisis was largely a media-constructed event, though it was aided by politicians who have bought into the globalization story for basically domestic political reasons: it provides an excuse, when necessary, for them to offload blame and to discipline their citizens in the name of continued 'international competitiveness', justifying austerity and so on.[9] In addition almost every 'City commentator' has a vested interest in claiming a global aspect to the crisis and its aftermath, since this bolsters the scope of their activities. But also – and perhaps most disappointingly – many academic commentators fell for this story, since they are themselves mesmerized by the prospects and spectacle of a new epochal rupture, one that allows them to indulge their skills as critical analysts of profoundly changing events (Thompson 2009).

Never ones to miss an opportunity for hyperbole and exaggeration, for all of these parties a 'global crisis' sounds so much better than an ordinary and boring multi-domestic or inter-national one.

Further comments on the notion of 'crisis'

Crises always expose the underlying character of situations and events. They are intriguing – even attractive – occasions, since they provide a glimpse into the very structure of the system. Indeed, there is probably a subliminal desire for crises: they enable decisive action to be taken, leadership to be exercised, hands to be wrung, mistakes to be exposed, blame to be apportioned. They break the normal pattern of the mundane.[10]

Crises are also periodic 'events'. But what exactly is an event? Things are always happening, but events seem something more, something beyond the ordinary – an unexpected eruption (see Chapter 1). In the social world, events display two related aspects: first, they break ongoing processes by establishing 'differences' between before and after; second, they draw together 'dispersions', seemingly creating a momentary unity among a range of different instances and contexts – but at the same time precisely preserving that dispersion by exposing its distribution. Summing up, events might be described as an occasion for the 'dispersed unity of differences'.[11]

How are any of these remarks pertinent from the point of view of the recent (and ongoing) financial crisis? First, the crisis exposed the real nature of the monetary system. The extreme measures adopted by the authorities – the 'nationalization' of large sections of the financial system, as a series of private institutions were taken into public ownership in the USA and the UK in particular (but also in Belgium, the Netherlands, Switzerland and elsewhere) – indicates a basic structural truth of capitalism. The only way to gain control of the financial system and the money supply is for there to be a socialized financial system. This may sound paradoxical, but in a capitalist world where credit is the basic form of money, controlling the money supply is always crucial, but also problematical. The money supply (credit) is crucial because the economic agent who has money has command over resources. As a result there is always an intense political struggle over controlling the money supply – between the 'public authorities', on the one hand, and private economic actors in the financial system, on the other. This was exposed very acutely during the debate about 'monetarism' in the 1970s and 1980s in the UK. The monetarists argued the authorities could 'manage' the economy simply by controlling the money supply. But central bankers knew differently. Though they never quite couched it in these terms, the central bankers knew they could not control the money supply. That was in the hands of private economic agents – who, of course, jealously guard this capacity at all costs.[12]

To control the money supply would have meant socializing the financial system, the complete opposite of the monetarists' policy prescription of liberalization and deregulation. But therein lies the paradox. Instead, the central bankers tried to manage the financial system and influence private economic actors – and the economy beyond – via an interest rate policy. But interest rates affect the demand for money in the first instance, not its supply. Thus the authorities never implemented 'monetarism' proper because they knew they could not. Rather, they adopted an interest rate-based policy, which was clearly only partially successful.[13] As we have seen subsequently, however, private economic agents relished their renewed capacity to 'control the money supply' by indulging in an orgy of credit creation as interest rates were pushed lower and lower (see Chapter 8 for a discussion of the consequences of these actions).

This orgy of credit creation was brought to a sudden halt by the 'credit crunch'. Indeed, credit creation (money supply) almost stopped. This provided the opportunity – and indeed the very necessity – for the authorities to confirm the basic truth of the above remarks by nationalizing large sections of the financial system so as to try to kick-start the money supply process again. In extremis, deep structural characteristics are revealed. And as a consequence of this nationalization administrative means of distributing credit emerged. Indeed, this administrative mechanism was written into the very terms of the nationalization moves. The commercial banks and other financial institutions involved were instructed to allocate credit in various ways: to existing mortgagees (delay or abandon foreclosures) or to lend to small businesses.[14] And many more claims along these lines – for administrative allocation of credit in a very general sense – subsequently emerged. Thus we have seen other vulnerable financial institutions seeking help, and large industrial companies radically undermined by the recession claim their share of support. All this is a consequence of partially nationalizing the financial system; administrative methods for the creation and allocation of credit take over from the market.

Second, this was a genuine event in that it galvanized all parties into action. And in a 'period of the exception', the location of sovereign power was once again (ex)posed.[15] So it was nation states that came to the rescue of their financial systems, not some general global response.

And this also exposed the basic dispersion of the international financial system. These responses were different and particular: specific to the characteristics of each national financial system. At its basis the international financial system remains just that – still an inter-nationalized one, organized between national economies. It is the implication of this different reading of the nature of the financial system and its crises for regulatory reform that the next section explores.

What is to be done?

As John Kay (2009) reminded us, national economies, international financial markets and businesses are complex, dynamic, non-linear systems, about which it is almost impossible to make specific predictions. It is foolish to pretend otherwise. Thus the argument here is that if financial crises are fundamentally 'irrational' – driven by 'excessive exuberance', 'animal spirits', 'bandwagon effects', 'bubbles', Ponzi schemes, exotic calculative technologies and the like – then we should prepare ourselves in quite a different manner than so far for the next crisis – because there will be one.[16]

Given the analysis so far, the first lesson to be learned is that further 'global' rules to try to tame the financial system are very unlikely to be fully successful. This is not an argument against strong regulatory rules, but only against these *always* being conceived as necessarily global in scope because the financial system is thought to be global. If it is not – and indeed will continue not to be so – then a different response is called for. Analysis of the financial system conducted earlier and elsewhere – and of the 'real' economy beyond – suggests the trajectory of development is largely supranationally regional in organization and not global, and with continued strong nationally based characteristics (e.g. Agur 2008; Hirst *et al.* 2009: Chapter 6). If this is so, supranational regional and nationally based responses would be more sensible. This would allow for these to be tailored to the specific conditions and features of such regional or national financial confutations, it would enable agreement on what to do to be reached more easily since fewer players are involved, and it would encourage 'regulatory innovation', since different regulatory frameworks would arise. Some (managed) regulatory competition is no bad thing. In a moment we address what could be thought to be one of the major drawbacks of this structure: it might allow or further encourage clever financial operators to find and exploit the gaps left within it, precisely the problem experienced with past regulatory structures. But as a first step, a thorough 'audit' of what the main financially affected countries have done in their individual responses to the crisis should have been conducted. This would have provided the necessary information base on what each country had already installed in terms of domestic regulatory structures before the crisis hit, how robust they proved to be and what has since been done to reform them. The objective here would be to initiate a period of 'mutual learning' – not in some top-down manner driven by the (now largely discredited) global institutions of financial governance, but a bottom-up one, by listening to the range of different responses that were extant and later introduced at the national level.

Clearly, the present financial crisis is deep and very serious – indeed, for the banking sector in particular it has been the worst crisis since the 1930s, and it has spilled over into the real economy of those countries most closely affected. But financial crises come and go – this is not the first such crisis and neither will it be the last. And here we need to reflect upon the typical 'financial crisis cycle', as it could be termed. It is a little difficult to know where exactly to analytically break into this cycle, but for convenience we do this with the phase involving 'financial innovation', since this is a central part of the recent concerns. Financial innovation raises many fears as it takes hold, which are often well documented and discussed at the time. Warnings are offered as to their likely downside effects but these warnings are, of course, never properly headed by authorities or regulators (for reasons outlined in a moment). But this leads to a second phase as the crisis largely brought about by these innovations strikes. As they are ingested into the system and become features of its regular operation a crisis arises. This results in a great deal of firefighting (as recently, and at present) to try to gain control of the crisis and prevent it spreading. It leads to a lot of hand wringing, immediate soul searching, recriminations and so on ('Why did no one see this happening or heed the warnings?'). As the crisis subsides this is followed by a longer analytical diagnostic and post-mortem phase. What were the reasons for the crisis? Who or what was to blame? What lessons can be learned and what can be done to prevent a further crisis? This is a difficult phase because there is never agreement about causes or consequences. However, alongside this phase the 'authorities' begin to act, putting into place a discussion about measures needed to prevent another crisis of this type. This phase requires a political mobilization for it to gather momentum among the affected parties. And this is the most difficult and lengthy phase because getting agreement about what to do is never easy. Eventually some consensus is reached, which usually means a very watered-down and minimalist set of regulatory responses are agreed and gradually implemented – lowest common denominator politics takes hold. But meanwhile, of course, the system has moved on and a new set of financial innovations have taken hold, so the responses to the previous crisis now being gradually implemented look as though they are unnecessary, or addressing yesterday's problem. And the fact that the authorities are still grappling with the regulatory consequences of that previous round of innovations means their focus is not on the existing round or the threats now posed. And so the cycle continues.[17]

To introduce a personal note here, I was once at a conference where I asked a panel of regulators and Central Bank governors what could be done, if anything, to break this cycle, and their response was intriguing. The chairman of the session replied that this was an 'existential question' and that such existential questions could not be answered! On reflection, however, I think this answer should be taken seriously. Perhaps the mindset of such bank governors and regulators is so focused on traditional responses that they cannot jump out of that mindset and see that the system is actually 'existential' in the sense that it is at least in part 'irrational'.[18] It is not, therefore, fully amenable to systematic and calculative responses where the International Monetary Fund (IMF)'s Financial Stability Forum, the Bank of International Settlements (BIS)'s Basel Committee or the Group of Twenty (G-20) simply begins another round of negotiations for a comprehensive and consistent set of new global regulatory norms and rules to be adhered to by everyone (as suggested in Mattli and Woods 2009, for instance).

Rather, what is needed is a realization that financial insecurity is going to continue to be a fact of life, involving as it does 'excessive exuberance', 'animal spirits', 'bandwagon effects', crowd behaviours and so on. If this is so, what is needed is to organize a highly flexible regulatory regime of 'distributed preparedness for resilience', one that does not presume a single centre from which a new elaborate global regulatory regime emanates (Collier and Lakoff 2008).[19] This approach would have to pay particular attention to the necessarily fragmented nature of financial regulation – given the range of characteristics and initiatives as suggested earlier – in an attempt to forestall any exploitation of the gaps within it (Perrow 2007). But it would need to recognize that the crisis represented only a temporary dispersed unity of differences, as suggested above, not a permanent one, so that the underlying distribution of differences continues. To address this would involve a lot of contingency planning and attempts to coordinate the disparate array of 'local' (supranationally regional or national in our case) organizational and partial initiatives, requiring the application of improvisational skills and ingenuity. This approach – which

Collier (2008) terms 'enactment-based assessment' – is contrasted to the traditional 'archival-statistical approach', which relies on assembling knowledge from already known risks and past patterns of events. The task would be to map the vulnerabilities and network the relationship between them.[20] This regulatory world would always need to expect the unexpected (Weick and Sutcliffe 2007).

While it will be difficult for those states that have socialized large sections of their financial systems to return these to private ownership quickly, this is not necessarily a priority. It may be that a newly formulated regulatory regime will require a continued presence of public ownership of significant parts of the financial system, if nothing else because of, as the analysis above indicated, the difficulty of kick-starting the credit/money production process without it (see Chapter 8). This may be the only effective way to deal with the continued dispersed character of the international financial system and to prepare for the resilience necessary to deal with new unexpected eruptions as they happen, because these will happen whatever is done.

Of course, a response along these lines is unlikely. More likely is for the traditional financial crisis cycle to kick in once again, and 'business as usual' to re-emerge (Thompson 2009). But imaginative thinking about the future to try to create a robust alternative conception is absolutely necessary, even if the precise terms of what has been suggested here prove wanting. However, this can hardly be worse than the recent debacle. Discussion of these issues continues in Chapter 5, Chapter 6 and Chapter 7.

Conclusions

The argument of this chapter has been that the 'global' financial crisis was not really global at all, but one confined to a relatively few countries centred across the North Atlantic (between North America and what has been termed 'greater Europe'). But this did not stop the spillover from this area to much of the rest of the world, in terms of a wider economic contagion and downturn. Contagion proved rife, though such contagion is not new in the international economic system, so, of itself, it cannot be used as an indicator of the onset of a new specific phase of international capitalism called globalization. But do these linguistic differences matter much? In fact they are conceptual differences not just linguistic ones. This chapter has argued that getting the conceptual terminology right is important because it indicates to the policy conclusions that might be drawn from any analysis. If the international economic system is not a globalized one in the terminology developed above – but rather an inter-nationalized one where there are strong elements of irrationality – then the regulatory response should be centred on national economies (or supranational regional configurations) rather than necessarily at the global level. This led to suggestions of how to develop a 'bottom-up' regulatory response based upon catastrophe management and a distributed preparedness for resilience. The implications of such a characterization and suggestion are the subject of the following three chapters, which take up the analysis of the financial system, as outlined here, in more detail.

Notes

1 For particular application of this technique by the World Bank, see Essama-Nssah (2006).
2 For a thorough analysis of the use of gravity equations in modelling international trade, see Rauch (1999).
3 In the equations for investment flows (FDI, equity) the distance variable (D) is a highly significant one, with negative impact on investment (and the same goes for international trade) (see Hirst *et al.* 2009: 175, Table 6.8).
4 This is referred to as the 'home bias' effect. In the case of trade see Disdier and Head (2008), and for financial markets see Bong-Chan *et al.* (2006) and Cai and Warnock (2004).
5 For instance, after an initial shock China emerged more or less unscathed (Wolf 2009). But perhaps a caveat should be introduced here. In some markets – derivatives trading, for example – there would seem to be single global price. But the 'meaning and significance' of that single price varies dependent upon the particularities (institutional, cultural, social) of the financial systems in which they are registered or located. The effects of different national financial systems cannot just be wished away in terms of the sense made of prices, or their impact and consequences. Prices as such do not govern everything. This is a mistake made by Marxist analyses of globalization, for instance, which stress the complete commodification of global trade and investment transactions, and the formation of a single global price for such commodities (Lysandrou 2005).
6 On the first 'global financial bubble' (of 1720) see Frehen *et al.* (2009).
7 Brunnermeier suggests an interesting measure to cope with contagion in these settings, designed to indicate to the 'value at risk' of any organization's balance sheet, which is covaried with other organizations in the network ('CoVaR'). This is designed as part of a better assessment of systemic network stress (Adrian and Brunnermeier 2009). Haldane (2009) constructs various measures of network characteristics based upon the extent of foreign assets and liabilities between the main financial centres.
8 These issues were posed acutely in early 2014 when the private virtual currency 'Bitcoin' hit the headlines. This is basically a speculative vehicle with little further economic consequence. But its 'value' was swinging erratically as exchanges dealing in it collapsed (Mt. Gox) and several others suspended trading (Vircurex) after hacking incidents. If it survives, regulatory attention will inevitably be directed at the activities associated with this and other virtual currencies.

9 A clear case of this was Gordon Brown (the UK prime minister at the time of the crisis) who, in an interview with the BBC Radio 4 *Today* programme on 23 January 2009, argued that the financial crisis was solely the result of irresponsible lending in the US. He also reiterated *14 times* that this was a 'global financial crisis', presumably something being faced in the same way by everyone. We are all, as a result, shared victims of a common unexpected process, where there is nothing individual governments can do about it because it is a 'global' phenomenon.

10 Thus, echoing a point made above, the media loves them; it chases them, helps construct them, and revels in them: 'breaking news', 'global tremors', 'the worst day on Wall Street since ...', etc. Crises are enthusiastically embraced by the media when they erupt.

11 An additional – and related – aspect of 'events' would be to stress their specific political character. According to Badiou (2001) and Rancière (1999), genuinely political events are those that declare a radical equality. They announce an equality where there had previously been a deep inequality. They right a wrong (Chapter 2 above). In the context of the financial crisis being discussed here, this would manifest itself in the way such events seem to demonstrate a unity in the diversity they display, and the way they open up an opportunity to put right things that had, up until then, been going very much awry.

12 In the contemporary crisis the emphasis on private control of the money supply was signalled by the call from several leading UK monetarists for the government to once again borrow from the commercial banks to create money (to prevent a potential deflationary spiral from emerging). From the *Financial Times* of 2008:

> Money being destroyed by the collapse in bank lending to the private sector must be made good by bank lending to the public sector ... If banks' claims on the private sector fall, the initial effect on the other side of the balance sheet is a matching decline in their deposit liabilities (i.e., the quantity of money). In these circumstances there is a risk of a debt-deflationary spiral. If so, the right policy response is for the government itself to borrow from the banks ... If the government borrows from the banks on an appropriate scale ... we believe that a wider recovery can be reconciled with reductions in the private sector's indebtedness to the banks.

Further reflections on possible monetary policy under extreme circumstances are developed in Chapter 8, where central banking activity since the financial crisis is analysed.

13 Thus the authorities in effect conducted a 'Keynesian' monetary policy, not a 'monetarist' monetary policy. Indeed, in the 2009 crisis interest rates have been forced down to almost zero, where monetary policy stops. In principle this could enable the government to purchase anything at zero cost to itself (since it can borrow at zero cost) and to spend as much as it likes. But as developed at length in Chapter 8, the authorities chose not to exercise this option. Instead they went for a more conventional route of borrowing from the private sector, hence encumbering the public sector with significant amounts of debt, which could have been avoided.

14 However, one of the problems more generally has been whether the nationalized banks – let alone the non-nationalized ones – have acted to pass on any easing of credit conditions to their customers. Generally they

failed to do this – a consequence of having ownership but not full control in the case of the nationalized banks, which may be an emergent pattern in the financial system. Further nationalization plus the exercise of control (or 'governance') may be an answer. Chapter 8 updates these comments and pursues their longer-term implications.

15 Thus, Gordon Brown almost became a 'Schmittian sovereign' for a while ('He who decides in the exception' (Schmitt 1998)) – in his *New York Times* column on 12 October 2008, Paul Krugman described Brown's decisive action in the UK as the potential saviour of the world financial system!). This is somewhat of an exaggeration, of course, since the very existence of the UK state was not in question.

16 In part this 'irrationality' can be illustrated by the way that options contracts (which are important in the derivatives markets) are priced – in fact necessarily 'mis-priced'. Two key assumptions for valuing options are that the volatility of returns is constant and their distribution is log-normal (Black and Scholes 1973; Merton 1973; Brooks *et al.* 1993). In practice neither of these assumptions is likely other than by pure chance: usually returns are volatile, and unexpected combinations of events disrupt their distribution. This means that strictly speaking options can only be 'correctly' priced ex post: when the contract has matured (because then the actual volatility and distribution would be known). These problems have given rise to a complex debate about options pricing (e.g. Mehrling 2005; MacKenzie 2006; also Chapter 5 and Chapter 6 of this book).

17 See Reinhart (2008) and Reinhart and Rogoff (2009) for the way the 'financial crisis cycle' has reproduced itself over many centuries, and the failure of the regulatory authorities to come to terms with this.

18 An existential moment in this context would be a crisis that lacks purpose, meaning or authentication, leading to anxiety, disorientation and confusion in the face of the seeming randomness, absurdity and volatility of events.

19 Here the lessons from natural disaster planning are introduced. And although in its own terms this has been problematic (e.g. in the case of the flooding in New Orleans in 2005), in principle it provides an important alternative conceptual apparatus for thinking about crisis management (Grossi and Kunreuther 2005).

20 This problem is almost recognized by Martin Wolf (2008) when he laments the failure of conventional economic analysis to spot the oncoming crisis:

> The difficulty was that we all tend to look at just one bit of the clichéd elephant in the room. Monetary economists looked at monetary policy. Financial economists looked at risk management. International macroeconomists looked at global imbalances. Central bankers focused on inflation. Regulators looked at Basel capital ratios and then only inside the banking system. Politicians enjoyed the good times and did not ask too many questions. What of commentators? They tended to indulge the fantasy that the above knew what they were talking about … One big lesson of this experience is that economics is too compartmentalized and so, too, are official institutions. To get a full sense of the risks, we need to combine the worst scenarios of each set of experts.

5 The global regulatory consequences of an irrational crisis

Examining 'animal spirits' and 'excessive exuberances' as features of the financial system

Nothing sedates rationality like large doses of effortless money.
(Warren Buffet, Chief Executive, Berkshire Hathaway – quoted in
Financial Times, 3 March 2009, p. 8)

When it comes to the all-too-human problem of recessions and depressions, economists need to abandon the neat but wrong solution of assuming that everyone is rational and markets work perfectly.

(Paul Krugman, *New York Times*, 2 September 2009)

Introduction

There have been many explanations of the 2007–8 financial crisis and what to do about it. By and large these explanations have been offered by traditional economics, which despite its many failings in the run-up to the crisis has quickly recovered its analytical composure (despite the warnings from the likes of Krugman quoted above). The feature that most strikes the reader about these conventional accounts is the underlying assumption that the crisis can be both explained by – and put right with the aid of – the usual rationalistic assumptions of conventional economic analysis and policy-making (such as utility maximization, rational expectations and the efficient market thesis).[1] From this perspective the crisis was just a random error. There are some exceptions to this, of course. The crisis has offered a space for rather unconventional approaches to be more seriously considered, giving these a voice they might not otherwise have had. The behaviourist school, for instance, has had a relatively 'good crisis' (Shiller 2000; Akerlof and Shiller 2009), and Keynes and Minsky are once again back in favour and on the intellectual radar (Cooper 2008; Davidson 2009; Minsky 2008; Skidelsky 2009), or so it seems.

In addition, the event has allowed financial journalists a perhaps unexpected opportunity to display their skills in narrating the crisis in various respects (e.g. Augar 2009; Fox 2009; Tett 2009). In fact, it is these journalistic accounts that have most forcefully broken with the analytical framework of conventional economics and its rationalistic assumptions, to adopt a much more unorthodox position in attempting to expose both the shortcomings of conventional economic models and the possible way forward in terms of sensible regulatory reform.

This chapter takes up the challenge of analytically assessing the reasons for the crisis associated with these economic models, developing some preliminary points made in the previous chapter. It provides an alternative conception of how the financial system works – at both the domestic and international levels – and pursues the consequences of this analysis for outlining the contours of a regulatory regime that might be installed at the global level that is quite different from current policy prescriptions. It does this in three stages.

First, it scrutinizes the underlying assumption of the models used in pricing financial instruments – particularly options contracts, derivatives and collateralized debt obligations (CDOs), which have been the key financial innovations over the last 30 years.[2] At the heart of these models lurks a series of overly rationalistic assumptions that have continuously proved inadequate to the task of effectively assessing the risks involved in these markets. It is suggested that these failings have been a key element in the evolution of the crisis – indeed, that they were centrally responsible for its catastrophic character.

Second, the chapter examines several central terms that have been associated with the unorthodox descriptions of the crisis. Among the most important of these is the idea that the financial system is driven by 'animal spirits' and 'excessive exuberances' rather than a rational calculative logic (see also Chapter 6). These two categories appear as part of an alternative terminology framework for describing the financial system (FS), and beg the question as to whether it is more an existential system than so far seriously considered. The aim is to locate the sources of these animal spirits and excessive exuberances within a radically alternative conceptual framework for financial decision-making.

After investigating these terms the chapter considers the global regulatory consequences if the financial system were indeed as chaotic and catastrophic as suggested by the previous analysis. What can be done in a regulatory sense, if the financial system is endemically prone to bubbles, Ponzi schemes, bandwagon effects, herding behaviour, 'overheating' and the adoption of exotic financial instruments the consequences of which few, if any, can fully understand?

The final main part of the chapter investigates the behavioural and regulatory consequences of conceiving the financial system as one infected by a virus rather than acting like a machine (see MacKenzie 2006; see also Mirowski 2002). This views the financial system as prone to events that are akin to a tsunami, a hurricane or an earthquake; catastrophic natural disasters that cannot be completely foreseen or properly calculated for in advance but which seem inevitably prone to reappear in one form or another (see Reinhart and Rogoff 2009). If the system is 'irrational' why should another round of rationalistic top-down policy prescriptions installed at the global level have any long-term positive impact?

The rationalistic terms of modelling options, derivatives and CDOs

Anyone wishing to appreciate the incredible range and complexity of modern financial instruments such as options, derivatives, swaps, forwards and so on, could do worse than consult Satyajit Das's monumental four-volume study (Das 2006). This probably represents the high point of that genre of instruction manuals dealing with how to play the 'financial engineering' game.[3] And while this is not a book for the lay reader – it is meant for the academic and the practitioner – even these might be overwhelmed by the sheer scale, detail and number of new exotic instruments invented over recent years (the book expanded from three volumes and 3,000 pages of the second edition in 2004, to four volumes with 4,700 pages for the third edition in 2006).[4] No wonder those charged with managing and regulating the risks involved with all these new developments were completely bewildered by their task. But what this book avoids (along with other similar products such as Chance 2008) is any serious consideration of the underlying assumptions of the models that it elaborates, something concentrated upon here. The argument is that these nowhere near confront a possibility that the FS is an 'existential' one.[5] If the characteristics of the FS are so thoroughly 'irrational' after a certain level of activity is reached – they are driven by 'excessive exuberances', 'animal spirits', 'bandwagon effects', 'bubbles', crowd behaviours, exotic calculative technologies and the like – then we should prepare ourselves in quite a different manner than we have so far for the next crisis, because there will be one. While post-Keynesian economics recognizes some of these features of the FS, it still clings to an underlying attitude of rationality on the part of economic agents, so calculative responses to temporary irrationality are possible (e.g. see Marchionatti 1999, who champions 'bounded rationality'). It is the behaviourist school that has come closest to recognizing the potentially existential nature of the FS and its crisis events, but as yet has not developed a distinctive response in terms of governance or regulatory initiatives.

Options and derivatives

To examine the modelling assumptions one needs to return to the articles by the founding names in the financial options and derivatives game such as Robert C. Merton (1973), and Fisher Black and Myron Scholes (1973), or to one or other of the critical commentaries such as MacKenzie (2006), or to more laudatory accounts such as Mehrling (2005). Here we do not deal with all these assumptions in comprehensive detail but rather pick on several of the most important, to trace key conceptual presuppositions that underpin option pricing results.

We begin with the famous Black and Scholes article of 1973. This model of the options market for an equity investment makes the following explicit assumptions:

- it is possible to borrow and lend cash at a known constant risk-free interest rate;
- the price follows a geometric Brownian motion with constant drift and constant volatility;
- there are no transaction costs;
- the stock does not pay a dividend;
- all securities are perfectly divisible; and
- there are no restrictions on short selling.

While subsequent developments – several of which are discussed in a moment – relax many of these assumptions, the Black–Scholes model has become the benchmark for options and derivatives trading.[6] And while these subsequent developments might seem to have solved many of the problems associated with the model, I argue that this is not as obvious as it might at first seem. I concentrate on the issue of 'volatility', since this is a key element in the model and in the markets it is aiming to comprehend.[7]

The basic model assumes constant volatility as indicated above. In response to the criticism that this is totally unrealistic, the usual story is that the model can be extended to cope with non-constant volatilities (and interest rates). Part of the popularity of the model is that it is seen to be robust and able to adjust to deal with these issues. For instance, rather than considering volatility of stock prices (or interest rates) as constant, these can be considered as variables, and thus added sources of risk. This is reflected in hedging these to mitigate the risk caused by the non-constant nature of the parameters. Alternatively, rather than assuming a volatility a priori and computing prices from it, it is possible to use the model to solve for volatility, which gives the implied volatility of an option at given prices, durations and exercise prices, so that a transformation from the price domain to the volatility domain is obtained. Rather than quoting option prices in terms of currency per unit, option prices can thus be quoted in terms of implied volatility, which leads to the trading of volatility in option markets. Indeed, this is what options trading has become; the trading of volatility in the asset, not the asset as such (Wigan 2009).

All this sounds quite comforting from the point of view of how volatility can be handled in the model, but several important issues remain. A key further assumption is that whatever the volatility considered in the model, this remains 'deterministic'. Thus there is always some assertion of a definite pattern to volatility that can be rationally incorporated into the model – if not determined 'in advance' and thus not 'predetermined'. Take the idea of 'solving for volatility' in the subsequent model developments. This involves 'operationalizing' the idea of implied volatility – defined as the volatility that, when used in a particular pricing model, yields a theoretical value for the option equal to the current market price of that option. At one level, then, implied volatility is a forward-looking measure – it embodies now what is anticipated from the future – so it differs from historical volatility because the latter is calculated from known past prices. But, once again, all this is based upon an expectation and an anticipation – it is based upon a hunch as to the pattern of future volatilities. This seems a necessary feature of any 'rational expectations' base model. And nor does the first response just mentioned – a resort to hedging – increase confidence, since this just displaces the problem on to hedging operations, which parallel the problems identified already.

Another way to try to deal with the problem of volatility is to approach this through the idea of stochastic volatility. In this case the underlying security's volatility is treated as a random process, governed by 'fundamental determining variables' (so-called 'state variables') such as the price level of the underlying asset, the tendency for volatility of which is thought to revert to some long-run mean value. But here again we have an assumption not dissimilar to the idea of 'constant volatility': in this case that the underlying security's volatility reverts to a long-run ('stable') mean value. And there seems no way around this.

So, the problem remains: to 'price' an option now requires assumptions about the future of volatilities, which of course may not be the actual outcome at all. And herein lies the rub, so to speak, because we can never actually accurately anticipate the outcome volatility either of the underlying security or, as a result, of the option itself. We never know what the actual volatility is until after the event; until the option has matured, so to speak. And this basic problem is reproduced in the case of indexes of options, which have become one of the main developments in financial markets since the original formulation of Black–Scholes models dealing with a single security (see for instance Brooks *et al.* 1993). Again, a range of not dissimilar assumptions needs to be made: that, for instance, the volatility of the underlying securities takes a log-normal form – it is a Gaussian distribution.[8]

It is these explicit and implicit assumptions built into the models that of course determine their outcome values. But actual events continually confound predictions, since single assets are unexpectedly volatile and volatilities of indexes are not log-normally distributed because actual combinations of unexpected events continually disturb these. Two important possible consequences follow from this that are important in explaining – at least in large part – the reasons for periodic financial crises and the necessary expectation that further crises will appear in the future if such modelling assumptions are maintained.

The first possible consequence would be that 'correct prices' of options contracts cannot be properly valued in advance of their actual maturity. Thus, if this were to be the case, prices are always necessarily 'wrong' in some way, since they cannot be determined 'in advance', so to speak. We can only retrospectively reconstruct correct prices after the event, when we know the actual pattern of the volatility. This obviously presents a 'problem' from the point of view of rationalistic calculation and attempts at the control of actual markets. Price signals are always necessarily 'wrong' in some sense.[9]

But the other possibility is to suggest – as is done by those theories that stress the 'performativity' of markets, particularly of financial markets – that this problem is 'disguised' or rendered redundant by the fact that the predicted prices that emerge from these models become the actual prices operating within the markets themselves. The models do not map the market, they create it (see MacKenzie 2006; MacKenzie *et al.* 2008). And this potential 'solution' to the volatility problem has an appealing plausibility. Attractive though this might be, however, it leaves the financial system exactly where it was in the case of the first possibility just discussed. It is 'indeterminate' in the face of the radical uncertainty associated with a truly volatile future. If we take the 'prices' that result from the output of Black–Scholes-type models at face value, as 'actual prices', we are still beholden to – or 'at the mercy of' – those models and their basic indeterminacy. The financial system becomes almost an existential one – beyond complete rational meaning and sense-making.

What other possible solutions to this seemingly existential problem are possible? An interesting – though ultimately unconvincing – approach is to use cognitive modelling and complexity theories as a way of operationalizing the problem (e.g. Orléan 1989; Sornette 2003; Sornette and Woodard 2009). Orléan pins his hopes on modelling a different form of rationality: 'mimetic rationality' associated with mimicry, so that market operators mimic their counterparts.[10] This leads to herding behaviour on the part of market participants and speculative bubbles in asset prices. Again, this seems an attractive alternative to the conventional 'rational expectations' approaches just discussed. But a close scrutiny of its modelling strategy reveals that it is once again beholden to a set of rationalistic assumptions similar – indeed directly comparable to – the traditional approach just criticized ('These bubbles generated by rational expectations will be called *rational bubbles*', Orléan 1989: 73, emphasis in the original). It is rational to imitate. And this goes for Sornette's associated attempt to explain financial crises with the use of complex feedback mechanisms drawn from a particular way of viewing natural disasters.

Sornette's argument is that financial crashes are 'outliers', which have their own statistical properties. This departs from the standard finance theory view that big price rises are just small ones writ large, with no particular distinguishing or predictable features. The specific statistical character of crashes means that they must be analysed separately from other market movements, but it also means that they can be tracked, and to some extent predicted. Before crashes, market movements can be approximately described by a process known as log-periodicity. Broadly speaking, log-periodicity is a series of oscillations that become more and more rapid before a crash. Log-periodicity is significant because it seems to emerge only in the lead-up to a crash and not at other times; hence its presence is an important sign that a crash may be imminent, and hence predictable.

But exactly how is this modelled? The difficulty is that Sornette uses the standard 'random walk' setting for volatility measurement, even after demonstrating that large price changes take place far too often for market movements to be truly random, given the market's average return and standard deviation. Thus, a problem with Sornette's approach is that random prices are supposed to be a sign of market efficiency – and randomness is the major plank of the evidence for market efficiency used – when we know that such randomness is unrealistically demonstrated by his own empirical evidence. In addition, Sornette is keen to promote the idea that financial bubbles as analysed along these lines are predictable (Sornette 2003: Chapters 9 and 10). But he rather rashly uses his log-periodic model to suggest that the world economy, as well as the financial market, may cease to grow – or even slump heavily – in the middle of this century: the end of the 'growth era' will be around 2050. A hazardous prediction indeed, and he seems to have got it wrong by about 40 years. This should undermine any easy confidence in the predictive qualities of a log-periodic approach.

Sornette's approach is closely linked to another feature of the response to these recognized difficulties with conventional volatility analysis. This is to rethink randomness (and volatility) as 'wild' or spontaneous, and thus not 'mild' or normal. Pioneered by Benoit Mandelbrot (1997; Mandelbrot and Hudson 2008), this forms one of the foundations for the idea of 'chaos' as a modelling framework for the financial system, associated with the frequency of large, often unexpected changes. But, as MacKenzie (2006: 105–18) has demonstrated, this approach was largely ignored by conventional economic analysis and options pricing modellers. It does, however, form the basis for the analysis of 'natural hazards' (Malamud 2004; Zanini 2009), something returned to in a moment.

CDOs

The final instrument to consider is that of collateralized debt obligations,[11] at the core of which lies the difficult issue of correlation. A low correlation between the default risks associated with credit derivatives implies that defaults are essentially idiosyncratic events, with the consequence that only the bottom-most tranche of a typical CDO is at significant risk. On the other hand, high correlation means that if defaults happen they tend to cluster, and the clustering of defaults puts investors in the higher, apparently safer, senior tranches at risk of loss (MacKenzie 2008). The way this is modelled in financial markets is usually via a technique known as the 'single-factor Gaussian copula'. The term 'copula' indicates to the connectedness of default risks, the term 'single-factor' to the idea that each debt issuer is subject to the same single underlying variable (such as the state of the economy) in determining their exposure, and 'Gaussian' to the idea that connectedness itself takes the form of a multidimensional standard bell-shaped curve.[12] Thus, once again, it is a traditional normal distributional logic of risk assessment that informs this approach.

Modest correlations of 0.3 were typically used in the financial markets before the crisis. But this seemed to have woefully underestimated the (*ex post*) 'actual' correlation, which could have been nearer 1.0 given the way events unfolded (MacKenzie 2009). Thus, once again, financial analysts made a wrong call: their faith in, and desire for, lower risk overwhelming even the 'rationalistic' calculative logic of their own models.

A question all this discussion poses is what sort of analytical approach might be adopted that would be better for thinking about the international financial system and its reregulation? If the conventional modelling frameworks discussed above are wanting, what alternative frameworks would better suit the task? To approach these questions the next section sets out some terms and modes of analysis that, it is suggested, are crucial for such a reassessment.

Dealing with the sources of animal spirits and irrational exuberances

Keynes (1973: 161) defined animal spirits as 'a spontaneous urge to action rather than inaction, and not as the outcome of a weighted average of quantitative benefits multiplied by quantitative probabilities', so that 'a large proportion of our positive activity depends on spontaneous optimism'.

Akerlof and Schiller (2009: 3, and footnote 3 and 177–8) point out that animal spirits have a long pedigree, originally associated with medieval theories of mental energy and life-force, attached to conceptions of bodily circulatory flows and movements producing an urge for spontaneous and intuitive action. But in respect to the modern economy it has acquired a slightly different meaning, referring to a restless and inconsistent element in human behaviour, associated with ambiguity, uncertainty and indecisiveness.

In turn this is linked to irrational exuberances, which, for Schiller (2000: xii), are experiences of 'wishful thinking on the part of investors that blinds us to the truth of the real situation', which can easily lead to a 'speculative bubble: a situation in which temporarily high prices are sustained largely by investors' enthusiasm rather than by consistent estimation of real value'. This is turn is linked to 'excess volatility' (Schiller 2000: 183–90): anomalous and persistent stock price movements that are not correlated in any discernible way with underlying asset values.

These definitions may be fine as far as they go, but they do not press the matter vigorously enough. We need a more rigorous explanation for the continued existences of these 'spontaneous urges', 'procliv-ities for ambiguity', 'wishful thinking', etc., in the arena of human decision-making. The next three sections try to develop such an explanation by exploring several theoretically oriented approaches that delve into the psychological sources of human decision-making. What we are seeking here is a set of alternative theoretical resources to help understand the basic irrationality of the FS and why there is a continual misapprehension of this.

George Bataille's 'economy of excess'

One possible source is with George Bataille's idea of the 'economy of excess'. Bataille (1984, 1997) contrasts what he terms the 'restricted economy of utility' – the kind of economy considered up to now, which is concerned with welfare, 'goods', happiness, productivity, profitabil-ity and so on – to the notion of a 'general economy of excess'. This economy concerns itself with the tragic, with extravagance, and aban-don, with the destruction of wealth, unproductive expenditure, prof-itless exchange, with ritualistic, sacred and symbolic activity. While the restricted economy concentrates upon the price mechanism and market exchange, the general economy concentrates upon the gift, symbolic transactions and the general embodiments of wealth. With the restricted economy, economic activity can be measured and is the subject of a calculation. It involves well worked out and specified contracts. The activity of the general economy of excess, by contrast, cannot be measured in this way or subjected to a rationality of cal-culation. There are no contracts (or, at best, only loose implicit con-tracts) within this general economy. While the restrictive economy is driven by scarcity, the general economy is driven by sacrifice – a kind of aimless energy. Thus the FS may be one concrete manifestation of this general economy of excess in action. What Bataille offers is a dual economic mechanism that should be considered operating in parallel: one as a calculative and restrictive economy, the other as the 'irrational' (or as embodying an alternative kind of rationality) and general excessive economy.

Flahault's 'Promethean spirit'?

A second possible source is to consider François Flahault's formula-tions about the basic underlying Promethean characteristics of human action: the idea that with enough will and ingenuity anything is pos-sible. Flahault works on the boundaries between the philosophical and the social, between the psychological and the actionable, at the intersection of the calculable and the irrational (Minson 2010). This makes him an interesting figure from the point of view of trying to work out that 'existential' moment in relationship to the operation of the FS. His arguments are presented here in an attempt to uncover what 'animal spirits' might mean, and why 'excess' could be seen as a necessary feature of all human activity. This is done in respect to two books: *Malice* (Flahault 2003) and *Le crépuscule de Prométhée* [The Twilight of Prometheus] (Flahault 2008).

The first of these outlines his basic position, while the second can be used to address the implications of his position for the nature of the FS, which is picked up in the later book. Clearly, the FS is a complex entity, the workings of which cannot be reduced to a single, easily digestible transcendence or 'human failing' – the issues that Flahault works on. But I argue that Flahault provides resources to think the limits of calculative actionable endeavour in the financial system (and, indeed, in the economy more generally). As we will see, the issue is how and where to draw the line at a point of these intersections, so that the 'psychological' and the 'structural' aspects of the FS might be reconcilable (CRESC 2009: 63).

Flahault (2003) argues that 'beings' are unavoidably both malevolent (evil) as well as capable of goodness (rational and enlightened). These twin aspects he attributes to them as subjects of two related modalities of life: what he calls the 'subjects of knowledge' enabling a differentiation between, and an adjudication over, what is good and evil; and the 'subjects of existence' enabling a similar differentiation between, and an adjudication over, life and death. This double form of subjectivity arises because humans are finite beings. Only non-beings, he argues, are infinite, absolute and boundless (i.e. Promethean). As a result, in these terms at least, it is only non-beings that could be simultaneously infinitely perfect and infinitely just, guaranteeing at the same time complete order and acting as the all-powerful sovereign.

Beings, on the other hand, exist at the cost of a definition or a demarcation: they are the subjects of the double articulation just mentioned and are not infinite, absolute or unbounded. But they would dearly love to be! And here is where the 'problem of transcendence' arises; the desire to transcend this human condition is inherent in the human condition itself. The claim to immortality is excessive for human beings, he argues. This involves a dependency on a non-being that transcends itself. But the attempt to transcend – to be accountable and reportable to the real world order – combats the attitude of the tendency to excess without being able to completely tame it. To 'live' requires us to struggle against and give up on a first-order sense of limitlessness and boundlessness. In turn, of course, this enables us to 'imagine' this condition of being 'beyond the limit'. But to support this sense of being requires others to respond to this state of affairs: to live with it and amongst it. So there is an inevitable sociality associated with 'beingness'. (Hence Flahault's necessary connection to a social moment in the analysis of the political and economic order – he is not simply a naked individualist.)

We have, then, an oscillation between the limited, the demarcated and the differentiated, on the one hand, and the unlimited, the unnameable, the confusion, the destruction and chaos, on the other. But this raises a problem within Flahault's work about how to move from a seemingly thoroughly individualistic 'psychologized' sense of the determination of the inner self to the reality of the external world – whether this be an evil or a good world. His answer is that it is stories and narratives that provide the vehicle for this transference. Such stories and narratives – which often provide a privileged position of narration for an internal moral spectator within the text – confirm our ability to imagine the unlimited and of an absolute existence that allows us to 'claim everything', tempting us to exercise these powers in excess (the *hubris*). It provides us with the ability to work with a sense of absolute justice, on the one hand, and the withholding of this compliance in the real world, on the other – both at the same time. Thereby, imagined stories enter the real world, which provides a place to test our own performance against that imagined world – so as to achieve completeness. These formulations nicely link up with a current interest in the role of 'convincing stories' in sustaining an exaggerated prospect for the future of the FS in the bubble run-up to any crisis (Froud *et al.* 2006), and the importance of the category of 'performance' in understanding how that mechanism works (e.g. MacKenzie 2006).

For Flahault this is what the Promethean spirit offers – an unconditional assertiveness, absolute possibilities, the limitlessness of independent action. In his 2008 book he links this to the idea of *homo-economicus* and the excess of exchange: a limitless positive common good arises from market exchange. Instead of a predation we have only fair exchange: only equality, not inequality. The Promethean denial of interdependence is manifest for Flahault in two different registers: cognitive and existential – so this links to the potential existential nature of the financial system, or aspects of it.

As far as the existential illusion is concerned – which given the concerns above is of more interest here – Flahault argues that J.-P. Sartre (in *Being and Nothingness*) adopts a similar Promethean view of Man as expressed through his definition of freedom: freedom is precisely the void that forces the human reality to *do*, as well as (or perhaps, instead of?), to *be*. In developing this position, Flahault takes a slight detour to discuss the nature of common property in economics.

Traditionally 'pure public goods' involve two conditions: non-rivalry (the consumption of one party is not lessened by the consumption of another) and non-exclusion (access is free if marginal cost is zero). To these criteria Flahault adds two others: this property must be enjoyed, i.e. experienced, and in being experienced this must result in an effect, i.e. an intangible feeling. These two criteria link the 'to do' with the 'to be' aspects of the existential illusion. Common property is not just a thing that exists, it must also be experienced: it must be both a 'to be' (an existence) and a 'to do' (an experience) to overcome the void. So, in the face of an injunction that all economic decisions are made in connection to a fully calculative logic, Flahault would empha- size the need not to overstate the role of intentions as against actual experiences. For him the first of these (intentions) invokes the logic of knowledge of the phenomenon ('calculative rationalism' – and is forward looking), while the second (actual experiences) invokes the logic of interactions – whether social or physical (and the 'potential- ity of the irrational' in respect to those interactions – and is backward looking) – and in so doing he returns to unite the subject of know- ledge with the subject of experiences with which we first began this investigative outline of his position.

The Promethean moment in human nature leads to a 'plasticator' image of the possibilities of transcendence: we become semi-fluid creators, who can model ourselves free of constraint derived from any pre-given natural attributes. At its extreme such a 'getting carried away' with ourselves leads to a metaphysics of autonomy, seemingly leading to existential acts of pure decisionism unencumbered by rea- son or consequence. That is Flahault's legacy for an analysis of the FS, to which we return in a moment. And the consequences of 'decision- ism' for financial calculation are pursued in Chapter 7 later.

The 'time of the project' and financial regulation

Supposing we were to say as a first hypothesis that another financial crisis was 'inevitable': that the irrationality of the financial system means it behaves in a manner that results in something rather like the catastrophic events akin to a natural disaster – and that it looks like this destiny is forever to repeat itself. Does this not just disarm us and prevent us from doing anything to change that possibility? Does destiny necessarily contradict 'free action'?

One response to this provocation – the traditional one – is to say: 'No … it is not inevitable, the future is still open and we still have time to act to prevent the worst reoccurring'. Nothing is a predetermined destiny. We can realistically appraise the possibilities of such a disaster and then take action to prevent it happening. Such an approach is comforting because it does not accept that the 'inevitable' will happen – there is no 'inevitable' – and it lulls us into a deep (but potentially false) sense of security as a result. It all becomes a matter of rationally assessing the possibilities and deciding whether or not – or which way – to act as a result, depending on a calculation of the likelihoods.

One the other hand – and much more radically – we might accept that the catastrophe is inevitable but act retroactively to 'undo it', so to speak. This means accepting and recognizing it as inevitable in the future so as to be able to confront it in the present. Only in this way, perhaps, can we solicit real action so as to counteract this outcome in the present. We may need a radically pessimistic prediction at the level of future possibilities so as to mobilize to counteract it in the present – otherwise it will actually become inevitable that the catastrophe does indeed hit.

This implies a new notion of time: the 'time of the project'. This concept of time invokes 'a closed circuit between the past and the future: the future is causally produced by our acts in the past, while the way we act is determined by our anticipation of the future and our reaction to this anticipation' (Dupuy 2005: 19). This is how we might confront the prospect of the catastrophic crisis: first perceive it as fate, as unavoidable, and then, projecting ourselves into it, adopting its standpoint, we should retroactively insert into its past (the past of the future) counterfactual possibilities upon which we then act today. ('If we were to have done this and that, the catastrophe we are in now would not have happened.') Therein lies Dupuy's paradoxical formula: we have to accept that, at the level of possibilities, our future is doomed, the catastrophe will take place, it is our destiny – and, then, on the back of this acceptance, we should mobilize ourselves to perform the acts that will change destiny itself and thereby insert a new possibility into the past. It is towards a formulation of this 'time of the project' that the rest of this analysis is directed.

The project is to press actions in the present that change the seeming destiny of the inevitable by first recognizing that inevitability. I would argue that only by doing this – indulging in this kind of 'event sequence', which foregrounds another financial crisis as an inevitable catastrophe – can such an event be (potentially at least) avoided. Of course, once one has done this, the whole process repeats itself but in another register. It is a never-ending process, but the acts next time require a different project to address the 'new' problem/potential catastrophic event that has emerged out of the present one.

What kind of regulatory responses?

Supposing, then, that the FS is similarly prone to catastrophic events like earthquakes and tsunamis. For all the reasons outlined above we know there are going to be more of these events sometime, but we do not know exactly when, where or how they will strike. Catastrophe planning confronts this issue in its regulatory guise, which we come on to in a moment.

But it is necessary to stress that the following suggested schema is not meant to be a complete substitute for more orthodox accounts of regulatory reform – examination of rules governing ratings agencies, constraints on executive compensation, rules for valuing assets on balance sheets, the construction of regulatory capital ratios for banks, reducing the extent of leverage, counter-cyclical (rather than pro-cyclical) measures, greater transparency and so on. These are all sensible. But if we simply try to avoid recreating the initial conditions that led to the crisis, this is unlikely to be successful. Many of these conditions are here to stay, one suspects (securitization, derivatives trading, large cross-border positions), which means that systemic risks will continue, and will continue to be underestimated. What is suggested here should be seen as a necessary complement to these approaches.

In the previous chapter I drew attention to the need to think this afresh in the light of the existential nature of the FS and its basic irrationality, something justified more clearly in the immediately preceding analysis. In Chapter 4 I argued that there is a need to organize a highly flexible regulatory regime of 'distributed preparedness for resilience', one that does not presume a single centre from which a new elaborate global regulatory regime emanates. Here the lessons from natural disaster planning would need to be introduced (Collier and Lakoff 2008). In principle it provides an important alternative conceptual apparatus for thinking about crisis management (Grossi and Kunreuther 2005). Such an approach is not the same as modelling volatility in markets as akin to natural disasters in the style of Sornette's theory discussed above, but to use some of its intellectual apparatus to think about responses to disasters. This favours a view of financial disasters as akin to the 'expected unknowns' rather than the calculable: we know there is going to be another earthquake along the San Andreas fault in California, and a tsunami in the Indian

Ocean, but we do not know exactly when and where these events will strike or how severe they may be, so we have to prepare for these 'expected unknown' events as best we can.[13] This approach would have to pay particular attention to the necessarily fragmented nature of financial regulation in an attempt to forestall any exploitation of the gaps within it. But it would need to recognize that the crisis represented only a temporary dispersed unity of differences, not a permanent one, so that the underlying distribution of differences continues. And these are differences that exist between national jurisdictions in the main (Hirst *et al.* 2009). As suggested in the previous chapter, to address this would involve a lot of contingency planning and attempts to coordinate the disparate array of 'local' organizational and partial initiatives, requiring the application of improvisational skills and ingenuity. This approach – which Collier (2008) terms enactment-based assessment – is contrasted to the traditional archival-statistical approach, which relies on assembling knowledge from already known risks and past patterns of events. The task would be to map the vulnerabilities and network the relationship between them. And this regulatory world would always need to expect the unexpected. It relies upon a de-idealized picture of non-completeness, tracing the delicate and thin threads between agencies in the regulatory domain.

It is in the context of mapping the vulnerabilities and networking their relationships that an alternative conception of the kind of international public space that might be developed to address this problem could be conceptualized. This means developing the idea of networks further as a new kind of global public space (one that is neither necessarily market nor state centred – see Haldane *et al.* 2007; Haldane 2009).

One of the main ways the financial crisis, centred on the banks originally operating mainly in countries stretching just across the North Atlantic, seemed to have morphed into a genuinely global economic depression has to do with 'contagion' between markets in different areas of the economy and in different countries. Contagion expresses the translation of volatility of prices in one market into volatility in another one (Allen and Gale 2000). The nature of this contagion was discussed in the previous chapter.

Conclusions

What are the consequences for global regulatory initiatives of conceiving the financial system as if not thoroughly irrational, then at least in part? If we cannot rely upon conventional economic analysis and its modelling framework to provide robust answers to this

question a completely different analytical approach may be necessary. Here we have discussed the basis of this in terms of the need
to understand what excessive exuberances and animal spirits mean,
and, more importantly, where they originate from in the human
decision-making psyche. Given this analysis, the implications are
not to roll out yet another rationalistically organized global regulatory initiative from the top, by such bodies as the G-20, the BIS or
the IMF's Global Stability Forum (as is the case at present). Rather,
attention needs to paid to a different 'bottom-up' process, based
upon loosely suturing together local and nationally based regulatory
regimes, to network the vulnerabilities of these to create a prudential system of decentralized preparedness for resilience in the face
of the inevitability of another financial disaster. To confront this possibility in the present is the only way to cope with it in the future.
The following chapter pursues the nature of financial irrationality
further.

Notes

1 The complacency within orthodox opinion is demonstrated by Woodford
   (2009), who argues that there is now a general agreement among macroecon-
   omists that dynamic stochastic general equilibrium models have become the
   accepted norm. See Blanchard (2009) for a more reflective account.
2 The object of critique here is not, then, neoclassical economics as a whole
   but only those models of financial product pricing that were at the forefront of the recent surge in the financialization of economic activity.
3 One matched by the four-volume, 2,600-page *Encyclopaedia of Quantitative
   Finance* (Cont 2010).
4 In 2000 there were 104,000 classes of options traded on the Chicago Board
   Options Exchange (MacKenzie 2006: 201).
5 The term 'existential' is put in quote marks to indicate its shorthand
   descriptive character. Later, quite what this might mean in an analytical sense is developed. But as a shorthand description it is meant to
   indicate that the system lacks overall purpose, meaning or authentication, leading to a sense of anxiety, disorientation and confusion in
   the face of the seeming randomness, absurdity and volatility of events.
6 The basic Black–Scholes Model (1969–70) is:

$$\partial w / \partial t = rw - rx \quad \partial w / \partial x - \tfrac{1}{2} \quad \sigma^2 x^2 \partial^2 w / \partial x^2$$

   where w is option price, x is stock price, σ is volatility of stock, r is riskless
   rate of interest, t is time. This is a 'European option', where the stock pays
   no dividends and can be exercised only at expiry – the model was subsequently revised to extend it to deal with 'American options' and other more
   complex matters. I concentrate upon Black–Scholes here whereas the classic model is often referred to as the Black–Scholes–Merton model to indicate the importance of Merton's (1973) contribution. In this contribution

Merton 'generalizes' the Black–Scholes model to some extent by reconciling American-type and European-type option contracts, dealing with dividend distribution before the contract matures, and introducing interest rate variation into the model. But as far as I can judge he does not deal directly with the main issue taken up in a moment, which is asset price volatility in various forms. Indeed, he endorses the idea of its stability: when discussing the variables on which an option price depends he remarks: 'It does depend on the rate of interest (an "observable") and the total variance of the return on the common stock *which is often a stable number* and hence, accurate estimates are possible from time series data' (Merton 1973: 161, emphasis added). Note the tentative nature of this assertion.

7 So an important distinction to keep in mind is the obvious one between the markets themselves and the modelling of the products traded in those markets. Quite how these are linked (if at all) is the key, and something discussed later in the main text.

8 A Gaussian normal distribution is a bell-shaped distribution of events that is assumed to be highly stable, so no single element of what is being measured can significantly affect the average. This is combined with the idea of a random walk; each event is discrete and not impacted by what has gone before. The combination of these two features does not allow for scalable variability or increasing error rates, something that 'bubbles' and herding behaviour clearly imply.

9 This is complicated because at the point of 'maturity' of an options contract its price should be zero! What is hinted at here, however, is that closing an option 'before' maturity is the issue.

10 Such a resort to mimetic rationality conceptions is also a central feature of some quasi-Marxist approaches to explaining the financial crisis, see Marazzi (2008).

11 CDOs are financial products constructed out of previous bonds, such as a bundle of mortgage-backed securities or credit card liabilities, the income stream from which passes to the CDO. These are ordered into tranches from bottom to top, where any default is felt by the bottom tranche first. CDOs are also traded as derivatives of CDOs (CDO2s, CDO3s).

12 The Gaussian copula function is:

$$\Pr[T_A < 1, T_B < 1]\Phi_2\left[\Phi^{-1}(F_A(1)),\Phi^{-1}(F_B(1))\gamma\right]$$

where Pr is the joint default probability for A and B; T_A, T_B are survival times between now and when A and B might default; F is that which couples the individual probabilities associated with A and B; F_A, F_B are probability distribution functions for how long A and B are likely to survive; γ is the correlation parameter between A and B defaults.

13 This echoes Donald Rumsfeld's comment when US Defense Secretary in February 2002: 'There are known knowns. There are things we know that we know. There are known unknowns. That is to say, there are things that we now know we don't know. But there are also unknown unknowns. There are things we do not know we don't know.' Although this was pilloried in the popular press, it is not as stupid as suggested – see Wikipedia entry 'known unknowns'. Expected unknowns as expressed here are rather like Rumsfeld's known unknowns.

6 Sources of financial sociability

Networks, ecological systems or diligent risk preparedness?

Introduction

How is financial sociability to be conceived? This chapter outlines several features of the financial system that pose this issue, though initially in a somewhat oblique manner. One of its main arguments is that to understand such sociality requires coming to terms with a controversial claim as regards the financial system: that it demonstrates many irrational properties. Thus a preliminary problem is to explore further the character of this irrationality. This is the task set for the first three main sections in particular, which widen the treatment of this to be found in Chapter 4 and Chapter 5. In the following section I address the relationship between rationality and irrationality as analogously analysed by Carl Schmitt in *The Nomos of the Earth* (2003 [1950]). Here Schmitt crucially links the *nomos* of a rational calculative 'inside' with an anomic 'outside' that is somehow beyond calculation and therefore 'irrational' in his terms (see also Chapter 7). Clearly, to sustain the force of any similar argument in the context of the financial system requires specification of exactly what rationality means in both contexts, something examined at the end of the second and third sections of this chapter, which then moves on to examine the history of the term 'finance' to point up the particularity of its modern usage: as a verb indicating to the generalized mobilization of creditors and debtors in an arrangement where there is no final redemption of debts. This is the source of financial crises, it is suggested, which, as a consequence, cannot be eliminated from the financial system through better modelling, regulation or management. Crises are endemic so the problem is to come to terms with this 'irrationality', something I will pursue later. It is in the fourth section that the issue of financial sociality as such is addressed head on. Here four senses of such sociability are invoked: it being conceived as a matter of contract, as a matter of interrelatedness, as a matter of habit and repetition, and as a matter of will and passion. And it is this latter sense of sociability that drives much of the irrationality of the financial system, it is suggested.

Once these preliminary observations have been made the chapter moves on to investigate the concrete failings of orthodox financial calculations in the light of this analysis of irrationality in its various guises. The key problem has been to deal with risk. The fifth section of this chapter plots the move from a concern with the risk facing individual agents to that of systemic risk assessment – broadly involving a move from value at risk for an individual organization (VaR) to the covariance of value at risk as between organizations (CoVaR) in conventional terminology. And this is where a consideration of the ideas associated with evolutionary models, networks and complexity as a way of understanding the financial system arises. Andrew Haldane (2009) provides an introduction to this in his Bank of England speech, which, along with his other writings (particularly Haldane and May 2011), is referred to in passing. However, it is argued that such an approach does not quite do justice to the kind of irrationality highlighted earlier in this contribution, though it represents a genuinely worthwhile antidote to the prevailing orthodoxy in terms of regulatory responses to the financial crisis. Finally, this section develops an alternative scenario for regulatory advance – 'diligent risk preparedness' – which draws upon the ideas presented earlier in the main body of the text and in Chapter 4 and Chapter 5. In this chapter we deepen this notion and allude to its connection to both agent irrationality and the systemic irrationality of some institutions and systems.

Schmitt's irrational other and the possibility of 'decisions'

In *The Nomos of the Earth* (2003 [1950]), Schmitt argues that for there to be a *nomos* there must be an 'outside' (the domain of the exception) that is anomic.[1] Schmitt presents several historical instances of a *nomos* (and its anomic other), but the one occupying the greater part of his analysis is the Eurocentric global order ushered in by (he argues) the discovery of the New World in the sixteenth century, and which came to an end towards the early part of the twentieth century, as the European system of a 'nation-based settlement' (*jus publicum*) ended with the prospect of 'total war' between the main European powers (which threatened to engulf everyone else). But the reference to Schmitt is not to re-rehearse his thesis in any detail (indeed, at all) but rather to use it as a way of opening up a discussion of the nature of the financial system.[2] At first glance this might seem a purely gestural and fanciful tactic, but I argue that it presents a powerful analogy that it will be profitable to examine.

The point about the reference to Schmitt is to suggest that a similar issue may arise in respect to financial calculation as it does in respect to the structure of his global *nomos*. Schmitt forcefully argued that without an anomic 'other' there could be no *nomos* in the first place. It is the anomic features (and fear, in his case) of a chaotic other that provides the basis for an accommodation between the parties within the terrain of the *nomos* – producing at least a *modus operandi* there (though not necessarily a *modus vivendi*). Without such an anomic 'outside' the chaos would immediately penetrate the 'inside' and undermine the conditions of its existence – it would cease to be and collapse as a *nomos* (indeed, this is exactly what he argues was the consequence of undermining the European-based and organized global *jus publicum*, as the contours of the Great War took shape in the early part of the twentieth century). And although Schmitt is mainly noted for his discussion of sovereignty and the exception, it is his idea of the decision that is important to the argument here. A *nomos* makes the decision possible; it both enables and establishes a juridical order (as at the same time it is outside of this, of course). But securing such a decision-making capacity requires a 'force', and this is somewhat problematical, since there is an issue of what comes 'first' in Schmitt: the boundary between the *nomos* and the Other, or the force?

So, how might this analogously transfer to the financial system? The issues it poses are several. First, Schmitt was concerned about the impossibility of making decisions if the conditions of the Other prevailed. This relates to the way calculation operates in the financial system. Calculation – as decision-making – is undermined in the realm of the Other, it ceases to exist. Automatic, computer-driven 'decision-making' – as in the case of index trading in the financial system for instance – actually implies non-decision-making in this Schmittian sense. It inhibits the operation of an active decisionist framework. It confirms a realm of technological neutrality where decisions are no longer made. Only the *nomos* confines and limits the conditions for a decision (it is thereby equivalent to the domain of sovereignty). This domain of sovereignty – the exceptionality of the exception – makes decisions responsible ones and justifiable ones, rendering them visible so their consequences can be assessed and a (limited) liability established. Handing decisions over to a quasi-automatic mechanism driven by a technological fix is a recipe for disaster, since it prevents the operation of genuine decision-making. It replaces the technique involved in the art of decision-making, with technology. The artisan is replaced by the computer. Automaticity is substituted for a considered choice.[3] But the relationship between the problematic nature of automatic trading/decision-making as embodied in machines, on the one hand, and the previously argued at least partly irrational decision-making of human agents, on the other, is considered near the end of this chapter and in the one that follows.

So the general question becomes whether the place of the 'unordered other' is a necessary condition for an 'ordered *nomos*' in the financial system. Or to put it slightly differently, for there to be a 'domain of the calculable' does there need to be an 'other of the un-calculable'? Does the 'rationalistic' require the 'non-rationalistic' as a condition of its existence? Within the financial system, economic calculation presumes a certain rationality among contracting and calculating parties, but does this also 'require' a terrain of the 'non-calculable' to make it work?

Further, this relates to the difficulty mentioned above about the role of 'force'. Force would seem to be necessary to secure a *nomos* and decisions. But where does it come from, so to speak? What is suggested here is this is always a becoming, always a distribution, always a scattering, always a repartitioning – but of the will. Force is a rather confusing intensity of the will, constantly being mobilized to discover new techniques of performance. This will is constantly in play across the frontier between the *nomos* and the Other, the boundary of which is, as a result, never completely stabilized. The role of the will in establishing a particular, rather disturbing, form of financial sociality is elaborated below.

The rest of this chapter takes these propositions and queries as its point of departure, so to speak. In general, the thrust of the argument is that there is an irrational and incalculable domain in respect to the financial system that makes possible a calculative and rational response to it.[4] The one presupposes the other, so that the irrational cannot simply be wished away. And it is precisely in respect to periods of crisis that these relationships are exposed, so the task is to examine this domain of the other in respect to the recent financial crisis.[5] Of course, there are many definitions of rationality, so one needs to be careful in specifying what is meant by it. Here I take a rather instrumental definition based upon a classic means/ends structure: decisions are made on a one-off basis, after a full calculation of the options possible, according to preferences and clear objectives, and with the aid of intention and reflection.[6] One can complicate this of course: the distinction between 'procedural' and 'substantive' rationality comes immediately to mind, where 'bounded rationality' is the clear (behavioural) lead complication in this respect. But these are still predicated on a basic rationality to their boundedness. In fact, one of the founders of the bounded rationality position, Herbert Simon (1985) – while discussing these complications – makes a reference to the issue being foregrounded here: what he calls 'radical irrationality' (pp. 301–3). But he carefully avoids tackling it head on.[7]

On the other hand, we could extend the idea of rationality to include intentional rationality or value rationality – the aspect of rationality stressed by Weber. This comes closer to the idea of the 'irrational' as used in this chapter. But I would suggest that the role of intentions and values driving decisions and behaviours should not be confused with 'rationality' as understood above, but considered as an aspect of the wider category of 'thinking'. People make decisions and behave as a consequence of thinking, but not necessarily as a consequence of their rationality. As we shall see, these could be better described as different 'modes of rationalization': characterizations of why things were done the way they were (Lentzos and Rose 2009: 236).

A final point to make in connection to this preliminary assessment of (ir)rationality is to distance it from the currently fashionable behavioural finance school of economic analysis (Barberis and Thaler 2003; Shefrin 2000; Shiller 2003; Shleifer 2000). This position is overtly model-driven, so it simply replaces one set of formal rationalistic assumptions with another, broadly taking a bounded rationality approach to its modelling framework, something criticized above. And although it embraces psychological insights, these are behaviourally, not socially driven, as discussed below and in Chapter 5. In addition, that behavioural approach is exactly that – exclusively about *behaviour* – while the approach being put forward here combines behavioural matters (but considered in a somewhat different manner) with institutional characteristics and the impersonal logic of calculative methods.

By contrast, the conception of irrationality developed here is a radical one, based upon the force of will, not a bounded set of otherwise still rationalistic behavioural rules. Further to this examination, what would be the global regulatory implications and consequences for the financial system if it were, if not thoroughly then at least partially, 'irrational'? These are the issues pursued later in this book. But first we need to consider the circumstances of finance, as such, so as to isolate the particularities of modern financial arrangements.

This will add a crucial aspect to the overall picture of its potential irrationality.

What is finance?

Like many things the term 'finance' can be traced back to the Greeks for its origin. But while it operated for the Greeks as a word with various meanings, it was only in the early fifteenth century that it became a more generally recognized conceptual category with some consistency of meaning and interpretation. From 1400 onwards, for instance, it operated as a noun describing the raising of resources – usually associated with a single venture or project. And its etymological root was important in this context – finance and 'final' are linked etymological categories. The finance associated with each venture would be 'finished' at the end with a final settlement. Thus, finance was associated with a single event or project, incurring a debt that would be 'peacefully' and fully paid off or settled at the end of the venture. It was very important that it did not end in 'turmoil'.

In the late eighteenth century – while still operating as a noun – it began to be associated with the systematic management of money. But from the early nineteenth century it crucially moved from being a noun to a verb – the activity of financing: the generalized bringing together of creditors and debtors. And associated with this was a further crucial move: the systematic deferral of payments and the possibility of the rolling over of debt and therefore the accumulation of debts. Herein lies the origin of modern finance – and its problems – because this involved another key consequential activity: the search for liquidity. Once debts could be rolled over, individual agents were faced with the possibility of liquidating their original positions in anticipation of raising further finance to cover their debts and defer any 'final payment'; indeed, there need be no final 'final payment' under these circumstances, but only if liquidity can be generated and found. As Keynes pointed out, however, while liquidity was a possibility for individual agents, it was not possible for the 'community as a whole'. Who or what would provide the liquidity for the community or system as a whole? Thus, for instance, while each national Central Bank might provide liquidity in the form of lender of last resort (LOLR) facilities for its particular monetary jurisdiction, who or what is to provide such LOLR facilities for the system of national Central Banks as a whole? If the answer is a 'global Central Bank' – apart from the difficulty of establishing such an institution at the global level – this just displaces the problem, since who or what would provide an LOLR facility for any such single global Central Bank? There is no obvious answer. Thus the search for liquidity by individual agents is fraught with difficulties. It leads to the drive to make all assets commensurable by rendering them into money in the first instance (liquidity), and then for organizing the interchangeability of all assets more generally. This in turn feeds the system of endless debt deferral – and thus of endless debt creation – which is the ultimate source of financial crises (Schularick and Taylor 2009).

Financial crises are impossible to avoid in a modern financial system that has broken with the original feature of finance – namely that of the bringing to an end the financing cycle of each venture with a final clearance of debts. In the absence of this 'peaceful' mechanism we have the turmoil created by endless debt and liquidity creation. But how can some surrogate mechanism for this ultimate 'clearance' of debts be secured? This is what the turmoil of crisis does. It 'devalues' the outstanding accumulation of debts, to bring into being a new realignment of creditor and debtor relationships. In turn this enables the whole cycle to begin again. But the point about this analysis of what modern finance is, and what it means, is to stress the 'necessity' of a financial crisis: it is built into its systemic structure. It is a necessary feature of the nature of modern finance. Under these circumstances the problem of regulation and management of the financial system shifts. It is not a matter of the total 'elimination' of such crises – this is impossible – but one of the management of their inevitable reappearance and the minimization of any disruption they might produce. In turn this shifts the focus of regulatory attention to systemic risk rather than risks associated with individual agents or institutions. The terms of such a management task are outlined later. Before that, let us turn to the characteristics of financial sociability and subjectivity, the last of our preliminary remarks setting out the sources of potential financial 'irrationality'.

Conceptions of financial sociability[8]

How is the nature of financial sociability or sociality to be understood? How is this conceived and constructed? Just as in the case of sociability more generally, there are four aspects to this, the latter three of which I argue seem the most pertinent in the case of financial sociability. These conceptual aspects have an immediate impact on how (financial) subjectivities are thought to be constructed and their consequences for shaping the (financial) world.

The first manner in which sociability is thought of is *as a consequence of a contract* – the 'social contract'. Thus, in this case parties inaugurate the social field through an initial contract, convention or pact. Such a contract is thought in various ways, but it always involves agreement on the basis of reasoning by those concerned or who later 'join'. And it is this emphasis on the role of reasoning and rationality that provides the most obvious link to the way the financial system is thought about; as a realm of rational calculability that secures its sociality. The importance of the contract analogy, or the concrete practices of contracting, has increased over time as more and more aspects of social existence are either subject to such contracting, or conceived to be dependent upon it. This moves from the grand social contracting of, say, Rousseau and Rawls, through to various forms of contract between leaders and the 'people', to the mundane micro-contracts now being asked of parents and pupils as a condition of their being admitted to schools.[9] And, of course, contracting in a legal sense has also mushroomed in modern societies, as more and more relational activity is formalized and subject to rule-bound adjudication.

Which leads neatly into the second main way sociability is conceived, that is, *in terms of interrelatedness*. Here it is the language of relationships, connections, combinations, interactivities, flows, chains and entanglements that expresses the necessary interrelatedness that makes up our sociality. Such a conception seems particularly appropriate in respect to the financial system, whether this be in the form of financial risks seen as the consequences of interrelated flows, or movements of financial capital and products; the combinations of institutions, markets and models that encourage fervent innovation, for instance, or the everyday practices and rituals of the financial system embodying power and authority. All these are thoroughly 'relational'. And this goes for approaches that stress fragmentation and disunity, or the way risks are aggregated and pooled into relatively closed silos (e.g. Tett 2010). From these perspectives the issue is to unlock such obstacles to sociality, or to see only loose connections between its constituent parts, but connections that exist nonetheless.

This stress on the interrelatednesses that typify the financial system, and which structure financial subjectivities, can also account for the way the anthropological sensibility has found a new and productive voice in respect to investigations of the everyday life of financial markets and the financial system. It provides a comparative advantage for anthropological and ethnographic approaches, the stuff of which has always stressed interconnection and relationality, now argued to be on display with a vengeance in the financial workplace and through the instruments of financial circulation and innovation (Ho 2009; Riles 2011; Zaloom 2012). What is more, it neatly chimes with another current trend – of which I will have more to say in a moment – which conceives the financial system as akin to an ecological network of radical complexity and reflexivity. Although this is typified by non-linearity and complex feedback mechanisms, it is a system of interrelatedness nevertheless.

A third distinct approach to thinking about financial sociality is to consider it *a consequence of habit or repetition*. Thus the financial system is redolent with conventions of this kind, which manifest themselves in day-to-day behavioural norms: ritualistic and routinized operational activities. While this might be considered as a case of 'interrelatedness' discussed above, it seems worthwhile separating it out and treating it as a distinct category. This notion of repetition would neatly fit with a view of financial analysts as merely sitting at workstations and repeating operations more or less automatically.

While these three conceptual positions – contracting, interrelatedness and habit/repetition – remain the most robust theoretical approaches to thinking about how 'the social' is made and remade, there is another, if rather neglected one. This has to do with the social being inaugurated and continually reinforced or reforged as a consequence of will and passion (see Chapter 2 in particular).

The liberal sentiment has always remained suspicious and hesitant about this, which explains its relative neglect. But will and passion – along with chance, fortune and determination – speak to a different conception of that which is involved with sociality. This combination is less associated with rational agreement (as typifies the social contracting approach, for instance) and more with irrationality, excessive exuberance, blind enthusiasm, momentary feverish drives, etc. It involves the dissipation of a certain psychic energy and the destructiveness or ostentatious display of wealth for its own sake.

In respect to the financial system it connects most closely with the ideas of excessive exuberances, cascading, herding, Ponzi schemes, Minsky moments and the like. Indeed, I would suggest it provides an underlying explanation for these attitudes and features.

One of the reasons this position is rather neglected, and one difficult to fully recognize and embrace, is because it seems to imply a fatalistic resignation: there is nothing that can be done to prevent the eruption of these emotions, since they are written into our psyches or the existential nature of social existence. Now, while there is an element of truth in this, I would suggest it is not the case that fatalism is its necessary consequence. Perhaps it was Hobbes who was instrumental in first drawing attention to this role of will and passion in forging a certain sociality (associated with the death and destruction consequent upon religious conflict in seventeenth-century Europe), but he also suggested a solution, if perhaps a temporary one. What was needed, according to Hobbes, was a leviathan, whose role was precisely to exercise his will to control that of his subjects – to instruct their wills and educate their passions. Their passions were to be caged by what we might think of as a 'benevolent dictator' or even a 'democratic sovereign' (Hunter 2010). But it needed an authoritative sovereign power of some sort to rule over the passions (recall, also, the discussion of Schmitt's decisionism above and the analysis of the formation of a nation-based international system in Chapter 2). And the lesson for the financial system is similar: it also needs an authoritative regulator or regulatory structure to 'rule over' the passions and wills that continually erupt in respect to financial excess. The problem with this, however, is that although the passions may be caged (for a time at least), they cannot be completely tamed: there is always the prospect that the regulatory cage will rust, that the keepers become complacent or neglectful of their charges, so that sooner or later the 'animal spirits' will escape to wreak their havoc once again.

But there have been other suggested solutions. An influential one was provided by Albert Hirschman in his book *The Passions and the Interests* (1977 – see also Myers 1983 for a more economics-inflected treatment of a similar argument). Hirschman argued that late seventeenth- and early eighteenth-century Enlightenment philosophers and worldly men of letters established the notion of the 'interests' (self-interests) as a way of taming the passions and establishing a relatively peaceful milieu for capitalism to flourish from the eighteenth century onwards. For Hirschman, it was the interests that trumped the passions, and that would keep them under control.[10] But the trouble with this is that the passions have never quite gone away. And when the passions combine with the interests, instead of being trumped by them, the consequences can be dramatic and uncomfortable.

Finally, there is another solution, one outlined before and that I develop a little further below. This is to construct a system of distributed preparedness for resilience, one designed precisely to be on continual guard against the destructiveness wrought by financial excesses, but which recognizes the continued threat of will and passion rather than wishing these away. Here three key potential analogies with other domains, where regulation or management of essentially unexpected events is involved, could be examined. These are that:

(1) The financial system might be profitably considered as one that works in a similar way as do natural disasters such as earthquakes, tsunamis or volcanoes: catastrophic events that cannot be completely foreseen or properly calculated for in advance, but which seem inevitably prone to reappear in one form or another (cf. Reinhart and Rogoff 2009; Aradau and Munster 2011). Clearly, natural disasters are not the same as financial crises: they exist in quite different domains with very different properties. But their consequences can profitably be considered as analogous in terms of disruptions and reactions. Natural disaster planning is thus one intellectual resource that could be brought into play to help understand how to manage or regulate the financial system (Collier and Lakoff 2008; Malamud 2004; Grossi and Kunreuther 2005; Weick and Sutcliffe 2007; Zanini 2009; Thompson forthcoming).

(2) Alternatively, the financial system could be considered analogously to an epidemiological system in which viruses invade and epidemics and pandemics strike as a result. In this case the lessons to be learned from the way public health authorities manage epidemics, and such like, provide an alternative potential intellectual resource (Epstein 2009; Price-Smith 2009).

(3) Finally, there may be similarities within the financial system to 'irregular forces' that inhabit the peripheries of military conflicts. How do the regular forces 'manage' or 'regulate' the irregulars such as privateers, buccaneers, partisans, raiders, etc.? What are the relationships between regular forces and irregular ones (Schmitt 2007 [1975])?[11] The financial system is – potentially at least – subject to a similar problem in that it is inhabited by irregular institutions, instruments and events: hedge funds, private equity, sovereign wealth funds, exotic financial instruments, etc., which are always threatening to escape official recognition or regulation by the authorities. This relates to the way 'private governance' is invading the international financial sphere, since this represents another potential set of irregular forces. The key role of the notion of the partisan for reterritorializing 'global' finance is the subject of the following chapter.

Thus, these approaches would not conceive of the financial system as acting like a machine (see MacKenzie 2006; see also Mirowski 2002) but as operating closer to an 'irrationality' as considered in its existential form. Let us now consider the concrete practices of financial calculation that might support this view.

What's wrong with modern finance theory and practice?

This section takes up some of the points made in the two previous chapters about the limitations of financial calculation and currently deployed models in finance theory. There is some overlap here, but it is worth reiterating the main points, since these are crucial to the overall argument of this section of the book.

According to Michael Woodford (2009), modern macroeconomics has seen a convergence of views centred around the 'efficient market hypothesis' (EMH). This theoretical position posits that all unfettered markets clear continuously, thereby making disequilibria, such as bubbles and crises, highly unlikely. Indeed, in terms of the EMH framework, economic policy designed to eliminate bubbles would lead to 'financial repression', resulting in higher interests rates, the unnecessary rationing of credit and the loss of profitable investment opportunities. That such views about a cozy consensus could have been announced just as the deepest meltdown in financial activity since the 1930s was maturing is perhaps testament to the complacency of conventional economic analysis. But it has not completely shaken the conventional belief in the virtues of such a framework among the mainstream macroeconomic modelling community. Rather the crisis has been interpreted as a simple 'random error' within a still robust EMH framework for economic analysis (e.g. Minford 2010). On the other hand, the crisis has had some impact on the regulatory and policy-making community, as will be discussed in a moment.

One of the key features of this EMH framework in its view of the underlying systemic stability of the economy as a whole is that this leaves little room for the separate consideration of the operational stability of the financial system. Once systemic macroeconomic stability is secured, this also provides the necessary conditions for systemic financial stability: these two levels are fused together. But in the wake of the 2008–9 crisis an earlier position has come to challenge this view, namely that associated with Hyman Minsky's 'financial instability thesis' (Minsky 1982, 2008). Minsky's argument was that the more stable the macroeconomic conditions, the more unstable the financial system becomes: systemic macroeconomic stability breeds systemic financial instability. This is because, as the macroeconomy seems to stabilize and present continuous growth prospects (the 'long moderation' of roughly 1995–2007), financial players in particular are encouraged to take on more and more risks, which precisely destabilizes the financial system and then the general economy beyond. It lulls financial players into a false sense of security. And this is precisely what seems to have happened in the run up to the 2008–9 financial crisis.

That modern finance theory is flawed has been extensively documented since the crash of 2007–8 (e.g. Triana 2009). And the likes of Taleb (2004, 2007a, 2007b), Mandelbrot (1997), Mandelbrot and Hudson (2008), Sornette (2003) and Sornette and Woodard (2009) (to mention just a few of the most prominent critics) have been pointing out these flaws for many years. But their critiques are mainly (1) about the shortcoming of an assumption of the normal distribution of asset prices in the financial markets – they are more 'wild', or subject to 'herding' behaviour, or 'fat-tailed', etc.; and (2) their alternative specifications remain largely within the 'rationally calculable' framework, although without the key assumption just mentioned (but with ad hoc distributions – see Jackwerth and Rubinstein 1996 for a systematic presentation of several options). Of particular importance is 'risk management' under these circumstances. The pricing of risk became the central feature of modern financial economics. Two key mechanisms for calculating risks are the Black–Scholes–Merton (B–S–M) model of options pricing and the Gaussian copula (G-C) function for the likelihood of correlated defaults, discussed in Chapter 5. Both of these proved insufficient to the task. The B–S–M option pricing model assumed the volatility of assets to be a random walk (when they proved to be 'fat-tailed'), while calculations using the G-C severely underestimated the degree of correlation between asset classes because the attention was focused on individual risks rather than systemic ones (Izquierdo 2001 – see also Chapter 5, and below). However, this could all have been quite easily recognized if even the most perfunctory attention had been paid to historical precedents. As early as 1637 the Dutch 'tulip mania' demonstrated how excessive behaviours can easily flourish (Goldgar 2007; Shiller 2003), and empirical testing of the B–S–M model of volatility demonstrated its shortcomings in tracking actual options prices and the fact that the B–S–M is not necessary to establish 'fair prices' anyway (Moore and Juh 2006; Mixon 2009). But 'irrational' adherence to the EMH prevailed.

The lessons from this episode are several. First, macroeconomic and financial systems need to be separated out but considered alongside each other in terms of their stability properties; and second, there is a problem of the systemic risks that continue to pervade just the financial system. Systemic risk is associated with the way the entire financial system is interlinked or interdependent, so that a problem in respect to a single financial institution (or small cluster of institutions) can cause a cascading and paralyzing failure across the whole system. While single markets or institutions may be exposed to systematic risk, this can be mitigated by diversifying into a portfolio so as to minimize this on an individual basis, and hedging. But systemic risk poses the issue of interdependencies across markets, which cannot be tackled simply by aggregating individual exposure to market risks. There are several approaches to deal with this, all of which have received a renewed interest in the post-crisis period (deBrandt and Hartman 2000; Allen *et al.* 2010; May and Arinaminpathy 2010; Stiglitz 2010).

In the international arena the gradual replacement of the Basel II regulatory requirements by a new Basel III system represents the leading edge of this change in emphasis. The Bank for International Settlements (BIS) is charged with regulating the big international banks, and under its pre-crisis Basel II system this concentrated on prudential capital requirement for individual banks, which were left more or less to themselves to assess the extent of this, as they were charged with implementing their own internal risk assessment models, providing them with an incentive to minimize the prudential equity capital held in their account books, so as to maximize the profitable use of thereby freed resources. As a result, systemic banking risks escalated.[12] The new Basel III system is designed to address this by concentrating on the interrelationship between bank risks ('stress testing' at the systemic level) and by beefing up necessary capital adequacy ratios accordingly (Fender and McGuire 2010). Whether this initiative is enough to prevent further systemic banking collapse remains unclear (Orléan 2010): the capital requirements still look to be minimal, and the system is not to be fully implemented until 2019. In addition – as developed in Chapter 8 – it may be that the particular asset classes used to provide capital adequacy are no longer relevant.

A second, closely related approach to this, is to concentrate upon modelling 'contagion' between one financial market and another, or between one market in one economy and one in another (Dungey 2008a; Stiglitz 2010; Chapter 5 earlier). Contagion represents the extent of externalities or spillovers between such markets, and in principle can estimate the likely systemic impact of a disturbance emerging in a single market on the system of interrelated markets as a whole. This approach involves operationalizing the covariance between 'values at risk' (CoVaR) across markets and institutions (Adrian and Brunnermeier 2009). The Basel II system (the precursor to the Basel III system just mentioned) concentrated upon VaR for each single bank considered separately.

What these points raise is the appropriate regulatory response to financial crises. Here, two general strands of analysis can be discerned. The first represents the conventional wisdom and is concerned to regulate out possible crises – or that is its implicit objective. It provides a one-size-fits-all, top-down approach, conceived to be organized at the global level and implemented from a single 'calculating centre', such as the BIS (Basel II and III) or the G-20. Harmonization and bench-marking are the key mechanisms, emphasizing the same best-practice adoption by all. Diversity is to be eliminated as far as possible, or ruled out as the basis for a regulatory response. But as the case of the Euro demonstrates clearly, such harmonization and the adoption of a single standard can encourage fierce contagion when things go wrong.

On the other hand, we have approaches that emphasize 'systemic ecologies of interrelatedness', often setting the financial system within a different paradigmatic universe: to view it as akin to a net-work operating in the context of an ecological system (Holling 1973; Haldane 2009; Haldane and May 2011). Systemic risks are modelled, as a result, in a 'non-rationalistic' and 'non-mechanical' operational framework involving complex adaptive feedback mechanisms display-ing non-linear reflexive network properties.

Whether this could ever be successfully or fully operationalized, or provide the necessary stabilizing regulatory outcome conditions, remains at issue. By and large it still represents a 'top-down' process driven by an all-encompassing calculative logic emanating from a single calculative centre. It rather proposes another technical fix for what is at heart a political problem of the mobilization and adaptation of 'bottom-up' distributed initiatives arising from a series of centres – the branching together of which requires continual political mobiliza-tion and attention (Jasanoff 2010).

And this is where an alternative related imagery to both of these arises, which combines elements of each approach. Clearly, it would be inappropriate to dismiss top-down efforts to initiate 'global' regu-latory responses entirely, just as it would be counterproductive to com-pletely replace these by only bottom-up ones. Rather, what is needed is something inbetween (see, for instance, University of Warwick 2010, which stresses the diversity to be seen and encouraged at the national and supranational regional levels, as well as at the global level). This would recognize the necessity of diversity being a fact of life, and learning to live with it. It would acknowledge an inevitable unease, precariousness and vulnerability associated with financial dealings (which could be rendered in respect to personal feelings or in terms of – crucially – connections). And managing precariousness and vulnerabilities raises issues of resilience: if we cannot completely do away with possible dreadful consequences, we can at least be alert to them and learn to live with them (Collier and Lakoff 2008). It is in the context of mapping the externalities and vulnerabilities, and networking their relationships, that an alternative conception of the kind of international public space that might be developed to address this problem could be conceptualized. This means developing the idea of networks further as a new kind of global public space (one that is neither necessarily market- nor state-centred – see Haldane *et al.* 2007; Haldane 2009; Kleindorfer and Wind 2009). But given will and passion – and a certain 'irrationality' that arises as a consequence of these – the presumption is that crises cannot be entirely eliminated either.[13] In terms of concrete regulatory initiatives, as well as stressing CoVaR-type modelling exercises, 'expected loss matrices' and the construction of 'living wills' would be useful in trying to prevent the sudden and chaotic deaths of institutions and to ensure some survival mechanism in the event of a crisis (Goodhart 2010).[14] Such is the task set for diligent risk preparedness.

Notes

1 In the Schmittian use this means a part of the earth that is *not* governed by any order, standards or norms, but which is purposeless, fatalistic, chaotic and, as a consequence, barbarous. The implications of this type of Schmittian analysis for a specification of how a revamped calculative regime would appear – involving the reterritorialization of financial activity (under the umbrella of his notion of the 'partisan') – is discussed at length in Chapter 8.

2 In fact, for various reasons, I am not as sympathetic to Schmitt's writings in this latter period as I am of his earlier writings on the Weimar period. This has mainly to do with the fact that in the Weimar period Schmitt was still concerned with democratic politics, even if in a very conservative style, a concern absent from his writings of the latter period. This also applies to Schmitt's *Land and Sea* (1997 [1954]), which, while important to the argument presented later in the chapter, is not explicitly discussed here. But it reappears in Chapter 8 where it supports an analytical take on the notions of artisans and partisans that are deployed there.

3 This is the site of considerable debate of course, broadly organized around the possible way that the social and the technological can be combined, as in the work of Michel Callon, for instance (Callon 1998).

4 Note the seeming 'functionality' of this point. In fact, although 'functionalism' is thought to be one of the cardinal sins of social scientific analysis, I remain relaxed about such a charge.

5 A parallel – though different – set of arguments to the ones developed here can be found in the IPS Forum on the financial crisis: see Kessler (2009).

6 This is operationalized in economic analysis as the maximization of an objective function, subject to constraints.

7 '[Y]ou may feel that I have not gone far enough in my skepticism about reason in political behaviour. Surely even the concept of bounded rationality does not capture the whole role of passion and unreason in human affairs' (Simon 1985: 301). He goes on to agree this is the case, but then steps aside from examining its implications by resituating it within the domain of reason: 'Let me take a more conservative approach, which accords well with what we know about the mechanisms that link emotions to reason' (Simon 1985: 301).

8 This section owes much to Wickham (forthcoming).

9 The two leading ways 'social contracting' is discussed in contemporary political philosophy are the schemas offered by Rawls and Habermas respectively. Both of these tackle the issue of how 'the unruly multitude' is rendered into 'the sociable people', capable of political activity. The Rawlsian version involves a single event (the original position) where, operating under the veil of ignorance, reasoned deliberation produces a liberal constitutional settlement in which the 'reasonable liberal peoples' so constituted can, if they wish, cooperate with 'decent peoples' elsewhere to develop the *Law of Nations* (Rawls 1971, 1999; Thompson 2012: Chapter 2). By contrast, the Habermassian variant is not a single event but an ongoing historical and discursive reflexive encounter between the public and private spheres: a double 'co-originating' move made by reasonable persons to inaugurate and continually sustain the law (Habermas 1997, 2001; Thompson 2012: Chapter 2). Again, however, this involves reasoned deliberation.

10 I was reminded of the nuances of Hirschman's position on reading Jeremy Adelman's magnificent biography (Adelman 2013). Hirschman has always been something of an intellectual role model. I hope this was demonstrated by the discussion of my particular intellectual project in this book in the latter part of Chapter 1.

11 It is a key to Schmitt's analyses of the irregular forces that they are 'partisans': tethered to a definite territory and ultimately dependent upon the regular forces. They are not features of the other, footloose global warriors on a jihadist mission, for instance, which were discussed in Chapter 3.

12 As Andrew Haldane rather colourfully put it: 'Basel vaccinated the naturally immune at the expense of the contagious: the celibate were inoculated, the promiscuous intoxicated', *Financial Times*, 26 November 2009.

13 But nor are they normal accidents in Perrow's terms (Perrow 1999, 2010). According to Perrow, while normal accidents happen when there is a high degree of complexity and coupling between elements in a system (see Guillén and Suarez 2010) – echoing some of the formulations here – he suggests the recent financial crisis was a result of policy mistakes and regulatory failure (on accidents more generally see Weick and Sutcliffe 2007).

14 An expected loss distribution is the expectation, with respect to any distribution, of the loss that would be incurred when following the decision recommendation if it were further assumed the predicted probabilities failed. So it would assign the (probabilistic) prediction in hindsight once the true outcome was known. A financial living will is a detailed plan that would enable banks to stipulate in advance how they would raise funds in a crisis and how their operations could be dismantled after a collapse.

7 From artisan to partisan
What would it mean to be an artisan of finance?

> Although computer-based algorithms have been utilized in US equity markets for quite a while, the expansion into other markets and the proliferation of high-speed algorithmic trading ... could lead to unintended errors cascading through the financial system.
>
> (Financial Stability Oversight Council 2013: 11 – quoted in *Financial Times*, 'In search of a fast buck', 20 February)

Introduction

This chapter outlines a particular way of assessing the financial system and its participants. This approach arises in the aftermath of the financial crisis, and has to do with the nature of financial calculation and what it may have done to our understanding of financial sociability. It develops arguments made in the previous three chapters, and links these explicitly to the issues of the deterritorialization and re-territorialization of financial activity in our so-called 'globalizing' world. What can be done to redress the imbalance that has arisen between domestic economic and financial activity, and its 'global' counterpart? Would it be possible to reterritorialize such activity and, if so, how and in what forms? These are the issues pursued in the latter part of the chapter.

And while the recent economic crisis provides the background for this assessment, in line with the overall character and aim of this book the emphasis is less on the crisis itself and more on what sort of response might be made, which brings some critical reflection to bear on alternative financial arrangements – ones directed at social and public purposes – with an eye to their democratic accountability in the longer run. Two key categories operate in the analysis: the artisan and the partisan. These two categories stand for a re-engagement with, first, an anti-technocratic conception of financial activity and the persona of those who inhabit it (artisanal activity) and, second, an attempt to reterritorialize financial activity so as to reassert better control over it (to make it partisanal). Quite what these categories mean and the form they might take in a revitalized financial system is the subject of the earlier parts of the chapter. Later we turn to how some of this might be operationalized in several concrete settings.

The particular context for this discussion is the huge surge in high-speed – and ultra high-speed – trading in financial markets (Financial Stability Oversight Council 2013). In 2012 it was estimated that High-Frequency Trading (HFT) was responsible for almost 60 per cent of all US equity trades, 55 per cent of global futures trading, 40 per cent of global Forex trading and 20 per cent of global fixed-income bond trading. Although there had been a slight decline in the percentage accounted for in equity trading (as volatility in this market declined after 2009), the surge was in the other three areas of financial activity, as traders switched from less profitable markets (equity) to more profitable ones (futures, foreign exchanges and bonds). HFT involves the automated use of sophisticated computer programmes (algorithms) to take advantage of minuscule price discrepancies, executed in fractions of a second (Arnoldi 2012; MacKenzie *et al.* 2012). Although we have known about the use of new technologies in financial trading environments for some time (Ho 2009; Riles 2011; Zaloom 2012) – which itself has some disquieting consequences; anonymous transactions have displaced relationship-based finance in all spheres (Huault and Ranielli-Weiss 2013) – the development of HFT and UHFT represents another ratcheting up of the technological frontier.[1] It takes the trading environment into another realm of extreme technicality and represents a further move away from considered judgement towards a blind acceptance of what the algorithms determine (Bhidé 2010). As the epigraph to this chapter demonstrates, this can have further downside consequences in terms of unintended systemic risks, and it poses yet more challenges to already harassed regulators (Haldane 2011).[2]

In this world there are two basic forms of high-speed algorithmic trading: 'automated' and 'speculative' (Gomber *et al.* 2011; Viliante and Lannoo 2011). It is claimed that automated trading serves some social purpose, as it allows asset managers like pensions funds to 'rebalance' their portfolios quickly and efficiently. On the other hand, 'speculative' trading serves no particular social purpose: it is mainly undertaken by hedge funds and proprietary traders who make short-term trades in the various markets mentioned above in their search for yield on behalf of wealthy investors and banks. And inasmuch as traditional asset management bodies are increasingly employing the services of organizations such as hedge funds in an attempt to boost their own returns, these are also becoming complicit in the systemically riskier 'speculative' form of HFT. Thus the rapid development of HFT and UHFT is threatening to become ubiquitous, and the distinction between automated and speculative activity is breaking down. As will be discussed below, this bodes ill for the future of a socially functional financial system, something the ideas of the artisan and partisan are designed to confront.

The chapter proceeds as follows. The next section outlines the key notion of artisanal activity. This is followed by a section dealing with the intellectual resources that are marshalled to develop the general argument: namely cognitive capacities, financial sociability, the nature of decision-taking and the figure of the partisan. The implications of these analyses are then assessed, before the chapter moves on to clarify the organizational consequences of an artisanal type of financial structure. This is followed by a section dealing with three illustrative examples, before a final concluding section.

What is an artisan?

This section preliminarily outlines the characteristics of the artisan as a figure and a persona. It responds to the question 'what is an artisan?' We can approach this by a roundabout route by first outlining what Marx had to say about the artisan in the *Communist Manifesto* (written with Engels, first published in 1850):

> Of all the classes that stand face to face with the bourgeoisie today, the proletariat alone is the revolutionary class ... The lower middle classes, the small manufacturer, the shopkeeper, *the artisan*, the peasant, all fight against the bourgeoisie, to save from extinction their existence, as fractions of the middle class. They are therefore not revolutionary, but conservative. Nay more, they are reactionary, for they try to roll back the wheel of history.
>
> (Marx and Engels 1970: 44, my emphasis)

And:

> Hard-won, self-acquired, self-earned property! Do you mean the property of *petty artisan* and of the small peasant, a form of property that preceded the bourgeois form? There is no need to abolish that; the development of industry has to a great extent already destroyed it, and is still destroying it daily.
>
> (Marx and Engels 1970: 47, my emphasis)

This characteristic sentiment also pervades the analysis in *Capital, Volume I* (Marx 1867), where the artisan gets similar short shrift: see in particular Chapter 32 ('Historical tendency of capitalist accumulation'). And while the artisan is not an explicit object of analysis in *Capital*, its presence shadows that analysis: the artisan is one of those pre-capitalist characters that stands in the way of the full development of capitalism, and therefore of the proletariat. For Marx and Engels, as a result the artisan is necessarily politically conservative or 'reactionary'.

In fact there are several different personas that the artisan takes in Marxist scholarship that show a little more complexity and nuance as to the artisan's economic position (rather than its political one), which tend to work through job descriptions and occupancy categories.

First, there is the classic 'petty bourgeoisie' formulation just alluded to. The artisan is a craftsman (and it usually was a man) who owns his own means of production, living off his own labour but also that of the other workers he employs in the workshop: journeymen, his apprentices, and so on.[3]

Then there is the notion of the artisan as a component of the labour aristocracy: a category of privileged skilled workers who encourage the formation of bureaucratic and conservative trade unions, something that Lenin was particularly exercised about.[4]

Finally, there is the continuation of the skill component of labour within the modern factory system. In these conditions the skilled worker is able to maintain some of his independence and 'control' over the means of labour. This skilled factory worker struggles against the full rigours of the division of labour and mass production. It exercises some degree of collective autonomy. And it *resists the complete automation* of production.

It is this latter formulation that is developed in a moment. But I want to insist on a much more sympathetic relationship to the artisan than displayed by Marx, Engels or Lenin. As argued later, the persona of the artisan is an attractive one for various reasons. The emphasis on skill in labour is an intellectually rich attribute.[5] But as we will see, there are other good reasons for defending the notion of the artisan as well.

In the Western tradition artisanal craft production carries with it some rather attractive *ethical qualities*: skill, integrity, dignity, honesty, self-reliance and also a certain fortitude. What is important about the emphasis on skill in connection to craft production, however, is that it does not just involve codified and cognitive knowledge but also *tacit* knowledge and a necessary inventiveness in respect to its operationalization. You cannot just go to a handbook, template or manual to read off the method of doing things; you have to have a certain sensitivity to manipulate and mould the materials under construction, which almost comes from an intuition. It involves an intuitive knowledge as well as a cognitive one. Of course, this comes after a long apprenticeship – the artisanal craft producer goes through a thorough training in the shadow of the master craftsman. But this apprenticeship is not just there to develop reproducible productive skills, it is also there to train the attitude of the apprentice, to instil all those informal characteristics mentioned above associated with the 'moral training' of the artisan.

And this element of the informality associated with tacit skill means that there is *no set model* of how to do things or what to exactly copy. Each new crafted artefact is therefore 'unique' at some level: there is a necessary variation built into it, even though reproductions can be continually made. *Diversity and difference* are embodied in each additional, though similar, product.

On the other hand, artisanship also presents the possibility of expressiveness. It connects to a certain wilfulness, playfulness and excessiveness, even though it also – and at the same time – embodies modesty and restraint. It engenders a *hesitation* at each new encounter with the material on which the craftsman works. This 'now exactly what am I going to do and how am I going to do it?' moment in artisanal life means that each such act requires a *decision*: artisanal production is decisionist in character. It is not just a slavish repetition.

Some intellectual resources

This section develops some of the intellectual equipment useful for the task of linking artisanship to the financial system, which will be the explicit subject of the following section.

The first point to make concerns the relationship between cognitive orders and the notion of intuitionism that is developed in a moment.

Forms of cognition

In a masterly account of the formation of our modern scientific culture, Stephen Gaukroger's recent volume – dealing with period 1680–1760 – explores this aspect directly, as is indicated by its title: *The Collapse of Mechanism and the Rise of Sensibility* (Gaukroger 2011 – this is the second of a planned six-volume work taking us up to the twenty-first century). This is an erudite and complex book, one for the specialist, but it contains a key argument that I would like to borrow for my own purposes. While the early sections of the book deal with natural philosophy as conceived very much in rationalistic and mechanical terms, Gaukroger argues that in the later part of the period – discussed in Part V of his volume in particular – this was displaced by a new approach to cognition that dwelt upon sense and sensibility: 'rationalism' was replaced by 'sensibilism' as the mechanism that gave access to scientific knowledge.[6] Explanatory pluralism replaced an Aristotelian explanatory unity that had methodologically linked a structural reduction of the physical to some fundamental, microscopic level of matter. Not only were matter and the physical torn apart by this move, it launched a new form of appreciation where the imaginary and the senses were as important as mechanical linkages – if not more so – for scientific understanding. And, argues Gaukroger, this liberated scientific endeavour, from a confining and limiting structural impasse, inaugurated the open and plural terrain for scientific exploration that became such a defining feature of Western culture (and, one might add, its subsequent economic and political ascendency).

What is suggested here, therefore, is that rationality and rationalism need to be complemented by the imaginary and sensibility as resources for cognitive understanding, something returned to in the next section in the context of the financial system.[7] No doubt this drama between rationalism and sensibilism has been replayed many times – indeed, it still resonates today in the contest between neoclassical economics (more mechanistic and rationalistic) and Keynesian economics (more intuitive and sensibilistic).

The nature of (financial) sociability

The second resource developed here concerns how financial sociability is understood. How is this conceived and constructed? As noted in the previous chapter, there are four aspects to this, the latter three of which are the ones that seem the most pertinent in the case of financial sociability. These four arrangements are as a consequence of a *contract*, in terms of *interrelatedness* (involving connections, combinations, communications, exchanges, transaction, interactivities, flows, chains, relationality and entanglements), as the consequence of *habit or repetition*, and finally as a consequence of *will and passion* (Chapter 5 and Chapter 6). These conceptual aspects have an immediate impact on how (financial) subjectivities are thought to be constructed and their consequences for shaping the (financial) world. It is important to note, however, that these four aspects can significantly overlap: they are not separate approaches but complementary ones.

While the first three conceptual positions – contracting, inter-relatedness and habit and repetition – remain the most robust theoretical approaches to thinking about how 'the social' is made and remade, the fourth one is rather neglected. This has to do with the social being inaugurated and continually reinforced or reforged as a consequence of *will and passion*.[8] The liberal sentiment has always remained suspicious and hesitant about this, which explains its relative neglect. But will and passion – along with chance, fortune and determination – speak to a particular conception of that which is involved with sociality. This combination is less associated with rational agreement – which very much typifies the social contracting approach, with its emphasis on the role of reasoning and rationality in decision-making, and which in turn links to the way that rational financial calculability secures sociality (Zaloom 2003) – but more with irrationality, excessive exuberance, blind enthusiasm, momentary feverish drives, etc. It involves the dissipation of a certain psychic energy and the destructiveness or ostentatious display of wealth for its own sake. In respect to the financial system it connects most closely with the ideas of excessive exuberances, cascading, herding and the like. Indeed, it could be argued that it provides an underlying explanatory figuration for these attitudes and features.[9]

One of the reasons this position is rather neglected, and one difficult to fully recognize and embrace, is it seems to imply a fatalistic resignation: there is nothing that can be done to prevent the eruption of these emotions, since they are written into our psyche or the existential nature of social existence. As argued in previous chapters, this is not necessarily the case – and ways of answering its accusations were presented there.

However, this is the site for a very important theoretical clarification. There is a temptation to think of rationality and passion/will as polar opposites: that reason and emotion occupy quite different conceptual and operational spaces. In cultural studies the latter – the emotional terrain of feelings – is often summed up under the notion of affect, and there has been a 'turn to affect' in cultural studies more generally (e.g. Connolly 2002; Thrift 2004). Several matters are involved here, which it will be useful to untangle and clarify from the point of view of this chapter.[10]

The first involves the notion of emotion/affect itself and whether this is as distinct from rationality as is often claimed. In part this depends upon exactly what rationality is taken to be. For the purposes here I take a fairly loose definition, as in the notion of the 'arts of reasoning'. And this might be alternatively described as *thinking*.

people make decisions on the basis of thinking about them rather than just as a consequence of a momentary emotional impulse. Temporarily substituting 'thinking' for 'reason' is a tactical move to distinguish this conception of reasoning from 'rationality', understood in the traditional sense of an instrumental means to an end, considered via an intention and after attending to individual preferences. It is closer to the idea of different 'modes of rationalization': characterizations of why things were done the way they were (Lentzos and Rose 2009: 236). So, from this point of view, passions or emotions and reasons are more closely related than commonly considered: passions and emotions can be considered within terms of reasons and are not necessarily pitched against them (Árdal 1966; Frank 1988; Elster 1999).

The second clarification is to do with the relationship between the passions and (self-)interests. Interests are linked to rationality, as they are thought to be a consequence of rational thinking conceived in the traditional manner just described. But we can be more nuanced about 'interests' in the same way we were about 'rationality'. Self-interests, for instance, are not necessarily selfish and individualistic, determining behaviours that are indifferent to the common good and necessarily self-serving. For instance Hirschman (1977) and Holmes (1995) point to how the notion of interests was vital for limiting and controlling the passions in the early stages of capitalist development (see also Myers 1983).[11] Here the self-interests of the emergent commercial class served to establish a relative social peace from which all benefited. It helped to suppress the warring passions of religious strife and its associated murderous impulse.

Thus passions and emotions are not necessarily at odds with reason or rationality. However, under certain conditions (panics, extreme pressure and bewilderment), passions and emotions can overwhelm rationality and even reason. Given the notion of the way passion and will enter into the construction of financial sociability, the next step is to link it to features of the artisan. It speaks to the non-rationalistic character of artisanal activity, to the way intuition and sensibility are a necessary feature of craft practice, and the way a modest deployment of will and passion enter into craft production. We return to this in a moment.

Decisions, decisions, decisions …

As mentioned above the artisan is a quintessential decision-taker. So let us look at decisionism more closely.

It is well known that Carl Schmitt was a consummate theorist of the decision. Actually, Schmitt is perhaps better known for his theory of the exception and sovereignty, but it is his decisionism that is emphasized here. And this is tied up – in quite complicated ways – with his notions of space and territory. Schmitt works within the context of the *nomos* and the Other (Schmitt 2003). He was concerned about the impossibility of making decisions if the conditions of the Other prevailed – the permanent exception. This relates to the way *calculation* operates in the financial system. Calculation – as decision-making – is undermined in the realm of the Other; it ceases to exist. Automatic, computer driven 'decision-making' – as in the case of high-frequency momentum or index trading in the financial system, for instance – actually implies non-decision-making in this Schmittian sense. It inhibits the operation of an active decisionist framework. It confirms a realm of technological neutrality where decisions are no longer made (the repetition of automatic trading and the habits of the financial analysts). Only the *nomos* confines and limits the conditions for a decision (it is thereby equivalent to the domain of sovereignty). This domain of sovereignty – the exceptionality of the exception – makes decisions responsible ones, and justifiable ones, rendering them visible, so their consequences can be assessed and a liability established. Handing decisions over to a quasi-automatic mechanism driven by a technological fix is a recipe for disaster, since it prevents the operation of genuine decision-making. It replaces the technique involved in the art of decision-making with a technology. The artisan is replaced by the computer. Automaticity is substituted for a considered choice.[12]

The partisan and the nomad

The *nomos* is characterized as an undulated space: it is striated, full of ripples, folds, holes and mines. The space of the Other, by contrast, is flat and featureless, just like the sea and the sky (Schmitt 1997). Schmitt feels much more comfortable with the conditions of the *nomos* as a result.[13] It is where decisions can be made – indeed have to be made to negotiate its undulations and hazards. But what about the figure of the artisan? It does not appear in Schmitt's writings, as far as I can judge. But what does figure there is perhaps a related category – the partisan (Schmitt 2007). The partisan is part (p-artisan) of the irregular forces in any conflict – analogous to the irregular agents in the financial system (such as hedge funds, private equity, exotic financial instruments, etc.) that it is suggested are always threatening to escape official recognition or regulation by the authorities. This relates to the way 'private governance' is invading the international financial sphere, since this represents another potential threat by irregular forces (Thompson 2012 – see also Erturk *et al.* 2010). But, for Schmitt, the partisan is always tethered to a definite territory, despite its relatively freewheeling existence.

The partisan is not a disembedded, detached warrior or terrorist (Chapter 5),[14] but something beholden to the regular forces (of the territory).[15] Thus Schmitt would want to throw an authoritative sovereign's net or shadow over the irregular institutions, instruments and events of the financial system: to turn them into 'partisans' (if not artisans). There is a lesson to be learned here, of course, which is pursued in later sections. But it is worth noting at this stage that the partisans also have to make decisions (rather like their conceptual cousins the artisans) precisely because they are irregular, with a certain autonomy of operation, having to think in each new situation, and with no set routine or plan.

The desert, nomads and artisans

Much of this relates to another set of connections it is useful to strike in this context, which arises from a reading of Deleuze and Guattari's *A Thousand Plateaus* (2004). Among many other things, Deleuze and Guattari are interested in the idea/figure/persona of the nomad and of nomadology (see also Deleuze and Guattari 1986), and this is linked but differentiated by them from the artisan, which they also discuss at some length (see Chapters 12 and 14 in particular for the sources of these remarks; Moore 2012; Moore and Bottomley forthcoming).

Deleuze and Guattari invoke the artisan in a similar manner as described above: 'the artisan [is] one who is determined in such a way as to follow a flow of matter ... The artisan is the itinerant, the ambulant' (2004: 452). Thus, while the artisan seems mobile, it is the nomad who truly represents the freedom of the decision – but thereby somehow escapes the decision. Actually, this is ambiguous in Deleuze and Guattari because the nomad is a true figure of the desert (or for Schmitt, perhaps of the sea or sky?), and the desert is smooth, flat and featureless – or is it? What about dunes and ripples in the sand, and rocks and stones? Thus the desert cannot quite adequately represent the space of the Other. And it is important for the argument here at least that the state itself does not become nomadic – though this is precisely what contemporary globalization enthusiasts suggest: that the state has lost its analytical purchase as a stable tethered entity.

In fact, Deleuze and Guattari want to present the sovereign and the nomad as two poles between which the artisan slips, to both confirm sovereignty and otherness/exceptionality as well as to confront both of these as stable categories. Again, they seem to appreciate the figure of the artisan because it both underpins these established categories, as well as disrupting them. And the artisan occupies a different kind of space – a holey space. Such a holey space is full of potholes, hazards and disruptions that demand a hesitation to negotiate. In taking up such a space, the artisan is able to enter into relations with both nomads and the sovereign, while remaining independent of both.[16]

So decisions are only ever possible in holey space, because the artisan must constantly decide which variations to follow, as well as knowing when to suspend technique so that something unforeseen or unanticipated might emerge. The artisan understands what is at stake in taking such decisions, inasmuch as the consequences of a decision cannot be avoided – there is no way to exclude some consequences as undesirable and unintended, while claiming others on the opposite basis.

Implications and consequences

The previous sections elaborated the intellectual resources that provide access to thinking about the artisan of finance. But why might such a figure be an attractive one from the point of view of an analysis of the new financial persona? It is around the features that such a persona would bring into the frame that an answer could be given.

First, there is the idea of a 'long apprenticeship', or training associated with artisanal activity, and the ethical context that this brings to the final day-to-day activity of the work situation. It would be useful to think that this could be – indeed, should be – part of the process of formation of a new kind of financial analyst or worker.

Second, the artisan of finance must make decisions. It is not sufficient to rely on automatic, computer-driven (non-)decision-making (repetition), which so easily allows – 'encourages' even – herding behaviours, following the market, doing what others do, graphology, momentum trading, crowding, index trading, etc., which can so easily create financial bubbles and added systemic risks. The artisan of finance embodies technique and tacit skill – and does not just rely on an automating technology or model. It engenders a 'hesitation' before each such decision, allowing for consideration and reflection.

Third, and relatedly, the artisan cannot simply rely upon financial models or algorithms to provide a guide to what should be done, as there are no adequate models for artisanal activity. This mode of financial production needs to be recast as a result, to encompass considered judgement on each occasion of a product design, granting a loan or trading decision.

Fourth, the artisanal mode of financial production must embrace all those non-rationalistic features of financial sociability discussed above. This is not to say that conceptions of rationality in decision-making should be abandoned altogether – that would clearly be silly and counterproductive. Rather, as suggested in the previous chapter, this must be considered alongside the recognition of cognitive intuitionism and sensibility, and a commitment to exploring its practical and regulatory consequences (Gaffeo and Tamborini 2011).

Fifth, the artisan of finance is not a traditional financial entrepreneur. 'Entrepreneurialism' is innovatory activity, and it is often associated with figures such as Warren Buffet and George Soros. But most financial entrepreneurialism is a form of arbitrage – the linking together of already available possibilities in new ways to make small gains possible on differences between the prices of financial products in different markets or different times. Very little of it is really new and innovative. Indeed, it would be worth systematically investigating whether there have been any new products or ways of doing things in the financial sphere that had not already been anticipated by the gambling industry. To some extent artisanal activity is like the routine rolling out of financial products that are slight variations on already existing products, which happens in the household oriented financial sector in particular (Lopes 2013). This does not involve 'trading' in financial transactions, however (Godechot 2008).

Sixth, the artisan would also be a partisan. The reterritorialization of financial activity is an imperative for a properly functioning financial system, and the notion of an artisan provides some of the intellectual resources to help in this task. A possible example of such reterritorialization in practice is discussed in the final main section.

Seventh, outlining these contours of an artisanal mode of financial production enables us to appreciate in a quite concrete sense what its ethical qualities might entail. It provides a vivid but practical set of ethically grounded 'values' that are not abstractly attached to, or floated into, the realm of production, but which would arise there 'spontaneously' from the day-to-day practical activity of such craft-like operations.

Finally, is this invocation just a nostalgic desire for the recreation of an artisanal economy of craft-like production, but now reinvented for the financial sphere? Does it succumb to the critique by Marx and Engels of trying to 'roll back the wheel of history'? Without being able to do this justice right now, it is rather to the contrary; artisanal activity is necessarily forward-looking. In its hesitations, its inherent decisionism, its relationship to the imaginary (Beckert 2011), its break with the tyranny of models, artisanal activity promises to provide a way forward for a more stable, productive and efficient financial system.

What would be the operational characteristics of such a system?

This section discusses a series of organizational and operational features that would inform the kind of artisanal/partisanal financial structure being argued for here. Obviously, we are not going to jettison the use of computer technologies in the financial system altogether, or even elaborate algorithmic trading in various contexts. There would be a place for these in any artisanal/partisanal system, but one where their characteristics were embedded in a different organizational and operational context. The persona of the artisan/partisan discussed above provides the image of an organizational arrangement where its characteristics act as a metaphor for an alternative set of techniques and practices oriented towards locally based, socially useful, financial functions. The next section elaborates several indicative actual developments in the realm of finance that embody many of the features outlined here (and earlier). Of course, the existence of huge financial institutions with enormous power and influence – and which have a clear vested interest in 'more of the same' in terms of financial products and activity – represents a formidable obstacle to any of these developments. But this is addressed more fully in the next section.

Perhaps one of the most important clarificatory reorientations to be considered in the field of artisnal/partisnal finance is to restress the importance of organizational matters in an attempt to overcome a commitment among organizational theorists and practitioners, innovation scholars and knowledge experts, and the like, to celebrate what I would term a 'discombobulated firm' formulation. This is the idea that the firm is best considered as a dislocated agglomeration of relative independent features and functions, little more than a 'nexus of contracts' (Jensen and Meckling 1976; Aoki *et al.* 1990), or a Mobius-strip organization with no clear inside or outside (Sabel 1991), or an arena for dissonance and differentiation (Stark 2009: Chapter 2; Beunza and Stark 2012[17]), a loosely configured non-hierarchical quasi-structure of fragmented elements and weak connections, etc. And what is more, this idea has taken such a hold of the popular and scholarly imagination that these features are viewed as the necessary characteristics for any firm to be 'fleet of foot', to be entrepreneurial and innovative, to become a 'learning organization', etc. This attempted dissipation of the entity that is the firm takes many forms, but it has the effect of undermining and destroying any clear idea of ordered structure and organizational control:[18] too much autonomy is given to particular agents to make too many isolated decisions (as in the case of financial traders, for instance): the organization – *qua* its character as an organization – is hollowed out from within, so it loses its capacities to make sensible decisions, the consequences of which could be calculated for and assessed (du Gay and Vikkelso 2013). In fact, of course, it is just such an ordered internal system operating within companies that fosters genuine innovation, skills and real learning. Those organizations without a seemingly bureaucratic mentality of this kind, where employees do not know exactly where they are placed, what their precise responsibilities are, what they have to do, etc., are the ones who are not innovative and that fail to learn. Confidence for people to act – and to act sometimes beyond their normal mandate – is a consequence of a well-ordered and clear structure, not the inhibiter of this (Stinchcome 2001). And this relates directly to much financial dealing. Financial managers often complain bitterly that they have (or had) no idea what exactly goes on 'at the business end' of their company's activities: on the trading floors and in offices where financial deals and transactions are actually conducted. Either this is too complex or too rapid or too opaque for managers to appreciate. They complain they have 'lost control' over much of this business activity as a consequence, so that the overall exposure and risk positions of the companies are unclear. A technology introduced in part to enable managers to track this and keep them informed in real time has had the exact opposite effect. It has disabled managerial control.

So one should be rather sceptical of the discombobulated company formulation, and indeed work against its sentiment. Coherent organizational structure, an attention to resource constraints, clear boundary demarcations and so on – i.e. proper bureaucracy – needs to be re-emphasized. There should be more cognizance and less dissonance, more simplicity less complexity, more organization less differentiation.

A second fairly obvious set of comments relates more to what is actually done in the financial sphere, rather than its organizational forms. To try to reduce the 'nervous excitement' that often captures the trading floor environment, there needs to be less trading of risk or volatility and more trading in underlying instruments. So this means turning attention to the primary market and away from secondary market activity, away from debt instruments and towards credit instruments, less trading on 'news' and more judgement – all designed to try to keep ever-present 'feral spontaneity' in check.

The consequential issue becomes how to learn the techniques of handling money in an artisanal fashion. This is to master the artistry of money: managing and manipulating money, private credit and government debt in a way that forsakes technologies that leave the operators (a)part from the market, to ensure they become part of the market. And it obviously implicates the trading of money, financial instruments and their derivatives: so this is not an argument to entirely turn back financial operations to an era of, say, pit trading – though that obviously had the attraction of direct contact between market traders. But those days are gone. So how can some semblance of financial artistry be reconfigured in today's technologically sophisticated environment? In the next section several tentative suggestions are made that take up already fairly well-established examples, but designed to inflect them in a way that illustrates some of the more general points made in this and the previous sections. Thus, here we examine organizational and institutional illustrations of how an artisanal/patisanal financial configuration might look, ones derived from already small-scale examples that have managed to emerge and flourish within the existing hyper-frenetic financial system.

Illustrations and applications

Electronic money transfer in East Africa

Figure 7.1 shows the remarkably rapid growth of mobile phone usage in (developing) Sub-Saharan Africa over the 2000s. It is estimated that in 2012 half the population then had access to a mobile phone.

Among other things, this has transformed the way banking activities are conducted in many parts of East Africa in particular, which is what is concentrated upon here. Mobile banking is now commonplace in Kenya, mainly because of initiatives undertaken by the mobile telephone service provider Safaricom (Hughes and Lonie 2007; Ruddick 2011).[19]

In 2007 Safaricom launched its nationwide mobile banking service M-PESA (M for mobile, 'pesa' is Swahili for money), which allows

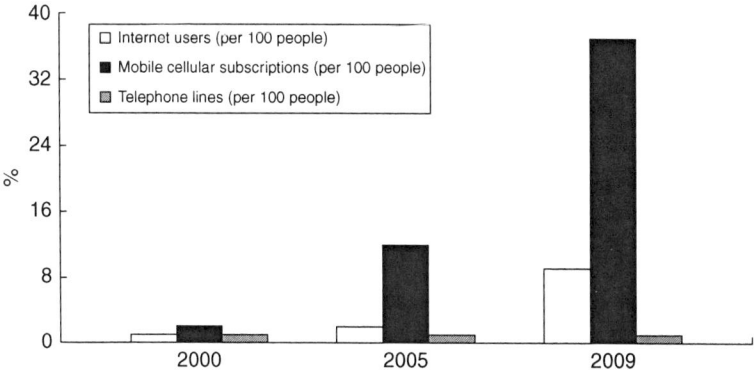

Figure 7.1. Telephonic infrastructure growth rates in Sub-Saharan Africa (2000–9)

Source: The World Bank, World DataBank: World Development Indicators (WDI) and Global Development Finance (GDF). Available at http://www.databank.worldbank.org (accessed 30 April 2012).

Kenyans to transfer money via SMS (http://www.safaricom.co.ke/ index.php?id=250, accessed 11 May 2012). This service does not require users to have bank accounts, which is a very important aspect in a country such as Kenya where many people remain unbanked. With M-PESA, the user can buy digital funds at any M-PESA agent and send that electronic cash to any other mobile phone user in Kenya, who can then redeem it for conventional cash with another agent. An M-PESA-enabled mobile phone can also function as an electronic wallet and can hold up to 100,000 Kenyan shillings on deposit there. And because the system is so safe – it is password protected so that if the phone is lost or stolen the funds are immobilized, and SIM cards can be easily replaced – this has also become a mechanism for conducting cross-border transactions within the region (and beyond). The system is not a debt-producing instrument, so it does not encourage borrowing – such a ubiquitous feature of other systems. It relies on providing temporary credits only: it remains very much a P2P transmission mechanism.

In effect, M-PESA is a development tool in the context of Kenya. It has over 13 million customers. The service has expanded into many online banking functions, enabling customers to access their bank accounts, transfer money between accounts, buy tickets, pay bills (including school fees), buy airtime, pay for taxi rides, etc. Similar services have now been rolled out by Vodafone affiliates in Tanzania,

South Africa and Afghanistan, and there are plans for further expansion into India and Egypt (http://www.en.wikipedia.org/wiki/M-Pesa; 'M-Pesa: Kenya's mobile wallet revolution', 22 November 2010, at http://www.bbc.co.uk/news/business-1179329; both accessed 28 April 2012). Why is this scheme being presented here? Several connections to artisanal organizational forms and activity can be made. It involves a cutting-edge technology but one directed at a real social purpose. A system of this type was unlikely to evolve in an advanced economy with an already sophisticated financial system, a dense network of branch banks and an extensively banked public. In the context of Kenya and East Africa M-PESA provided a simple, easy-to-use and relatively cheap alternative. This is also an option that puts the initiative squarely into the hands of the users. Of itself, it does not encourage the taking on of debt, something that typifies such schemes in already developed countries. It is fundamentally artisanal in character.

Public banking in North Dakota

North Dakota is home to one of the most successful publicly owned financial institutions in North America. Indeed, The Bank of North Dakota (BND) is the largest publicly owned bank in the USA – it is owned by the state – in terms of capitalization. North Dakota is a small, highly conservative state – it has a population of about 680,000 and has been mainly (though not exclusively) under Republican Party administration since the state was founded in 1889. So what is a publicly owned bank doing is such a seemingly hostile political environment?

The BND was incorporated in 1919. Its main deposit base is the state tax receipts – which are required by law to be deposited in the bank – and it manages the other state institutions' funds (it also takes some private deposits). Contrary to most US banks, it is not a member of the Federal Deposit Insurance Corporation (FDIC – though it has an account at the Federal Reserve), and it has had only limited dealings with Washington or Wall Street (its deposits are guaranteed by the state itself). In general it is prohibited from making loans to borrowers whose residence or place of business is outside of the state.

The bank was originally set up to encourage the farming industry: extending credit to agricultural businesses and supporting mortgage loans for the purchase of ranches. Its other main traditional business activity is in extending loans to students to finance their higher education.[20] During the 'long moderation' it did not get involved in the home loan mortgage business, and it avoided engagement with 'securitization' and all the exotic secondary financial instruments that were such a feature of the financial sector more widely. As a result, the bank emerged relatively unscathed from the financial crisis and has continued to make a (modest) surplus, which is transferred to the state and augments the state's own tax revenues.

There would be a lot to say about this bank, its history and its governance structure (Schneiberg 2013), but for our purposes it represents an example of what a modest, locally oriented bank might do. Of course, there are many examples of this kind of local secondary banking in Europe: often those operating in Spain (*cajas*) or at the regionalized state level in Germany (*Landesbanken*) are cited; these were originally set up with purposes similar to the BND. But what happened to many of these banks was that they became closely involved with all the general bad practices originally associated with secondary banking; they were infected by the mania for securitization, intrabank and sovereign debt lending, accepting suspect deposits, speculative mortgaging, etc., as their practices were 'liberalized' over the 1990s. Thus there is no guarantee that state-led local banking would necessarily deliver a better performance in terms of social purposes. This utterly depends on the manner of the bank's legal governance and the internal culture of the organization. It is precisely because the BND was so 'conservative' in terms of its practices and lending criteria, and its transparency, that it has survived and prospered in what might otherwise be considered a very unfavourable political environment. The BND is an example of artisanal – and partisanal – banking in action.

Local currencies in operation

In mid-September 2012 the 'Bristol Pound' was launched (http://www.bristolpound.org/index.php?com=pages&page=16, accessed 2 March 2013). This is the latest example of a slow and quietly growing movement to try to stimulate local economic activity by developing local currencies (Ryan-Collins 2011; Martignoni 2012; Naqvi and Southgate 2013).

Like other local currencies the Bristol Pound (BP) is to be offered at a one-to-one exchange rate with sterling, so there is no obvious purely economic incentive for its use. Its use relies on an 'ethical nudge': a shared concern with the fate of the local business community and the value afforded locally based economic activity. It will tie up a Community Interest Company (CIC) – which issues the currency

Table 7.1 Currencies in circulation (UK, 2013)

Paper instrument	Value in circulation	Population of area
BoE notes	£54.2 billion	63.7 million
S&NI notes	£6 billion	7.1 million
Bristol pound	£250,000	1 million
Brixton pound	£100,000	300,000
Lewes pound	£20,000	17,000
Totnes pound	£8,000	15,000
Stroud pound	£7,000	13,000

Source: Naqvi and Southgate 2013: Table A, p. 322.

Note: BoE = Bank of England; S&NI = Scotland and Northern Ireland.

and supervises the scheme – with the Bristol Credit Union, and crucially the local authority, which will accept the BP from businesses as payment for their local rates.[21] This removes a major obstacle to other local currency schemes that have lacked a mechanism via which local businesses can use any accumulated surpluses of the currency. This scheme was expected to begin with about 300 signed-up traders. Payments can be made in cash or by mobile phone or online over the Internet, so this scheme overcomes other obstacles to its use in that it embraces electronic payments, like the Kenyan example discussed above. Participants have to open an account with the credit union – a body licensed by the Financial Services Authority, which provides confidence in the process and affords the same protection as it does to ordinary bank accounts.[22] The city of Bristol is the eighth most populous city in the UK (nearly 450,000), and with the surrounding regional zone – also included in the currency scheme – this more than doubles to over a million. Table 7.1 shows the other UK local currency areas in existence (along with nationally circulating currencies), and by comparison the Bristol scheme is a real qualitative step up from these. By late 2013 there were already approximately 250,000 BPs in circulation (Naqvi and Southgate 2013). Of course, these schemes are paralleled in other countries. Figure 7.2 shows the extent of them in different parts of the world.

A number of analyses view ACs as offering a response to globalization and the debacle of the financial crisis (Pacione 2011; Parádi-Dolgos *et al.* 2011). There may be something in this, so we pursue it further here. As many authors have observed (e.g. Engelen *et al.* 2011), the possibility of there being serious financial reform originating at central governmental level in the UK is more or less an impossible dream. The central authorities neither have the political will nor the technical expertise to launch a thorough ongoing strategy of financial reform designed to meet a social purpose and one geared to local regeneration. If this is going to happen at all it will have to originate from initiatives at the local level. Thus it is understandable why local authorities are beginning to think seriously about anything that might have an impact on their plight. This is where ACs enter the picture. But there are objections to ACs. Here we mention just two of the most serious.

The first of these concerns welfare externalities.

> Local currencies do not affect welfare (as one may have expected *a priori*) by undermining fiat currency, but because they impose externalities on other regions (i.e., by lowering demand there). Their emergence may thus be detrimental for the overall economy. For example, suppose that there are two regions in a country which both (independently) introduce their own alternative currency pegged to the legal tender money at a fixed exchange rate. Aggregate demand in this case should be unaffected because the effects in each region cancel out. Still the economy overall faces additional costs as there will be some deadweight losses from using the alternative currency.
>
> (Pfajfar *et al.* 2011: 5)

However, this objection could be overcome if there are positive multiplier effects in either or both local regions. And this is a key to the underlying strategy for ACs. The New Economics Foundation (NEF) has developed a tool that calculates the potential multiplier effects arising from local currencies (NEF 2002). Local currencies are mainly directed at small independent businesses. It has been found that only 10–12 pence of every pound spent at big retailers, for instance, stays in the local area; the rest 'leaks' elsewhere. For local authorities, desperate to find some way of stimulating their local economies, keeping a higher proportion of this expenditure within the local area, so that it circulates among local businesses and shoppers, is an attractive proposition. Clearly, this requires a critical mass of active participants for it to develop. The Bristol experiment, if it is monitored correctly (though this is very difficult to do), could show whether there is in fact a 'local multiplier' of this character. But a reasonable criticism of ACs is that they could form a kind of 'local mercantilism'.

A second objection to ACs is that they represent a form of the privatization of money: they could be the unwitting forerunners of a (neo)liberal project for the progressive dismantling of state money and its replacement by 'competing (private) monies' (Hayek 1976).

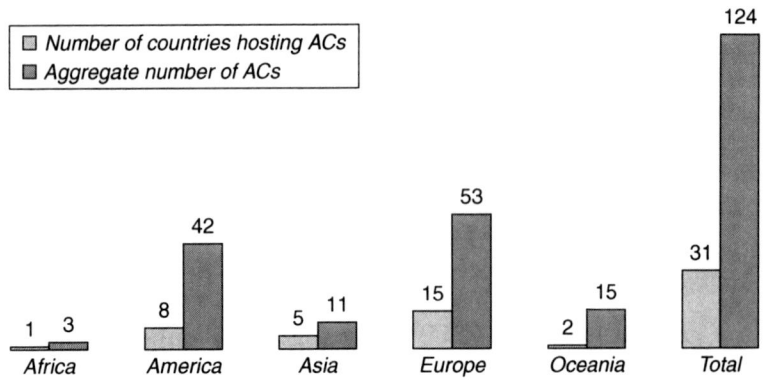

Figure 7.2. The distribution of alternative currencies (ACs) across the world
Source: Pfajfar *et al.* 2011: Figure 1, p.22.
Notes:
a This shows the regional breakdown for the number of countries hosting ACs as well as the aggregate number of ACs.
b The total number of countries per region in the data sets are – Africa: 11, America: 15, Asia: 15, Europe: 33, Oceania (Australia and New Zealand): 2.

Of course, as it stands, this is not a feature of the AC experiments discussed above, since these still rely on a one-to-one exchange rate with state money. However, in the wider AC movement there is an element of this as an implicit consequence of the introduction of local currencies, even an explicit objective in some cases. But to do justice and provide a response to this issue would require a longer argument and will be the subject of a subsequent analysis (see, however, footnote 8 in Chapter 4 above).

Conclusions

In the face of the debacle that was the financial crisis of 2007–8 and its continuing aftermath, radical responses are necessary. As it stands, most of these have been pitched at the aggregate level and involve proposals for state-led or globally coordinated regulatory reform. Few of these really address the fundamental questions of the kind of financial system that might replace the existing one, the kinds of operatives that would man such a system, and the organizational forms conducive to a social or public purpose being at the forefront of financial activity. In a tentative manner, this has been the objective addressed in the present chapter.

The organizational principles suggested to frame such a task are the ideas of the artisan and the partisan. It is artisanal activity that is the key here: a category that stands for a re-engagement with an anti-technocratic conception of financial activity and the persona of those who would work such a system. This is supported by an attempt to reterritorialize financial activity so as to reassert better control over it – to make it partisanal as well as artisanal.

Later on in the chapter, suggestive illustrative examples of what this might involve were examined. These represent existing financial activity that meets some of the characteristics of an artisanal type of financial system. The key to developing this would be to link these three areas up in some manner – a widespread money transfer mechanism that put control over the credit relationship firmly in the hands of the users, a well-financed publicly owned bank that took its responsibilities towards local business development seriously, and an alternative supplementary currency that worked to stimulate a virtuous multiplier effect on the local economy without simply diverting activity from outside its area of operation. Needless to say, the immediate possibilities of such a system being developed remain remote in the current political and economic climate.

A final point, to conclude, concerns an issue that has arisen in this and the previous three chapters, which have dealt with the 'irrationality' of various aspects of the financial system. It might be asked if – as argued earlier – humans are at least in part irrational in their judgements, whereas machines are 'logical' and take decisions away from the direct involvement of humans – that this might impart a better framework for rational decision-making overall. Machines – embodying rational modelling techniques – dispense with the messy and fatally flawed human decision-making. But this would be to misunderstand what has been argued here. The idea of irrationality – as defined in the chapters – pertains to three levels: human activity, the underlying assumptions and nature of financial modelling itself, and the organizational structure of the financial institutions and their relationships. It is all three of these levels that must be addressed if we are to think differently about financial regulation and governance, and reform its basic structure. We need more 'human decision-making' and more considered choice about this, not less.

Notes

1 Disquiet with securities trading strategies is not that new, however. It goes back to at least the early eighteenth century, when Daniel Defoe was a stern

critic (Defoe 1701). In the more modern period, Fischer Black extolled the virtues of automated trading for the operationalization of the efficient market hypothesis in the 1970s (Black 1971). And Domowitz (1993) provided an early survey and assessment of the use of computer technologies in financial trading environments.

2 See http://www.ft.com/cms/s/0/b77f05ec-a8ec-11e0-ab62–00144feabdc0. html#axzz2M2IWLbEg (accessed 23 February 2013). Of course there is huge controversy over the effects of HFT, and nothing is settled. For a report that is more ambiguous than the *Financial Times*'s byline might indicate, see 'Studies say no link between HFT and volatility', http://www.ft.com/ cms/s/0/38452490-da07–11e0-b199–00144feabdc0.html#axzz1j4CUW4r9 (accessed 23 February 2013). Longer-term assessments (Jain 2005; Hendershott *et al.* 2011) are more reassuring, but these are mainly based upon pre-crisis data and come from within the financial orthodoxy. And European regulators remain edgy. The new European Securities and Markets Authority has asked for clarification of trading strategies in a wide-ranging review, see: http://www.ft.com/cms/s/0/1126c474–5ed6–11e0-a2d7–00144feab49a.html#axzz2M2IWLbEg (accessed 23 February 2013). Meanwhile, the main industry players have formed a lobby group (under the auspices of the Futures Industry Association) to try to head off regulatory initiatives.

3 For the purposes of this chapter I run together the notion of the artisan and the craftsman. For a telling analysis of the value of the notion of craftsmanship in relation to modern sociality see Richard Sennett (2009). His analysis is pitched at the societal level, extolling the virtues of craftsmanship as a necessary means for fostering social cooperation. Sennett does not differentiate between craft and artisan; indeed he does not mention the artisan at all.

4 In part, Lenin's antagonism towards the artisan was because craft was associated with a particular form of organization: the Guild. In this chapter I am not defending this aspect of organizational artisanship, though Guild Socialism was an interesting formulation of the 1920s and '30s, and has acted as one of the precursors for the idea of 'associationalism', towards which this chapter is in part sympathetic and which could act as a modern organizational framework for thinking about the wider role of artisanship (see Hirst 1994; Smith and Teasdale 2012).

5 Particularly from the point of view of an academic: much academic activity (teaching, researching, writing) is a form of craft production, I would suggest.

6 Sensibilism refers to a body of discursive arrangements and approaches.

7 The necessary element of the imaginary to understanding the nature of sociality is stressed by Castoriadis (1987). In the context of the financial system, see Beckert (2011).

8 Will provides the link between an inner mental state and an outward action or conduct. A passion is an enthusiasm. Both of these may be exercised thoughtfully or more momentarily on a whim.

9 As should be clear, this is not exactly the same as the notion of 'animal spirits', which remains a strong feature of Keynesian and post-Keynesian analysis of the financial system (Marchionatti 1999; Dow and Dow 2011).

10 These comments are the result of engagement with the following critical literature dealing with affect: Papoulias and Callard 2010; Leys 2011a and 2011b; Connolly 2011; Altieri 2012; Frank and Wilson 2012; Leys 2012; and Rose 2012.

11 This might help illuminate Alan Greenspan's confession over the crisis that 'those of us who have looked to the self-interest of lending institutions to protect shareholders' equity (myself especially) are in a state of shocked disbelief' (quoted in Alan Clark and Jill Treanor, 'Greenspan – I was wrong about the economy. Sort of', *The Guardian*, 24 October 2008). Greenspan later retracted his self-doubt in an ABC TV News interview of April 2010, in which he reaffirmed his faith in Ayn Rand's philosophy of the free market as the embodiment of reason (available at: http://www.abcnews.go.com/ThisWeek/video/interview-alangreenspan-10281612, accessed 18 September 2014).

12 This is the site of considerable debate of course, broadly organized around the possible way that the social and the technological can be combined, as in the work of Michel Callon, for instance (Callon 1998). Indeed, continuing in this tradition, Latour and Lépinay (2009) – taking their cue from Gabriel Tarde's 'economic anthropology' – insist that economic calculation is only made possible by the passions, so that passionate interests are the handmaiden of economic calculation: there is no separation of the rational from the passionate (or what I have been calling above the 'irrational'). Clearly this relates to the earlier discussion about the differences/similarities between rationality and emotions. In part this may be a terminological difference, but it also expresses a conceptual one, the contours of which were outlined above. The position in this chapter is not Tardeian, since I am for keeping these two domains conceptually and operationally distinct, though at the same time recognizing that they can be closely interlinked.

13 'Appropriation' for Schmitt is always something that takes place in respect to the land and territory – seizing it and dividing it. Thus the sea and the sky presented problems for him, which he never fully resolved.

14 Nor strictly speaking a guerrilla, who is potentially everywhere but disguised – hence nowhere.

15 In the words of (Schmitt 2007: 53),

> The powerful third party delivers not only weapons and munitions, money, material assistance, and medicines of every description, he offers also the sort of political recognition of which the irregularly fighting partisan is in need, in order to avoid falling like the thief and the pirate into the unpolitical – which means here the criminal sphere. In the longer view of things the irregular must legitimize itself through the regular, and for this only two possibilities stand open: recognition by an existing regular, or establishment of a new regularity by its own force. This is a tough alternative.

16 Of course, things are always more complicated with Deleuze and Guattari. Really, as stressed by Moore (2012), such an artisanal figure distributes space (between the nomad and the sovereign) rather than occupying a fixed position in another space. But then the holey space is exactly that, a sort of non-space.

17 Beunza and Stark's analysis is considerably more subtle than indicated here. They introduce the notion of reflexive modelling to deal with the social entanglements of traders, trading practices, and the technical modelling that produce algorithms and their adaptations. Nevertheless, the suggestion here is that this underplays the role of pure automatic HFT in the financial environments discussed above, which represent the leading edge of a new round of systemic riskiness associated with current developments.

18 This relates to the idea of the 'enterprise entity' and 'enterprise analysis'. The characteristics of these are discussed at length in Thompson (2012: Chapter 5). Originally posed by Berle and Means in the 1930s, the notion of a company viewed as a definite entity (if not a unity) existing in its own right has fallen into relative decline, as a more proprietary conception of the firm emerged. In part this has to do with changes in fashion in the case of organizational theory as discussed above, but also in terms of corporate law, which views the firm as a multi-layered structure with many subsidiaries and holding arrangements. In addition this is reinforced by the rise of a 'shareholder rights' discourse in the business world: financial disbursements to shareholders ('shareholder value' extraction) is given an absolute primacy over the maintenance of an ordered internal structure designed for continued organizational and operational reproduction. This is paralleled in many other areas of social analysis, e.g. in terms of the state, where this is also increasingly seen as a disarticulated and fragmented entity made up of many disparate apparatuses of governance and rule, not anymore a single centralized entity (as in post-colonial state formulations in particular – see, for instance, Hansen and Stepputat 2002); and further in terms of the nation state, which is also being increasingly considered as having been hollowed out by the forces of globalization. All these conceptions are having the effect of undermining any possibility of the effectiveness of social organizations with capacities to act as such to secure their effective reproduction.

19 Hughes and Lonie show how a remarkably tenacious small team of employees and consultants established the system against considerable technical, organizational, social and political obstacles. Safaricom is a Vodafone subsidiary. The principles behind M-PESA were extended to Eco-Pesa in 2010 (Ruddick 2011). This is a B2B framework for payments in impoverished informal settlements (slums) to aid waste collection and disposal, and other local ecologically sound community developments.

20 Gradually the bank has moved into other areas of local business support and more recently into the energy sector, which is becoming a major activity in the state as 'fracking' takes hold to release gas deposits.

21 Businesses can also redeem the BP for sterling, but at a 3 per cent discount.

22 The UK has perhaps a surprisingly rich range of corporate forms that could encourage a wider social enterprise agenda: traditional Industrial and Provident Societies, Company Limited by Guarantee, Company Limited by Shares and Community Interest Company, as in the case of the BP. As yet these company forms do not challenge the ubiquity of the traditional limited liability company, either in terms of extent or size, but they provide a mechanism by which social objectives could be pursued and charitable objectives advanced, particularly in the context of the 'Big Society' idea popularized by the Coalition Government in the UK (Smith and Teasdale 2012).

8 Creating credit and rating it
Central Banks in post-crisis global finance

Introduction

In this chapter we return more directly to the theme of modern globalization. Again, this is centred on the financial system, but this time on the role of Central Banks in the post-crisis period, and of the consequent focus on sovereign debt that their actions have served to raise. One of the most intriguing developments since the crash is the way it propelled Central Banks (CBs) to the forefront of financial innovation and policy formation. As the political authorities abandoned activist macroeconomic management and set their treasuries and finance ministries the sole task of cutting public expenditure and organizing for austerity, the CBs took up any management of the economy that was permissible, or that they could get away with. And this was aided by their semi-autonomous status, granted to them by earlier political administrations' determination to see CBs independent of direct political control, able to pursue monetary policy as they saw fit, albeit originally set within the bounds of conservative inflation targeting. This is the legacy CBs such as the US Federal Bank (US Fed), the European Central Bank (ECB) and the Bank of England (BoE) inherited as they faced the consequences of financial meltdown and monetary turmoil in the wake of the crisis (I come back to the Bank of Japan (BoJ) in a moment). But far from this inheritance completely constraining CBs it actually presented them with an opportunity: whether by design or fortunate circumstances they have seized the possibility of turning themselves into the premier activists of economic management. We now have what Bowman *et al.* (2013) have termed a 'Central Bank-led capitalism' on an unprecedented scale. If, as a consequences of prolonged austerity, we add in the likelihood of very low growth rates for many years ahead (which seems feasible, see Alpert 2013) then we may be moving into a new and unusual era for advanced capitalism – *low-growth Central Bank-led capitalism.*

This chapter describes some of these events and tries to assess their possible consequences and implications. The approach adopted here builds upon a 'political arithmetic' that is theoretically parsimonious but empirically rich, as announced in Chapter 2 (see also Engelen *et al.* 2011; Bowman *et al.* 2013). It shows how Central Bank-led capitalism connects to the rest of the financial system, and how it is being accompanied by interesting and potentially radically different ways of assessing sovereign risk. Indeed, it is the issue of sovereign risk that is posed afresh by the rise of CB activism. Sovereign risk has become a major issue as CBs' balance sheets (BSs) have exploded in the manner described in a moment, and new ways of calculating such sovereign risk have emerged in its wake.

Central Bank BSs have proved crucial in designing and pursuing economic policies in the wake of financial crises. As we will see, CBs have purchased a wide range of financial assets in order to further major macroeconomic and financial stability objectives, which has implied a comparable increase in domestic liabilities. This has led to an unprecedented global expansion of CB BSs. But BSs of the current size could create broad policy risks, beyond the increased exposure of the CBs to market developments. These risks include inflation, financial instability, distortions in financial markets and conflicts with government debt managers. Critics of the CB BS explosion suggest that as huge monetary stimuluses have accumulated it becomes increasingly difficult for the CBs to reverse their monetary easing policy and shrink their BSs from their current size back down to pre-2008 levels. But the argument here will stress that this is not such a problem as it is often made out to be, for reasons outlined later in the chapter.

Thus this chapter acts as an antidote to all those who say, first, that not much macroeconomic activism can be discerned since the financial crisis – 'we are all doomed' by the continued global stranglehold of neoliberal ideology; and second, that there has been no, or little, innovation in economic policy-making since the crisis. In actual fact we have witnessed a very innovative period, one that continues, it will be argued. Quite where all this is going, however, remains unclear. Each CB has its own particular problems to confront – there is no effective 'global policy coordination' and nor is there likely to be. As stressed in previous chapters, for the moment at least this is wishful thinking. While the US Fed, the ECB and the BoE still retain a residual primary commitment to low inflation targeting, for the BoJ it is precisely the opposite as it tries desperately to increase inflation (interrupt its deflationary experiences and expectations). There are also increased informal concerns about 'deflation' in the Eurozone.

All this makes international capitalism inherently unstable, particularly in respect to financial and monetary matters (Kindleberger and Aliber 2011; Minsky 1982).

The rest of the chapter proceeds as follows: the next section outlines the evolution of CB BSs since the crisis. It concentrates upon the four main advanced country CBs already mentioned. After that we turn to the innovative policies that have been responsible for the explosion of BSs. This is followed by a section dealing with the relationship between CBs and assessments of sovereign risk. The responses to this from those institutions dealing with the ratings business are discussed in the penultimate section, where the characteristics of new metrics and those new institutions trying to muscle into the ratings business are discussed. The chapter ends with a conclusion outlining why this matters and what its ultimate consequences might be.

The empirics

Broadly speaking a Central Bank balance sheet provides a snapshot summary of the financial position of the CB at any one time. As BS assets must equal liabilities, for convenience in what follows we concentrate upon the asset side. As we will see later, however, 'reserves of commercial banks' appearing on the CB liability side is very important for an examination of the policy implications of the expansion of assets on the opposite side of the BS.

Figure 8.1 demonstrates what happened to the aggregate assets of the US Fed, the ECB and the BoJ between 2002 and 2012, and by way of contrast it includes the Chinese Central Bank (PBoC). We return to the PBoC in a moment, but first we concentrate on the three advanced country CBs.

In absolute terms the ECB's assets more than trebled. There were two main noteworthy episodes: the first in the latter part of 2008, and the second in the early part of 2012. The first was associated with the onset of the crisis, as the ECB tried to staunch the loss of liquidity in the Eurozone and support its banks, while the second had more to do with the sovereign debt crisis among, mainly, the countries in the south. But what this diagram illustrates is that far from being moribund, the ECB was very active. Despite a hugely constraining political and organizational environment, the ECB continually pressed against these obstacles and extended its mandate considerably.

If we now turn to the US Fed, the big push happened just after the original crisis during 2008. This mainly involved supporting the domestic banking and wider financial system via the policy of, first, the Troubled Asset Relief Program (TARP) – an emergency measure introduced to staunch the liquidity losses in the immediate aftermath of the crisis – and then quantitative easing (QE – more on this innovative policy later). The key elements for the expansion of the asset side are the mortgage-backed securities (MBS) that the Fed bought to prevent the holders of these going bankrupt as their value fell with the collapse of the US housing market. Subsequently this was overtaken by QE-driven bond purchases. But note that unlike for the ECB, there was no subsequent sovereign debt crisis to contend with.

Initially the Fed gave assistance mainly to US financial institutions, but not exclusively so. It supported Wall Street and the international financial system beyond. Again, this marks out the particularity of the US Fed's role. Keoun and Kuntz (2011) estimate that between 2007 and 2010 a trillion dollars was dispensed by the Fed.[1] Later estimates for overall 'global' support for distressed financial institutions – in the US and beyond – suggests this amounted to anywhere between US$7 trillion and nearly US$9 trillion. This just demonstrates the huge amount of public subsidy that has been pumped towards private financial interests: a veritable corporate welfarism of unprecedented scale.

These trends are mirrored in the case of the BoJ (Iwata and Takenaka 2012) though the cycle of expansion is different. The BoJ embarked on a formal programme of QE in 2001, which lasted until 2006 (this had to do with the much earlier onset of domestic financial disruption in Japan). As a consequence, between 1997 and 2005 its assets increased from 12.5 per cent of GDP to over 32 per cent. Subsequently, other polices were introduced (corporate financial facilitation, comprehensive monetary easing) so that, after a fall in the BS between 2006 and 2007, it began to climb again to be 30 per cent of GDP in 2012 (Iwata and Tanaka 2012; Figure 8.1).

But look also at the position of Chinese CB. The People's Bank of China (PBoC) has overtaken the Fed, BoJ and even the whole Euro system in terms of its assets in recent years, and has become the largest Central Bank in the world.[2] Thus the developments outlined in respect to the main advanced capitalist country CBs have not been confined just to these.

Additionally, we could add in the Bank of England, whose assets doubled between February 2009 and October 2012 (see http://www.bankofengland.co.uk/markets/Pages/balancesheet/default.aspx), and in a small open economy such as Denmark the experience was

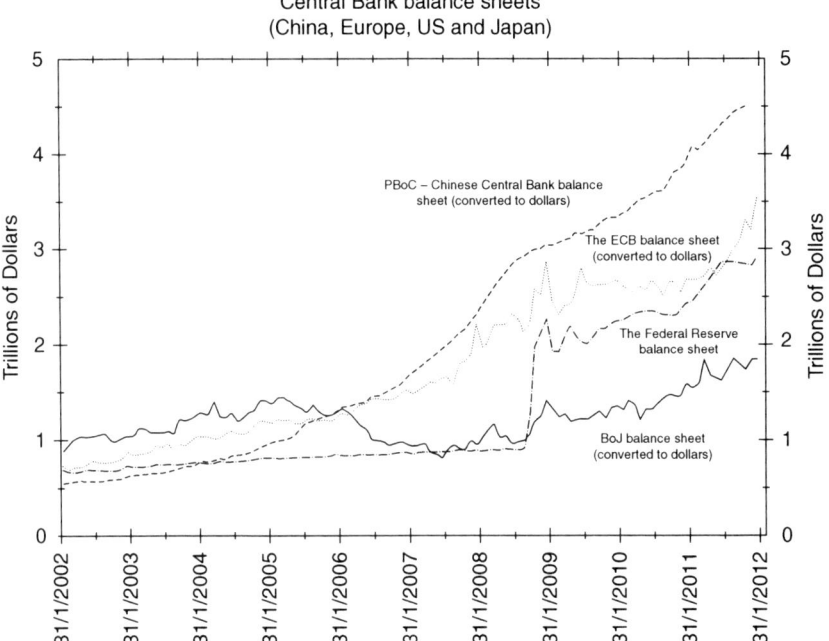

Figure 8.1. Assets of the ECB, the US Fed, the BoJ and the PBoC (2002–12, trillions of US$)

Source: Thomson Reuters Datastream.

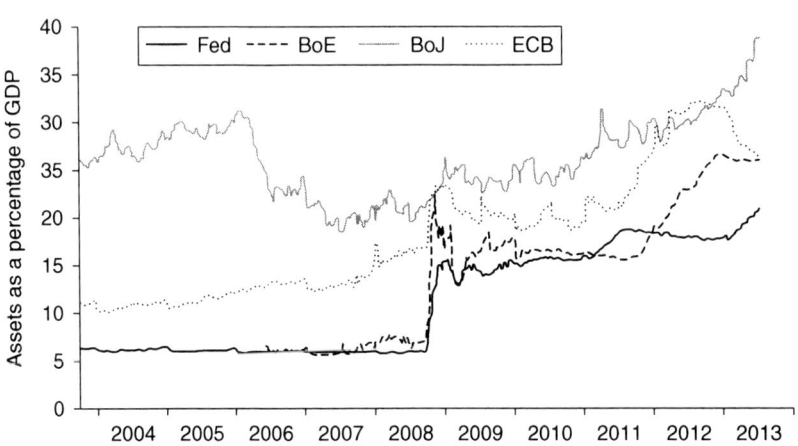

Figure 8.2. Balance sheets compared: ECB, US Fed, BoE and BoJ (2004–13, expressed as a percentage of GDP)

Source: Thomson Reuters Datastream.

similar, with the CB's assets growing 165 per cent between 2000 and 2012.

Finally, we have a comparison between the four main advanced CBs in Figure 8.2, expressing their assets as a percentage of country GDP. This illustrates the significance of the BoJ's interventions relative to the others, despite its smaller overall absolute size. The ECB also looks very exposed, the US Fed the least.

Again, this means the ECB will face a different set of problems in unwinding its position than the US Fed or the BoE (or the BoJ, see immediately below). Different policies will be in order to deal with different circumstances.

What have been the innovative policies?

The above data illustrated the consequences of CB actions, but what exactly were those actions? This section discusses several of the more important policy developments since 2008. But first we describe how the main CBs are institutionally configured.

The BoE is formally a limited liability company fully owned by the UK Treasury. The US Fed is in a more complicated legal position, since it is a federation of several (twelve) quasi-independent regional banks (Federal Reserve Districts), which have significant private institutional involvement, making the FRS a mix of public and private interests. However, the Federal Reserve Bank has legislative backing, is a properly constituted Central Bank and is banker to the US government.

In the UK the BoE's Monetary Policy Committee is the body responsible for conducting monetary policy – setting interest rates and determining the general conditions for lending and borrowing. The parallel body in the US Fed is the Federal Open Market Committee. But CBs also act as bankers to governments. For instance, as the government's bank the Fed acts as its fiscal agent: the US Treasury keeps an account with the Federal Reserve, through which incoming federal tax revenues and outgoing government payments are made. It also sells and redeems US government securities such as savings bonds and Treasury bills (TBs), notes and bonds, and it issues the nation's coin and currency. In the UK it is the BoE that directly issues TBs on behalf of the government. It also manages the country's foreign exchange and gold reserves. Both CBs also act as a lender of last resort.

The ECB is a corporate entity with shareholders and capital stock (€5 billion), which is owned by the Central Banks of all 28 EU member states. It is formally controlled by a Governing Council made up of representatives of the Eurozone countries. In a similar way to the other CBs it acts as the Eurozone's banker, issuing Euro currency, managing the foreign reserves of member states and the exchange rate of the Euro, and devising and conducting monetary policy. But it does not have explicit lender of last resort powers.

Returning to the policies pursued, an early caution is in order, since it could be argued that there is nothing necessarily radically innovative about these policy developments. In a moment we discuss 'quantitative easing' (QE) – which is the main claim to innovation in this environment, though it could be said it is nothing more than a revamped form of traditional 'open market operations' (OMO) by the CBs. While recognizing this as a possible argument, it is suggested here that what we have witnessed since 2008 exceeds traditional OMO in both its extent and range. OMO is essentially a short-term policy instrument designed to affect short-term interest rates, the amount of 'base money' in the economy, and massage the financing of governments. The sheer size of the recent interventions and their longevity is unprecedented – and amounts to more than the orthodoxy of financial policy. In addition, as we will see in a moment, the level and variety of 'subsidies for lending' vastly exceeds normal practice. We concentrate upon QE here for convenience.[3]

The immediate problem to which QE was the response is signalled in Figure 8.3. This shows the long-term trajectory of 'global' real interest rates (compared to an inflation-proof US TB issued by the Fed).

When interest rates reach the 'lower bound' of zero (or below), conventional monetary policy designed to stimulate economic activity ceases to work effectively: the authorities cannot reduce interest rates any lower (though see below for the case of the Danish Central Bank policy). So other policies need to be introduced. This is where QE arises.

QE – practised mainly by the US Fed, the BoE and the BoJ, but also the Swiss National Bank and elsewhere – involves the CB 'buying' bonds from the private sector financial institutions in the hope that this will, on the one hand, help 'repair their balance sheets' and, on the other hand, stimulate the commercial banks to extend loans so as to encourage economic activity generally. The mechanism through which this works varies between CBs depending upon the institutional nature of their national financial systems and their precise objectives. In one way or another, however, the selling of bonds by private sector institutions ends up as deposit in the commercial banks that would also have enhanced credit with the CB, thus affording them the possibility of extending their liabilities in the form of credit creation to the

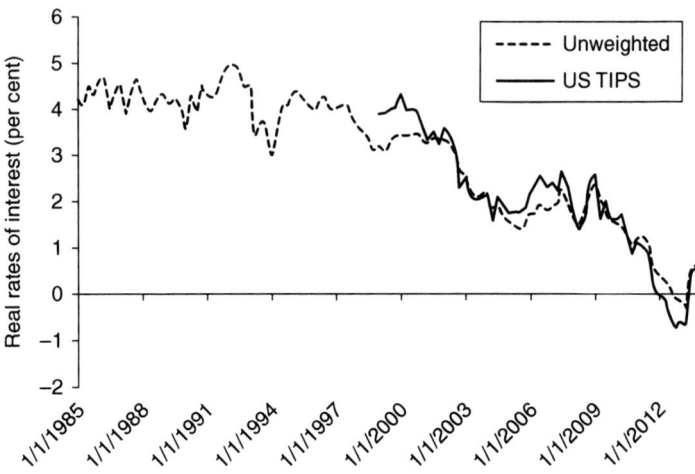

Figure 8.3. World real interest rates (1985–2012)
Source: King and Low 2014: Figure 3, p. 21.

private sector (to firms and individuals). This is the basic mechanism. But it can have all sorts of effects. There have been various rounds of QE – the first of which is generally recognized to have helped support share prices (thus shoring up the stock markets), while the second round is helping to restore balance sheets.[4]

But there is a key theoretical issue at stake in this, which illustrates its possible undoing. It is often claimed that this mechanism involves the CB simply 'printing money' – principally in the form of 'Central Bank base money' – because how else could it 'purchase' the private sector's assets/gilts? However, this is not altogether the case, or quite that simple. Under these circumstances the CB does indeed indirectly extend 'credit' to the commercial banking system (in the UK case via the non-bank financial institutions who actually sell the gilts) – which would appear as an increase in reserve balances on the liabilities side of the CB balance sheet referred to earlier – but it does not print money directly, nor extend credit directly to the household or commercial sectors. That is the job – indeed, the whole the rationale – of the commercial banks themselves.[5] The CB's policy of QE is based upon a hope and a prayer. In our financial world, it is commercial banks that directly 'control the money supply', not the CB (or, indeed – and God forbid – the government). Orthodox monetary policy dictates that commercial banks should have control over the money supply under capitalism – i.e. private economic agents and not the public authorities. To do otherwise would be tantamount to socialism, i.e. the administrative control over credit creation and allocation. This capacity to control the money supply by private agents – via the direct extension of credit money to households and firms (creating a deposit for them in their accounts at their commercial banks) – is jealously guarded by the financial system, and even QE could not fully challenge this nostrum. Under a monetized capitalism the agent who controls the money supply has control over economic resources, so it is clear what is ultimately at stake in this process.[6]

Thus, what QE amounts to is a very unorthodox form of the orthodoxy. The CB policy of QE may have indirectly helped to re-establish the strength and credibility of commercial banks' balance sheets, but there is no necessary link between this and the extension of private credit, i.e. an enhancement of the money supply in the form of loans to a private sector of households and firms. That is a decision left to the commercial banks themselves, and, indeed, much to the frustration of the governments and the relevant CBs, there is growing evidence that they have not done so. As shown in Figure 8.4, in the UK, bank lending to the private sector collapsed in 2007–8 and had not recovered by 2013. And despite the escalation of the monetary base consequent upon bond purchases, as Figure 8.5 shows, bank lending to the private sector across the main advanced countries has also stagnated. Of course this may be because there is no demand for loans by the private sector, which is deleveraging to restore credibility to its BSs, and increasing savings, which lie dormant in the financial system.[7] Again, this reinforces the idea that the policy is based upon a hope and a prayer.

The alternative would be to issue 'helicopter money' – where the CB simply drops money directly on to the general public by, say, sending them individual cheques – but this has been ruled out for fairly obvious reasons. Of course, this whole policy initiative is also predicated on a conception that increasing the (credit) money made available to the private sector will indeed stimulate consumption, commercial activity or investment, or whatever. That is also part of the hope and the prayer. The BoE has purchased £375 billion worth of gilts as part of its QE programme, which amounts to a direct subsidy to the private sector financial institutions. As mentioned above, in the US QE began in 2009, and has been successively extended in various phases. As of December 2012 'QE Infinity' began (sometimes known as QE 4) – infinite bond purchases until the US labour market recovered – see

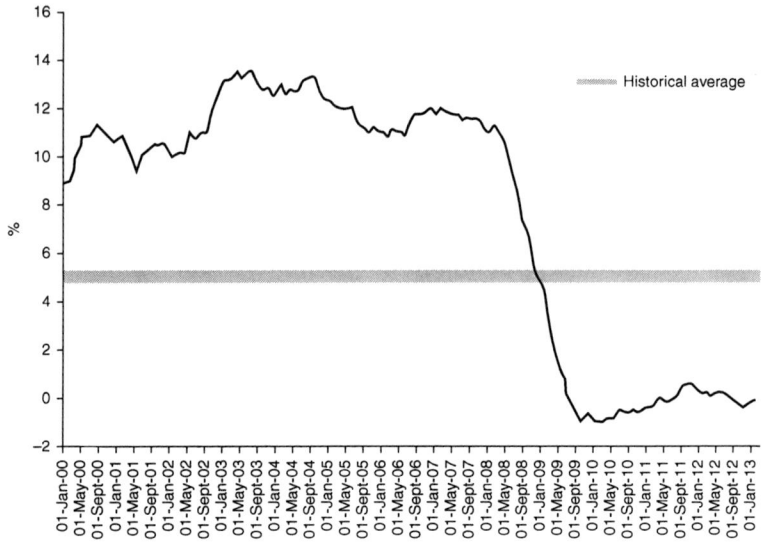

Figure 8.4. Bank lending to UK businesses and households (2000–13)
Source: NEF 2014: Figure 1, p. 6.

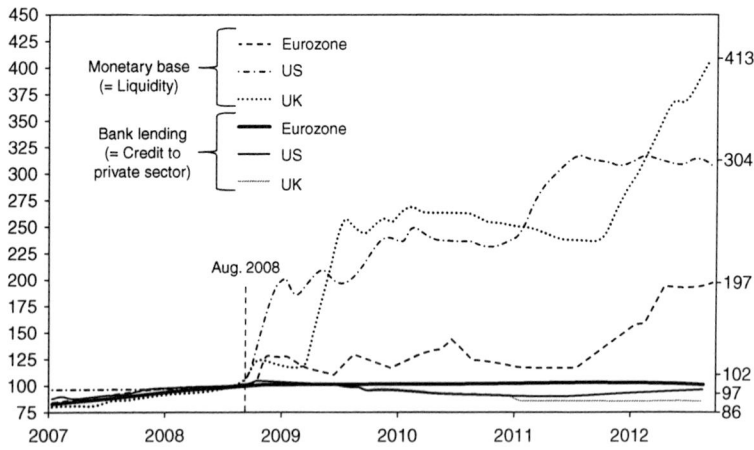

Figure 8.5. Monetary base and bank lending (2007–12)
Source: Koo 2013: Figure 10, p. 144.
Note: Aug. 2008 = 100, seasonally adjusted.

below. But by June 2013 labour market improvement was evident and the 'tapering back' of QE was broached by the Fed. The possible reversal of the programme threw into stark relief the potential difficulties of unwinding the CB BS position quickly and extracting the Fed from its entrenched support of the financial system, something returned to in a moment.

Thus, while a great deal of effort and energy (political, ideological and economic) has been expended on QE, it may have repaid sparse real economic dividends. But what it has done is hugely inflate the CB BSs – as shown above – because they have 'purchased' more and more privately owned assets in an attempt to 'kick-start' private sector monetary growth, and with it economic activity more generally. While the jury still remains out on what the ultimate effect of it will be on economic growth, it is towards a discussion of its consequences within the financial system that we turn in a moment. And what happens here may also ultimately affect economic growth, which is returned to in the conclusion. But first, what other policies have CBs resorted to?

Ever since Ben Bernanke voiced an official concern in 2012 with US unemployment (that had peaked at 10 per cent in October 2009 – see http://www.federalreserve.gov/newsevents/speech/bernanke20120831a.htm), CBs have toyed with a range of possible new policy mandates. As unemployment in the US fell to around 7.5 per cent in 2012, an official unemployment objective was established by the Fed at 6.5 per cent. In fact the US Fed has a 'dual mandate': to both establish stable prices and maximize employment, though the inflation objective had, up until the recent past, been considered its prime task.

The additional innovative part of this policy was to pre-commit the CB to maintain its policy stance on interest rates until the objectives for inflation, and particularly unemployment, had been met. But this explicit statement by Bernanke set off a debate among other CBs as to whether they should also target unemployment, like Bernanke was encouraging.[8] Or should they adopt an explicit growth rate target ('nominal GDP' targeting). Or should they engineer negative nominal interest rates? The BoE floated this idea in February 2013. And the Danish Central Bank (DCB) adopted this policy explicitly. Investors would now pay the Danish authorities to lodge their money on overnight deposits in Denmark. In Denmark's case this policy – and its general policy of keeping all interest rates at zero – or as near as possible to this – was designed to maintain the exchange rate between the krone and the Euro.[9] Thus, here the DCB's policy is principally directed at exchange rate stability, another possible policy target for CBs more generally and another indicator of the different objectives facing different countries in managing their economies. The exchange rate between the krone and the Euro is the foundation on which all of Denmark's macroeconomic policy is based. On the other hand the ECB – which also toyed with the idea of negative interest rates in May 2013 – views this as a policy for stimulating private demand in the traditional manner, not for stabilizing the Euro exchange rate.

Of course the BoJ has also adopted an implicit exchange rate policy, since in keeping interest rates very low the idea is to encourage spending and to see the yen exchange rate fall, so as to make Japanese exports more competitive. This is viewed as the way out of its deflationary malaise. Although this policy mix is often attributed to Prime Minister Shinzo Abe ('Abeconomics'), the newly appointed Governor of the BoJ, Haruhiko Kuroda (from March 2013), was the key player in devising the package.

But most 'innovative' CB policies have been associated with direct subsidies to the banks to try to stimulate lending, like QE discussed above. Further examples of this include the UK's 'Funding for Lending' (F4L) programme (another £80 billion) and its subsidy on mortgages to help buyers climb the housing ladder, announced in the April 2013 Budget.

Amongst all of this, however, what is left of inflation targeting, the original mandate for independent CBs? Very little, or so it seems. Inflation has slipped down the policy agenda, as CBs have seized the opportunity to exploit their new-found freedoms to experiment with policy-making. They may not know quite what they are doing, or what they should do. They may all have different objectives. But they have certainly been active. Some would say overactive, and they will reap the downside consequences later (e.g. Stockman 2013). But what might those consequences be? This we turn to in the next section.

Central Banks and sovereign risk

I outlined the functions of the CBs above to indicate that they are intimately tied to the financial functions of their respective treasuries, governments and financial systems beyond. They are part of an elaborate complex of institutions and mechanisms that are scrutinized for establishing the risks and rewards associated with sovereign debt, for instance. In this, of course, the overall fiscal position of the government is crucial, but so too is the state of its banking sector and CB.

Indeed, it is just this 'fiscal position' that the explosion of CB BSs indicates. At the end of the day, QE and all the rest represent a fiscal problem for the government and the public, since this is a debt that has to be 'repaid', even though it is formally on the books of the CB. The expansion of the CB BSs indicated above was a result of a decision about public expenditure, involving a huge transfer of debt from the private sector to the public sector, and with it a huge transfer of risk and a huge public subsidy to the financial system. Several possible consequences follow, which are only presented here in outlined form (Caruana 2012; Weidmann 2013).

First, will it be possible for the CBs to unwind their newly acquired financial positions as indicated by their BSs? This issue was posed acutely in June 2013 as the US Fed hinted at a policy of imminent phased withdrawal of QE. Of course this threw the US financial markets into instant turmoil. The prospect of interest rate rises upsets plans and expectations throughout the financial system. But this policy readjustment would have implications far beyond the US. The economic cycle in the US is in quite a different phase to that in Europe. Europe was still mired in deep recession in mid-2013 whereas the US economy was on a recovery trajectory. So despite anything else, this makes prospects of global policy coordination even more unlikely, since these two economic blocs are facing quite different current economic conditions. But these involve essentially short-term considerations. What about the longer term?

Economists would answer 'yes' to the longer-term prospect of successful unwinding because of their faith in the market mechanism: as conditions improve and the expansionary BS phase comes to an end the CBs can repackage their acquired debts and sell them, as market sentiment improves. They might even make a profit on these transactions. There may be something in this, as will be indicated in a moment, but the medium-term uncertainties are legion and the political cost may be prohibitive – fiscal conservatives are incensed by these policies (Stockman 2013). But there are three alternative policy options available here: explicitly wind down the position as just suggested; hold on to it and keep things as they are (why should the CB really worry about this since it is a sovereign risk and the CB will not default); or relatedly, wait for it to be eroded by inflation in the longer run.

What about the sovereign debt issue? This is related to what has just been said. Given the dangers associated with such a large and swift 'deterioration' of the CB BSs, might this not inhibit investors when thinking about acquiring further sovereign debt? The state of the CB BSs is also an indicator of the state of the sovereign BSs, since this is ultimately a form of public debt. However, as indicated by the discussion of the Danish case, things are complicated by several other factors.

At this stage it is important to bring in the credit rating agencies, since these are the bodies that actually establish the credit rating for sovereign debt. The three big CRAs are Standard and Poor, Fitch, and Moody's (who collectively control 95 per cent of the global credit rating business). These bodies are important because they have semi-official status as regulatory institutions, fulfilling a public purpose despite being privately owned (Sinclair 2005). The CRAs assess the risks associated with financial investment in both private corporations and sovereign debt. They rank various institutions and sovereigns – rating the debtor's ability to pay back the debt, make timely interest payments and the likelihood of default. Traditionally, the countries we have been dealing with above were 'Triple A-rated' by these agencies; as a result their debt was judged as 'riskless': they were the ultimate 'safe havens'. Recently, however, there has been some downgrading of their debt, as their fiscal positions deteriorated and growth prospects faltered (e.g. for the US and UK). But a problem here is that there is a growing loss of confidence in these bodies in the wake of their role in the run-up to the financial crisis. They failed to spot the emerging problems and were compromised by their dual role as both assessors of risk and advisors/consultants to the very financial institutions they were assessing. This disillusion-ment with the existing CRAs has provided a space for potential com-petitors to emerge in the credit rating business. And this is a further indicator of potentially quite rapid institutional change in this world. New bodies are marketing their indexes, claiming they are superior in their methodology in the new period of CB-led capitalism and are not compromised by past mistakes of the old era. Thus, while we may have another round of potential 'financial innovation' emerging, this time it is not one involving yet another exotic financial instrument or form of securitized debt obligation (for the foreseeable future that era is probably over), but, rather, a new and better index of sovereign risk, one suitable for a new era of 'sovereign debt crises', fiscal auster-ity and CB BS inflation.[10]

This rapid perceived increase in sovereign debt risk has led to the development of a vibrant market-led response to insure against such risks, particularly through the issuance of credit default swaps. A CDS is a bilateral agreement designed to shift credit risk between two par-ties. In a CDS, one party pays a periodic fee to another party in return for compensation for default (or similar defined credit event) by a reference entity. Whilst a CDS is a privately negotiated bilateral contract between two parties, these OTC contracts are increasingly being cleared centrally by a range of organizations according to publicly committed and transparent benchmarks. Originally, these products were developed in the context of commercial companies but from the late 1990s (after the Asian Financial Crisis in 1997) they rapidly spread to the sovereign sector.

According to the International Swaps and Derivatives Association (the trade body of the derivatives industry) the notional value of outstanding sovereign CDS in 2012 was nearly US$26 trillion (http://www.isdacdsmarketplace.com/market_overview, accessed 27 August 2014). The credit ratings company Fitch rates sovereign CDSs for 84 countries.[11] It uses daily CDS market quotes to construct a market-driven perspective on credit quality (via its CDS Implied Ratings modelling framework) which complements fundamental credit ratings analysis (Boy, 2013: 15).[12] Standard and Poor and Moody's do much the same.[13] And there are several other firms that calculate CDS ratings and operate central counterparty clearing facilities for credit default swaps. In this context the main countries against which CDS contracts were being taken in 2014 were Italy, Brazil, China, Mexico, Germany, France, Turkey and Russia, indicating the sensitivity of perceived sovereign risk associated with these countries (http://www.isdacdsmarketplace.com/exposures_and_activity/top_10_cds_positions, accessed 29 August 2014). But all these indices are based upon market prices. They share an approach that is committed to key ratios such as the debt to GDP indicator, and/or a 'mark-to-market' pricing valuation arrangement that tracks actual market prices for CDS.

As Nina Boy (2013) points out, the BlackRock Sovereign Risk Index, on the other hand, rejects these indicators as being inadequate (though it embraces them in part – see below) and adopts a 'research-led' methodology instead. BlackRock is a US-based company that claims to be the largest global asset manager, and the leading institution in developing a new role for sovereign debt assessment. Initially covering 44 countries, BlackRock's index produces a ranking of sovereigns according to their relative likelihood of default, devaluation or above-trend inflation, based on four conceptual categories (BlackRock 2011). These are 'fiscal space', which assesses the fiscal characteristics and prospects of a country; 'external finance position', which assesses the vulnerability to shocks emanating from abroad; 'financial sector health', which concentrates upon the state of the

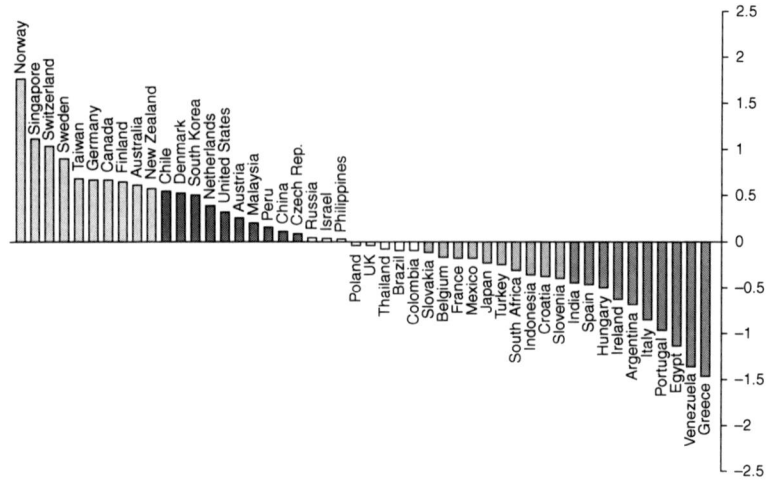

Figure 8.6. The BlackRock sovereign risk index (June 2013)

Source: http://www.blackrock.com/corporate/en-dk/news-and-insights/blackrock-invest-ment-institute-risk-index (accessed 7 October 2013).

domestic financial system; and finally 'willingness to pay', which deals with the likelihood of sovereign default. These features are combined into a weighted index (40:20:30:10 respectively), an example of which is given in Figure 8.6.

This index does not coincide with the list of countries 'most at risk' according to the ISDA list of sovereign CDS contracts reported above. The most creditworthy countries are not the most liquid but those most isolated from risks associated with external and internal financial shocks (Boy 2013: 18). Thus Norway, Singapore, Sweden and Switzerland take the prime spots and Chile and South Korea feature in the top ten.

Four consequences follow from this. First, BlackRock claims that a more intelligence-based approach to assessing sovereign risk is needed that dispenses with past correlations as indicators of future trends, and instead relies on intuition, simplicity and fast repositioning conducted on an almost day-by-day basis (Boy 2013: 19). CDS are beholden to an insurance-based logic based upon market prices which no longer perform adequately to represent genuine sovereign risk. And second, as Nina Boy has argued, this indicates a move away from bond markets and prices as the prime site for risk assessment (Boy 2013: 19). The bond markets are in effect rigged by the big issuers as their overwhelming presence skews calculations in their favour. Third, the development of these instruments raises fresh regulatory issues. The European Parliament, for instance, banned so called 'naked CDS' on sovereign debt in November 2011. In a naked CDS, the investors do not own the debt, betting they can purchase it later at a cheaper price if a default occurs. These 'short selling' vehicles were deemed to be purely speculative in character.[14] Fourth, this may not signal the end to innovation in the sovereign debt risk assessment game. For instance, in principle there would seem no reason why Catastrophe Bonds ('Cat Bonds') could not be extended to cover catastrophic sovereign default events (Thompson, forthcoming). 'Cat Bonds' were originally devised in the 1990s to insure against one-off climatic catastrophic events like Hurricane Katrina (2005). But it has proved possible to adapt these instruments to other contexts: to protect against catastrophic stock market crashes and against hedge fund collapses. Sovereign risks might be the next target.

Conclusions

So, what is the bottom line with respect to sovereign debt, economic growth and the possible new era? A lot of the BlackRock criticism of other calculative methods is, of course, marketing hype: it needs to justify its product and differentiate it from the competition. There is not going to be a rapid erosion of the traditional CRA's role and a complete undermining of its position. But ultimately, does it matter whether governments and their CBs are heavily in debt, or more heavily in debt than they used to be (other than in periods of severe national crisis such as war)? This issue was posed recently in a slightly different context, around the Reinhart and Rogoff dispute over the importance of different debt/GDP ratios for the prospects of economic growth. Reinhart and Rogoff had argued a debt/GDP ratio of over 90 per cent was historically associated with significantly slower growth rates (Reinhart and Rogoff 2009, 2010). This had been used by 'fiscal conservatives' to argue the need for severe austerity and a cutback in public expenditure. Subsequently it was discovered that there were several 'errors' in the original Reinhart and Rogoff analysis, in terms of coding the data (Denmark, along with four other leading OECD countries, were left out), in dealing with outliers, and with the presentation and interpretation of results (Herndon *et al.*

2013). The outcome is that it is disputable whether the '90 per cent rule' is robust, and that a causal relationship between high government debt/GDP ratio and low growth can be established (it might go the other way (Reinhart and Rogoff 2013) – note also that BlackRock has its own percentage rules, which seem equally arbitrary).

However, this tends to ignore a key point about the demand for government debt (Lysandrou 2013). In the aggregate investors are desperate for 'safe havens' and good quality public debt because there is a surplus of savings in the international system. In part, this is why Denmark can offer negative or zero interest rates and still attract funds: it is considered a super-safe haven. The private sector is amiss in providing this – it is not investing much, and so not issuing new shares; it has been 'buy-back big time' for corporate shares, as companies have been trying to boost 'shareholder value' and provide incentives and the right conditions for enhancing executive remuneration, and the corporate sector's BSs are in a complete mess. This means the supply of corporate paper has been diminishing and its reliability challenged. The only alternative 'relatively' safe havens are sovereigns, even though some of them are being slightly downgraded by the established CRAs. So there is no shortage of demand for government debt, indeed there is a deep market for it. This is also because, relative to their growing significance in terms of global GDP, the emerging market economies are much smaller issuers of securities, so demand has been concentrated on advanced country securities. Generally, this makes it easy for sovereigns to maintain very low interest rates. But its implication is clear. There are no real 'crises of sovereign debt', so CBs might be able to easily unwind their positions. And governments need not worry unduly about their fiscal positions. They could quite easily issue more debt, which would be eagerly absorbed by investors who have 'nowhere else to go'.

Finally, how long will real interest rates (Figure 8.3) stay at such historically low levels, which lie behind the developments and policies discussed above? In large part this is driven by two current structural features of the international economy:

(1) austerity in the advanced industrial economies, which supresses demand for loanable funds; and
(2) the 'glut' in world savings, which implies a huge excess supply of funds.

This is popularly known as the 'global imbalances'. In the 1970s it was Japan that provided the excess savings for the international system, with its ultra-high savings ratio. And this has now been replaced by China. As a consequence China and the US are caught in a recipro-cal dance: the US is the major deficit country with a low savings ratio, while China is the major surplus economy with a high savings ratio and a current account surplus. As a consequence China finances the US by buying US-issued assets. But how long will China continue to be the source of such funds? Here the lesson of Japan is telling. Japan has moved from being a traditional surplus economy to having a def-icit on its current account. In part this is because of its prolonged recession, but it also has to do with demographics. Japan's ageing population is beginning to 'dis-save'. And this demographic experi-ence will hit China in the not-too-distant future: on average, for every four grandparents in China there is now only a single grandchild, the result of many decades of the 'single child policy'. And in 2013 the working population declined slightly. So with an ageing popula-tion and fewer young to support it, dis-savings will inevitably appear in China, perhaps sooner rather than later. And there are enormous domestic pressures to stimulate consumption in the country. At the same time the appetite – and perceived need – for further auster-ity will eventually diminish among the traditional developed coun-tries, leading to a renewed stimulus for investment, consumption and demand more generally. Both these trends will encourage an 'adjust-ment' to the global imbalances, and a rise in interest rates. But this will also have profound consequences for managing such a transform-ational rebalancing in the 'global' economy of the future.

Notes

1 Clearly, this figure underestimates the final total for the US financial sys-tem as a whole, as it does not include support for Fannie Mae, Freddie Mac or AIG, for instance. It just records amounts extended to banks.
2 According to Yu and Lan 2013: 20,

> During 2008–2012, China's broadly defined money stock (M2) doubled in size, increasing from 47.5 trillion yuan (7.5 trillion dollars) to 97.4 tril-lion yuan (15.7 trillion dollars). As a result, the Chinese economy is heav-ily levered – outstanding bank loans more than doubled, climbing from 30.3 trillion yuan (4.9 trillion dollars) in 2008 to 67.2 trillion yuan (10.8 trillion dollars) in 2012; outstanding bonds also rose from 12.3 trillion yuan (2 trillion dollars) to 23.8 trillion yuan (3.8 trillion dollars); and trust funds increased from less than one trillion yuan (16 billion dollars) to 7.5 trillion yuan (1.2 trillion dollars).

3 In the US, QE was preceded by the Troubled Asset Relief Program (TARP), mentioned above – an emergency measure introduced in October 2008. QE proper began in March 2009. But sometimes TARP is designated QE

1, so the QE policy sequence often discussed in the literature would be shifted along by one digit for each phase.

4 In the UK the explicit mechanisms involve the sale of gilts to the CB by non-bank financial institutions in the first instance (pension funds, insurance companies). The idea is that they will then have an incentive to buy more financial instruments, which will prop up the stock market and lead to more economic activity, as investors take advantage of low interest rates and the rising price of assets to issue more of these and/or undertake further investments (McLeary *et al.* 2014; Joyce *et al.* 2012; Miles 2010; NEF 2014). For a critical assessment of the US case, see Randall Wray (2013).

5 For an outline of the way this works in the UK, see Ryan-Collins and Greenham (2012). This 'post-Keynesian' position was recently seemingly endorsed by the BoE (McLeary *et al.* 2014).

6 This can account for the basic 'failure' of the orthodox monetarist project of the 1980s in trying to control the economy by controlling the money supply. The only way the authorities could actually have directly controlled the money supply would have been by fully socializing the financial system, not something monetarism could have contemplated. Paradoxically, strict monetarism requires financial nationalization.

7 The success or otherwise of the various QE programmes in the US remains controversial. It has certainly worked to keep long-term interest rates low. In part this was aided by another novel policy development undertaken as part of QE 2, namely 'Operation Twist': the US Fed's policy of selling short-term treasuries to fund the buying of the long-term bonds. This 'twisted' the yield curve (short-term rates rose and long-term rates fell).

8 In the UK a huge fuss was made when the new Governor of the Bank of England (Mark Carney) announced a similar pre-commitment strategy to target unemployment (at 7 per cent) in August 2013. An interesting issue this raises is why target unemployment? This is a notoriously unreliable measure. Alternatives – perhaps better alternatives – would have been earnings, or productivity, or GDP growth, as suggested in the main text.

9 In May 2013 the overnight deposit rate was -0.1 per cent, and the benchmark lending rate just 0.3 per cent. The background to Denmark's financial problems is admirably sketched by Frances Schwartzkopff: 'ECB agenda tests Central Bank extremes in Denmark: Nordic credit', Bloomberg News, 10 May 2013 (http://www.bloomberg.com/news/2013–05–02/ecb-agenda-tests-central-bank-extremes-in-denmark-nordic-credit.html, accessed 23 June 2013).

10 The following sections draw heavily on the unpublished paper 'The Emperor's new clothes – or how do political-economic fictions fail?' by Nina Boy, 2013.

11 See http://www.fitchratings.com/web/en/dynamic/fitch-home.jsp, accessed 27 August 2014.

12 http://www.fitchratings.com/web_content/product/methodology/cdsir_methodology.pdf, accessed 27 August 2014.

13 See S&P/ISDA: CDS, Fixed Income Sovereign Indices, http://www.eu.spindices.com/ and https://www.moodys.com/researchandratings/market-segment/sovereign-supranational/-/005005/4294966293/4294966623/-1/0/-/0/-/-/en/global/rr; both accessed 27 August 2014.

14 http://www.eubusiness.com/news-eu/finance-economy-cds.dij, accessed 29 August 2014.

References

Abbott, A. (ed.) (2001) 'Things of boundaries', in *Time Matters: On Theory and Method*, University of Chicago Press: Chicago.

Adelman, J. (2013) *Worldly Philosopher: The Odyssey of Albert Hirschman*, Princeton University Press: Princeton, NJ.

Adrian, T. and Brunnermeier, M. J. (2009) 'CoVaR', Princeton University, NJ. Online, available at: http://www.princeton.edu/markus (accessed 30 September 2009).

Agamben, G. (1998) *Homo Sacer: Sovereign Power and Bare Life*, Stanford University Press: Stanford, CA.

Agamben, G. (2005) *State of Exception*, University of Chicago Press: Chicago.

Agnew, J. (1994) 'The territorial trap: the geographical assumptions of international relations theory', *Review of International Political Economy*, 1(1), pp. 53–80.

Agnew, J. (2009) *Globalization and Sovereignty*, Rowman & Littlefield Publishers: Lanham, MD.

Agur, I. (2008) 'The US trade deficit, the decline of the WTO and the rise of regionalism', *Global Economy Journal*, 8(3), pp. 1–32.

Akerlof, G. A. and Shiller, R. J. (2009) *Animal Spirits: How Human Psychology Drives the Economy and Why it Matters for Global Capitalism*, Princeton University Press: Princeton, NJ.

Albert, M. and Hilkermeier, L. (eds) (2004) *Observing International Relations: Niklas Luhmann and World Politics*, Taylor and Francis: London.

Albert, M., Jacobson, D. and Lapid, Y. (eds) (2001) *Identities, Borders, Orders: Rethinking International Relations Theory*, University of Minnesota Press: Minneapolis, MN.

Alesina, A. and Spolaore, E. (2003) *The Size of Nations*, MIT Press: Cambridge, MA.

Alesina, A., Spolaore, E. and Wacziarg, R. (2003) 'Trade, growth and the size of countries', HIER Discussion Paper Number 1995, January.

Ali, T. (2002) *The Clash of Fundamentalisms: Crusades, Jihads and Modernity*, Verso: London.

Ali-Yrkkö, J. (2010) 'The value creation of mobile phones – the case of Nokia N95' in Ali-Yrkkö, J. (ed.) *Nokia and Finland in a Sea of Change*, The Research Institute of the Finnish Economy: Helsinki, pp. 91–108.

Allen, F. and Gale, D. (2000) 'Financial contagion', *Journal of Political Economy*, 108(1), pp. 1–33.

Allen, F. and Babus, A. (2009) 'Networks in finance', in P. Kleindorfer and J. Wind (eds), *The Network Challenge: Strategy, Profit and Risk in an Interdependent World*, Wharton School Publishing: Philadelphia, PA, pp. 367–82.

Allen, F., Babus, A. and Carletti, E. (2010) 'Financial connections and systemic risk', NBER Working Paper No. 16177, July.

Alpert, D. (2013) *The Age of Oversupply*, Portfolio/Penguin: New York.

Altieri, C. (2012) 'Affect, intentionality, and cognition: a response to Ruth Leys', *Critical Inquiry*, 38(4), pp. 878–81.

Anderson, J., O'Dowd, L. and Wilson, T. M. (2002) 'Introduction: Why study borders now?', *Regional and Federal Studies*, 14(4), pp. 1–12.

Aoki, M., Gustafsson, B. and Williamson, O. E. (eds) (1990) *The Firm as a Nexus of Treaties*, Sage: London.

Aradau, C. and Munster, R. van (2011) *The Politics of Catastrophe: Genealogies of the Unknown*, Routledge: London.

Árdal, P. S. (1966) *Passion and Value in Hume's Treaties*, University of Edinburgh Press: Edinburgh.

Arestis, P. and Basu, S. (2003) 'Financial globalization: some conceptual problems', *Eastern Economic Journal*, 29(3), pp. 183–9.

Arestis, P., Basu, S. and Mallik, S. (2005) 'Financial globalization: the need for a single currency and a global Central Bank', *Journal of Post Keynesian Economics*, 27(1), pp. 507–31.

Arnoldi, J. (2012) 'Cheating models: algorithmic trading and the normative reconfiguration of financial trading', Aarhus University Business School. Online, available at: http://forskningsbasen.deff.dk/Share.external?sp=Sa40d7204-79a5-4c7f-be60-65d7cc53bd11&sp=Sau (accessed 29 September 2014).

Arrighi, G. and Silver, B. J. (1999) *Chaos and Governance in the Modern World System*, University of Minnesota Press: Minneapolis, MN.

Asad, T. (2003) *Foundations of the Secular: Christianity, Islam, Modernity*, Stanford University Press: Stanford, CA.

Augar, P. (2009) *Chasing Alpha: How Reckless Growth and Unchecked Ambition Ruined the City's Golden Decade*, Bodley Head: London.

Auvinen, J. and Nafziger, E. W. (1999) 'The sources of humanitarian emergencies', *Journal of Conflict Resolution*, 42(3), pp. 267–90.

Auvinen, J. and Nafziger, E. W. (2003) *Economic Development, Inequality and War*, Palgrave: Basingstoke.

Babus, A. (2007) 'The formation of financial networks', Discussion Paper 06-093, Tinbergen Institute, Rotterdam, Holland.

Badiou, A. (2001) *Ethics: An Essay on the Understanding of Evil*, Verso: London.

Baldwin, T. (1992) 'The territorial state', in H. Gross and R. Harrison (eds), *Jurisprudence: Cambridge Essays*, Clarendon Press: Oxford.

Barberis, N. and Thalar, R. (2003) 'A survey of behavioural finance', in G. M. Constantinides, M. Harris and R. M. Stulz (eds), *Handbook of the Economics of Finance*, Volume 1, Series 2, Elsevier: Amsterdam, pp. 105–1128.

Bataille, G. (1984) 'The notion of expenditure', in *Visions of Excess: Selected Writings, 1927–1939*, University of Minnesota Press: Minneapolis, MN, pp. 116–29.

Bataille, G. (1997) 'Part III general economy', in F. Botting and S. Wilson (eds), *The Bataille Reader*, Oxford University Press: Oxford, pp. 165–220.

Beckert, J. (2011) 'Imagined futures: fictionality in economic action', MPIfG Discussion Paper 11/8, Max Planck Institute for the Study of Societies: Cologne.

Benhabib, S. (2002) 'Unholy wars', *Constellations: An International Journal of Critical and Democratic Theory*, 9(1), pp. 34–45.

Berman, P. (2003) *Terror and Liberalism*, W. W. Norton & Company: New York.

Beunza, D. and Stark, D. (2012) 'From dissonance to resonance: cognitive interdependence in quantitative finance', *Economy and Society*, 41(3), pp. 383–417.

Bhidé, A. (2010) *A Call for Judgment: Sensible Finance for a Dynamic Economy*, Oxford University Press: New York.

BIS (2011) 'The impact of sovereign credit risk on bank funding conditions', CGFS Papers No. 43, BIS: Basel.

Black, F. (1971) 'Toward a fully automated stock exchange', *Financial Analysts Journal*, 27(2), pp. 28–35, 44.

Black, F. and Scholes, M. (1973) 'The pricing of options and corporate liabilities', *Journal of Political Economy*, 81(3), pp. 637–54.

BlackRock (2011) 'Introducing the BlackRock sovereign risk index: a more comprehensive view of credit quality', BlackRock Investment Institute. Online, available at: http://www2.blackrock.com/global/home/BlackRockInvestmentInstitute/index.htm, June (accessed 29 September 2014).

Blanchard, O. E. (2009) 'The crisis: basic mechanisms and appropriate policies', Massachusetts Institute of Technology Department of Economics Working Paper Series 09-01.

Bong-Chan, K., Stulz, R.-M. and Warnock, F. E. (2006) 'Financial globalization, governance and the evolution of the home bias', BIS Working Paper No. 220, Bank of International Settlements: Basel, December.

Bordo, M. and James, H. (2006) 'One world money, then and now', *International Economics and Economic Policy*, 3(3–4), pp. 395–407.

Bowman, A., Erturk, I., Froud, J., Johal, S., Leaver, A., Moran, M. and Williams, K. (2013) 'Central Bank-led capitalism?', *Seattle University Law Review*, 36, pp. 455–87.

Branch, J. (2011) 'Mapping the sovereign state: technology, authority and systemic change', *International Organization*, 66 (winter), pp. 1–26.

Brooks, R., Corson, J. and Wales, J. D. (1993) 'The pricing of index options when the underlying assets all follow a lognormal diffusion', in D. M. Chance and R. P. Trippi (eds), *Advances in Futures and Options Research*, Volume 7, JAI Press Inc: Stamford, CT.

Brunnermeier, M. K. (2009) 'Deciphering the liquidity and credit crunch 2007–2008', *Journal of Economic Perspectives*, 23(1), pp. 77–100.

Cai, F. and Warnock, F. E. (2004) 'International diversification at home and abroad', International Finance Discussion Paper 2004–793, Federal Reserve Board: Washington, DC.

Callon, M. (1998) (ed.) *The Laws of the Market*, Blackwell: Oxford.

Caruana, J. (2012) 'Why central bank balance sheets matter', BIS Paper 66, BIS: Basel, pp. 2–9.

Castells, M. (1996) *The Rise of the Network Society*, Blackwell: Oxford.

Castoriadis, C. (1987) *The Imaginary Institution of Society*, Polity Press: Cambridge.

Chakrabarty, D. (2000) *Provincializing Europe: Postcolonial Thought and Historical Difference*, Princeton University Press: Princeton, NJ.

Chance, D. M. (2008) *Essays in Derivatives: Risk-Transfer Tools and Topics Made Easy*, John Wiley & Sons, Inc: Hoboken, NJ.

Claire-Cutler, A. (2003) *Private Power and Global Authority: Transnational Merchant Law in the Global Political Economy*, Cambridge University Press: Cambridge.

Claire-Cutler, A., Haufler, V. and Porter, T. (1999) (eds) *Private Authority and International Affairs*, State University of New York Press: Albany, NY.

Clarke, J. (2005) 'New Labour's citizens: activated, empowered, responsibilized or abandoned?', *Critical Social Policy*, 25(4), pp. 44–63.

Collier, S. J. (2008) 'Enacting catastrophe: preparedness, insurance, budgetary rationalization', *Economy and Society*, 37(3), pp. 224–50.

Collier, S. J. and Lakoff, A. (2008) 'Distributed preparedness: the spatial logic of domestic security in the US', *Environment and Planning D: Society and Space*, 26(1), pp. 7–28.

Connolly, W. E. (2002) *Neuropolitics: Thinking, Culture, Speed*, Minnesota University Press: Minneapolis, MN.

Connolly, W. E. (2011) 'Critical response I. The complexity of intention', *Critical Inquiry*, 37(4), pp. 791–8.

Cont, R. (2010) (ed.) *Encyclopaedia of Quantitative Finance*, John Wiley & Sons: Chichester.

Cooper, A. F., Hughes, C. W. and Lombaerde, P. (eds) (2008) *Regionalism and Global Governance: The Taming of Globalisation?*, Routledge: London.

Cooper, G. (2008) *The Origin of Financial Crises: Central Banks, Credit Bubbles, and the Efficient Market Fallacy*, Harriman House: Petersfield, Hampshire.

Cooper, R. N. (2006) 'Proposal for a common currency amongst rich democracies', *International Economics and Economic Policy*, 3(3–4), pp. 387–94.

Creppell, I. (2003) *Toleration and Identity: Foundations in Early Modern Thought*, Routledge: London.

CRESC (2009) *An Alternative Report on UK Banking Reform*, Centre for Research in Economic Sociology and Culture: Manchester.

Das, S. (2006) *Swaps/Financial Derivatives: Products, Pricing Applications and Risk Management*, John Wiley & Sons: Singapore.

Davidson, P. (2009) *The Keynes Solution: The Path to Global Economic Prosperity*, Palgrave Macmillan: New York.

deBrandt, O. and Hartman, P. (2000) 'Systemic risk: a survey', European Central Bank Working Paper No. 35, November.

Defoe, D. (1701) (published anonymously) *The Villainy of Stock-Jobbers Detected, And the Causes of the Late Run upon the Bank and Bankers Discovered and Considered*, London.

Deleuze, G. and Guattari, F. (1986) *Nomadology: The War Machine*, MIT Press: Cambridge, MA.

Deleuze, G. and Guattari, F. (2004) [1980] *A Thousand Plateaus: Capitalism and Schizophrenia*, Continuum International Publishing Group: London.

Denton, R. E. (2005) 'Religion and the 2004 presidential campaign', *American Behavioral Scientist*, 49(1), pp. 11–31.

Devji, F. (2005) *Landscapes of the Jihad: Militancy, Morality, Modernity*, Hurst: London.

Disdier, A.-C. and Head, K. (2008) 'The puzzling persistence of the distance effect on bilateral trade', *The Review of Economics and Statistics*, February, 90(1), pp. 37–48.

Domowitz, I. (1993) 'A taxonomy of automated trade execution systems', *Journal of International Money and Finance*, 12(6), pp. 607–63.

Dow, A. and Dow, S. (2011) 'Animal spirits revisited', *Capitalism and Society*, 6(2), Article 1.

du Gay, P. (2012) 'Leviathan calling: some notes on sociological anti-statism and its consequences', *Journal of Sociology*, 48(4), pp. 397–409.

du Gay, P. and Vikkelso, S. (2013) 'Exploitation, exploration, and exaltation: notes on a metaphysical (re)turn to "one best way of organizing"', *Research in the Sociology of Organizations*, Special Issue on Exploration and Exploitation.

Dungey, M. (2008a) 'Contagion in currency markets: what do we mean?', La Trobe University, Australia.

Dungey, M. (2008b) 'The tsunami: measures of contagion in the 2007–2008 credit crunch', *CESinfo Forum 4*, pp. 33–43.

Dunning, J. H. (ed.) (2003) *Making Capitalism Good: The Moral Challenges of Global Capitalism*, Oxford University Press: Oxford.

Dupuy, J.-P. (2005) *Petite Métaphysique des Tsunami*, Seuil: Paris.

Eco, U. and Sebeok, T. A. (1984) *The Sign of Three: Dupin, Holmes, Pierce*, Indiana University Press: Bloomington, IN.

Eichengreen, B., Rose, A. K. and Wyplosz, C. (1997) 'Contagious currency crises', NBER Working Paper W5681, July.

Einaudi, L. (2001) *Money and Politics: European Monetary Unification and the International Gold Standard (1865–1873)*, Oxford University Press: Oxford.

Elden, S. (2009) *Terror and Territory: The Spatial Extent of Sovereignty*, University of Minnesota Press: Minneapolis, MN and London.

Elden, S. (2013) *The Birth of Territory*, University of Chicago Press: Chicago and London.

Elster, J. (1999) *Alchemies of the Mind: Rationality and the Emotions*, Cambridge University Press: Cambridge.

Engelen, E., Erturk, I., Froud, J., Johal, S., Leaver, A., Moran, M., Nilsson, A. and Williams, K. (2011) *After the Great Complacence: Financial Crisis and the Politics of Reform*, Oxford University Press: Oxford.

Epstein, J. M. (2009) 'Modelling to contain pandemics', *Nature*, 460(687), 6 August, p. 687.

Erturk, I., Leaver, A. and Williams, K. (2010) 'Hedge funds as "war machine": making the positions work', *New Political Economy*, 15(1), pp. 9–28.

Essama-Nssah, B. (2006) 'Building an applied general equilibrium model', Poverty Reduction Group (PRMPR), The World Bank, Teaching material for PAMS, 15–19 May 2006. Online, available at: http://siteresources.worldbank.org/INTPSIA/Resources/490023-1121114603600/1413109-11 35026571018/CGE_Modeling_052206.pdf (accessed 29 September 2014).

Fender, I. and McGuire, P. (2010) 'Bank structure, funding risk and the transmission of shocks across countries: concepts and measurement', *BIS Quarterly Review*, September, pp. 63–79.

Fernandez-Izquierdo, A. and Lafuente, J. A. (2004) 'International transmission of stock exchange volatility: empirical evidence from the Asian crisis', *Global Finance Journal*, 15(2), pp. 125–37.

Financial Stability Oversight Council (2013) *Annual Report 2012*, US Treasury Department: Washington DC. Online, available at: http://www.treasury.gov/initiatives/fsoc/studies-reports/Documents/2012%20Annual%20 Report.pdf (accessed 20 February 2013).

Flahault, F. (2003) *Malice*, Verso: London.

Flahault, F. (2008) *Le crépuscule de Prométhée: Contribution à une histoire de la démesure humaine*, Mille et une Nuits: Paris.

Forst, R. (2004) 'The limits of toleration', *Constellations*, 11(3), pp. 312–25.

Foucault, M. (1977) *Discipline and Punish*, Allen Lane: London.

Foucault, M. (1980) *The History of Sexuality*, Volume 1, Penguin: Harmondsworth.

Foucault, M. (1981) 'Omnes et singulatem: towards a criticism of "political reason" ', in S. McMurrin (ed.), *Tanner Lectures on Human Values Volume II*, University of Utah Press: Salt Lake City.

Foucault, M. (2003) *'Society Must Be Defended': Lectures at the Collège de France 1975–76*, Picador: New York.

Foucault, M. (2007) *'Security, Territory, Population': Lectures at the Collège de France 1977–1978*, Palgrave Macmillan: Basingstoke and New York.

Foucault, M. (2008) *'The Birth of Biopolitics': Lectures at the Collège de France 1978–79*, Palgrave Macmillan: Basingstoke.

Fox, J. (2009) *The Myth of the Rational Market: A History of Risk, Reward, and Delusion on Wall Street*, HarperBusiness: New York.

Frank, A. and Wilson, E. A. (2012) 'Critical response I. Like-minded', *Critical Inquiry*, 38(4), pp. 870–7.

Frank, R. H. (1988) *Passions within Reason: The Strategic Role of Emotions*, W. W. Norton & Co.: New York.

Fraser, N. (2003) 'From discipline to flexibilization: rereading Foucault in the shadow of globalization', *Constellations*, 10(2), pp. 160–71.

Frehen, R. G. P., Goetzmann, W. N. and Rouwenhorst, K. G. (2009) 'New evidence on the first financial bubble', NBER Working Paper No. 15332, September, NBER: Cambridge, MA.

Freud, S. (2004) [1930] *Civilization and Its Discontents*, Penguin Books: London.

Froud, J., Johal, S., Leaver, A. and Williams, K. (2006) *Financialization and Strategy: Narratives and Numbers*, Routledge: London and New York.

Gaffeo, E. and Tamborini, R. (2011) 'If the financial system is complex, how can we regulate it?', *International Journal of Political Economy*, 40(2), pp. 79–97.

Gai, P. and Kapadia, S. (2010) 'Contagion in financial networks', *Proceedings of the Royal Society A*, 466, doi: 10.1098/rspa.2009.0410, first published online 24 March 2010.

Gaukroger, S. (2011) *The Collapse of Mechanism and the Rise of Sensibility: Science and the Shaping of Modernity, 1680–1760*, Oxford University Press: Oxford.

Geertz, C. (1973) 'Thick description: toward an interpretive theory of culture', in Geertz, C., *The Interpretation of Cultures: Selected Essays*, Basic Books: New York, pp. 3–30.

Geuss, R. (2001) *History and Illusion in Politics*, Cambridge University Press: Cambridge.

Geuss, R. (2002) 'Liberalism and its discontents', *Political Theory*, 30(3), pp. 320–38.

Gibbon, P., Ponte, S. and Blair, S. (2008) 'Governing global value chains: an introduction', *Economy and Society*, 37(3), pp. 315–38.

Godechot, O. (2008) 'What do heads of dealing room do? The social capital of internal entrepreneurs', *The Sociological Review*, 56 (Special Issue 1), pp. 146–61.

Goldblatt, D., Perraton, J., Held, D. and McGrew, A. (1999) *Global Transformations: Politics, Economics, Culture*, Polity Press: Cambridge.

Goldgar, A. (2007) *Tulipmania: Money, Honour and Knowledge in the Dutch Golden Age*, University of Chicago Press: Chicago.

Gomber, P., Arndt, B., Lutat, M. and Uhle, T. (2011) *High-Frequency Trading*, Deutsche Börse Group/Gothe Universität: Frankfurt-am-Main, Germany.

Goodhart, C. A. E. (1998) 'Two concepts of money: implications for the analysis of optimal currency areas', *European Journal of Political Economy*, 14(3), pp. 407–32.

Goodhart, C. (2010) 'How should we regulate the financial sector?', in A. Turner, A. Haldane, P. Woolley, S. Wadhwani, C. Goodhart, A. Smithers, A. Large, J. Kay, M. Wolf, P. Boone, S. Johnson and R. Layard (eds), *The Future of Finance: The LSE Report*, London School of Economics and Political Science: London.

Gowan, P. (2009) 'Crisis in the heartland: consequences of the new Wall Street system', *New Left Review*, 55(2), pp. 2–29.

Gray, J. (2000) *Two Faces of Liberalism*, Polity Press: Cambridge.

Grossi, P. and Kunreuther, H. (eds) (2005) *Catastrophe Modelling: A New Approach to Managing Risk*, Springer: New York.

Gruber, L. (2000) *Ruling the World*, Princeton University Press: Princeton, NJ.

Guillén, M. F. and Suarez, S. L. (2010) 'The global crisis of 2007–2009: markets, politics and organizations', *Research in the Sociology of Organizations*, 30, Part A, pp. 257–79.

Gunaranta, R. (2002) *Inside Al Qaeda: Global Network of Terror*, Hurst and Co: London.

Gunder Frank, A. and Gills, B. K. (eds) (1996) *The World System: Five Hundred Years or Five Thousand?*, Routledge: London.

Habermas, J. (1997) *Between Fact and Norm: Contributions to a Discourse Theory of Law and Democracy*, Polity Press: Cambridge.

Habermas, J. (2001) 'Constitutional democracy: a paradoxical unity of contradictory principles?', *Political Theory*, 29(6), pp. 766–81.

Haldane, A. G. (2009) 'Rethinking the financial network', Bank of England, London, April. Online, available at: http://www.bankofengland.co.uk/research/Pages/economists/staff/andy_haldane.aspx (accessed 29 September 2014).

Haldane, A. (2011) 'The race to zero', Speech given to the International Economic Association Sixteenth World Congress, Beijing, China, Bank of England, London, 8 July. Online, available at: http://www.bankofengland.co.uk/publications/Documents/speeches/2011/speech509.pdf (accessed 23 February, 2013).

Haldane, A. G. and May, R. M. (2011) 'Systemic risk in banking ecosystems', *Nature*, 469, 20 January, pp. 351–5.

Haldane, A., Hall, S. and Pezzini, S. (2007) 'A new approach to assessing risks to financial stability', Financial Stability Paper No. 2, Bank of England, London, April.

Hansen, T. and Stepputat, F. (2002) (eds) *States of Imagination: Ethnographic Explorations of the Postcolonial State*, Duke University Press: North Carolina.

Hardt, M. and Negri, A. (2000) *Empire*, Harvard University Press: Cambridge, MA.

Hayek, F. A. (1960) *The Constitution of Liberty*, Routledge and Kegan Paul: London.

Hayek, F. von (1976) *Denationalization of Money*, Institute of Economic Affairs: London.

Held, D. (2004) *Global Covenant: The Social Democratic Alternative to the Washington Consensus*, Polity Press: Cambridge.

Held, D. (2010) *Cosmopolitanism*, Polity Press: Cambridge.

Held, G. and McGrew, A. (2002) *Globalization and Anti-Globalization*, Polity Press: Cambridge.

Hendershott, T., Jones, C. M. and Menkveld, A. J. (2011) 'Does algorithmic trading improve liquidity?', *The Journal of Finance*, 66, pp. 1–33.

Herndon, T., Ash, M. and Pollin, R. (2013) 'Does high public debt consistently stifle economic growth? A critique of Reinhart and Rogoff', PERI Working Paper Series No. 322, University of Massachusetts, April.

Hindess, B. (1996) *Discourses of Power: From Hobbes to Foucault*, Basil Blackwell: Oxford.

Hindess, B. (2006) 'Territory', *Alternatives*, 31(3), pp. 243–57.

Hirschman, A. O. (1977) *The Passions and the Interests: Political Arguments for Capitalism Before its Triumph*, Princeton University Press: Princeton, NJ.

Hirst, P. (1994) *Associative Democracy: New Forms of Economic and Social Governance*, Polity Press: Cambridge.

Hirst, P. (2003) 'The future of political studies', *European Political Science*, 3(1), pp. 47–59.

Hirst, P. and Thompson, G. (1996) *Globalization in Question: The International System and the Possibilities of Governance*, 1st edition, Polity Press: Cambridge.

Hirst, P. and Thompson, G. (1999) *Globalization in Question: The International System and the Possibilities of Governance*, 2nd edition, Polity Press: Cambridge.

Hirst, P. Q., Thompson, G. and Bromley, S. (2009) *Globalization in Question: The International System and the Possibilities of Governance*, 3rd edition, Polity Press: Cambridge.

Ho, K. (2009) *Liquidated: An Ethnography of Wall Street*, Duke University Press: New York.

Holling, C. S. (1973) 'Resilience and stability of ecological systems', *Annual Review of Ecology and Systematics*, 4, pp. 1–23.

Holmes, S. (1995) *Passions and Constraint*, University of Chicago Press: Chicago.

Holmström, B. and Roberts, J. (1998) 'The boundaries of the firm revisited', *Journal of Economic Perspectives*, 1(4), pp. 7–9.

Huault, I. and Ranielli-Weiss, H. (2013) 'The connexionist nature of modern financial markets: from a domination to a justice order', in P. du Gay and G. Morgan (eds), *New Spirits of Capitalism? Crises, Justifications, and Dynamics*, Oxford University Press: Oxford, pp. 181–205.

Hughes, N. and Lonie, S. (2007) 'M-PESA: mobile money for the "unbanked". Turning cellphones into 24-hour tellers in Kenya', *Innovations* (winter and spring), pp. 63–81.

Hunter, I. (2002) *Rival Enlightenments: Civil and Metaphysical Philosophy in Early Modern Germany*, Cambridge University Press: Cambridge.

Hunter, I. (2010) 'Kant's regional cosmopolitanism', *Journal of the History of International Law*, 12, pp. 165–88.

Huntington, S. P. (1996) *The Clash of Civilizations and the Remaking of World Order*, Simon and Schuster: New York.

Huntington, S. P. (2004a) 'The Hispanic challenge', *Foreign Policy*, 141 (March/April), pp. 31–45.

Huntington, S. P. (2004b) *Who Are We? The Challenges to America's National Identity*, Simon and Schuster: New York.

Ignatieff, M. (1997) *The Warrior's Honor: Ethnic War and the Modern Conscience*, Metropolitan Books: New York.

IMF (2008) 'Financial stress and deleveraging: macro-financial implications and policy', *Global Financial Stability Report*, October.

Ingham, G. (2004) *The Nature of Money*, Polity Press: Cambridge.

Ingham, G. (2006) 'Further reflections on the ontology of money', *Economy and Society*, 35(2), pp. 259–78.

IPS (2013) 'Territorialities, spaces, geographies', *International Political Sociology Virtual Issue*.

Ishaq, M. and Atiq Ur Rehman, M. (2013) 'Surmounting the individual: establishing a common currency in Asia – a case study of East Asian economies', *Global Economy Journal*, 13(1), pp. 63–88.

Iwata, K. and Takenaka, S. (2012) 'Central Bank balance sheets expansion: Japan's experience', Japan Centre for Economic Research Discussion Paper No. 134, January.

Izquierdo, A. J. (2001) 'Reliability at risk: the supervision of financial models as a case study for reflexive economic sociology', *European Societies*, 3(1), pp. 69–90.

Jackson, R. (2000) *The Global Covenant: Human Conduct in a World of States*, Oxford University Press: Oxford.

Jackwerth, J. C. and Rubinstein, M. (1996) 'Recovering probability distributions from options prices', *The Journal of Finance*, 51(5), pp. 1611–31.

Jain, P. K. (2005) 'Financial market design and the equity premium: electronic vs. floor trading', *The Journal of Finance*, 60(6), pp. 2955–85.

Jasanoff, S. (2010) 'Beyond calculation: a democratic response to risk', in A. Lakoff (ed.), *Disaster and the Politics of Intervention*, Columbia University Press: New York, pp. 14–40.

Jensen, M. and Meckling, W. (1976) 'Theory of the firm: managerial behavior, agency costs and ownership structure', *Journal of Financial Economics*, 3, pp. 305–60.

Joerges, C., Sand, I.-J. and Teubner, G. (2004) *Transnational Governance and Constitutionalism*, Hart Publishing: Oxford.

Joyce, M., Miles, D., Scott, A. and Vayanos, D. (2012) 'Quantitative easing and unconventional monetary policy – an introduction', *The Economic Journal*, 122 (November), pp. 271–88.

Juergensmeyer, M. (2003) *Terror in the Mind of God: The Global Rise of Religious Violence*, University of California Press: Berkeley.

Kant, I. (1990) [1919] 'To perpetual peace: a philosophy sketch', in H. Reiss (ed.), *Political Writings*, 2nd edition, Cambridge University Press: Cambridge.

Kay, J. (2009), *The Long and the Short of It*, The Erasmus Press: London.

Kearney, M. (2004) 'The classifying and value-filtering missions of borders', *Anthropological Theory*, 4(2), pp. 131–56.

Keoun, B. and Kuntz, P. (2001) 'Wall St. aristocracy got $1 trillion', *Bloomberg. com*, 22 August.

Kepel, G. (2004a) *Jihad: The Trail of Political Islam*, I. B. Tauris: London.

Kepel, G. (2004b) *The War for Muslim Minds: Islam and the West*, The Belknap Press: Cambridge, MA.

Kessler, O. (2009) 'Interrogating the current financial crisis: introduction', *International Political Sociology*, 3(4), pp. 449–68.

Keynes, J. M. (1930) *A Treatise on Money*, Macmillan: London.

Keynes, J. M. (1973) [1936] *The General Theory of Employment, Interest and Money*, Macmillan: London.

Khatib, L. (2003) 'Communicating Islam: fundamentalism as global citizenship', *Journal of Communication Inquiry*, 27(4), pp. 389–409.

Kindleberger, C. P. and Aliber, R. Z. (2011) *Manias, Panics and Crashes: A History of Financial Crises*, Palgrave MacMillan: Basingstoke.

King, M. and Low, D. (2014) 'Measuring the "world" real interest rate', NBER Working Paper No. 19887, NBER: Cambridge, MA, February.

Kleindorfer, P. R. and Wind, Y. J. (2009) *The Network Challenge: Strategy, Profit and Risk in an Interlinked World*, Wharton School Publishing/Pearson Education: Upper Saddle River, NJ.

Knapp, G. (1924) *The State Theory of Money*, Augustus M. Kelly: New York.

Knox, P. L. and Taylor, P. J. (eds) (1995) *World Cities in a World System*, Cambridge University Press: Cambridge.

KOF (2013) *KOF Index of Globalization*, Swiss Institute of Technology: Zurich. Online, available at: http://www.globalization.kof.ethz.ch/ (accessed 29 September 2014).

Koo, R. (2013) 'Balance sheet recession as the other half of macroeconomics', *European Journal of Economics and Economic Policies: Intervention*, 10(2), pp. 136–57.

Kriegel, B. (1996) *The State and the Rule of Law*, Princeton University Press: Princeton, NJ.

Kuru, A. T. (2005) 'Globalization and diversification of Islamic movements: three Turkish cases', *Political Science Quarterly*, 120(2), pp. 253–74.

Lane, P. R. (2012) 'Financial globalisation and the crisis', BIS Working Papers No. 397, December, BIS: Basel.

Lane, P. and Milesi-Ferretti, G. M. (2006) 'The External Wealth of Nations (Mark II)', CEPR Discussion Paper, Paper 5644, CEPR: London.

Latour, B. (2004) 'Whose cosmos, which cosmopolitics?', *Common Knowledge*, 10(3), pp. 45–62.

Latour, B. and Lépinay, V. A. (2009) *The Science of Passionate Interests: An Introduction to Gabriel Tarde's Economic Anthropology*, Prickly Paradigm Press: Chicago.

Lavallée, E. and Vicard, V. (2010) 'National borders matter … where one draws the lines too', Document De Travail No. 272, Banque de France, January.

Lawrence, B. (ed.) (2005) *Messages to the World: The Statements of Osama Bin Laden*, Verso: London.

Lentzos, F. and Rose, N. (2009) 'Governing insecurity: contingency planning, protection, resilience', *Economy and Society*, 38(2), pp. 230–54.

Leys, R. (2011a) 'The turn to affect: a critique', *Critical Inquiry*, 37(3), pp. 434–72.

Leys, R. (2011b) 'Critical response II. Affect and intention: a reply to William E. Connolly', *Critical Inquiry*, 37(4), pp. 799–805.

Leys, R. (2012) 'Critical response III. Facts and moods: reply to my critics', *Critical Inquiry*, 38(4), pp. 882–91.

de Lombaerde, P. (2007) *Multilateralism, Regionalism and Bilateralism in Trade and Investment*, Springer: Dordrecht.

Lopes, D. S. (2013) 'Metamorphoses of credit: pastiche production and the ordering of mass payment behaviour', *Economy and Society*, 42(1), pp. 26–50.

Loughlin, M. (2014) 'Constitutional pluralism: an oxymoron?', *Global Constitutionalism*, 3(1), pp. 9–30.

Lysandrou, P. (2005) 'Globalisation as commodification', *Cambridge Journal of Economics*, 29, pp. 769–97.

Lysandrou, P. (2013) 'Debt intolerance and the 90% debt threshold: two impossibility theorems', *Economy and Society*, 42(4), pp. 521–42.

Maalouf, A. (2000) *On Identity*, Harvill: London.

McGarvey, A. (2004) 'As God is his witness', in *The American Prospect Online*, 19 October 2004. Online, available at: http://prospect.org/article/god-his-witness (accessed 29 September 2014).

MacKenzie, D. (2006) *An Engine, Not a Camera: How Financial Models Shape Markets*, MIT Press: Cambridge, MA.

MacKenzie, D. (2008) 'End-of-the-world trade', *London Review of Books*, 30(8), 8 May, pp. 24–6.

MacKenzie, D. (2009) 'All those arrows', *London Review of Books*, 32(12), 25 June, pp. 20–2.

MacKenzie, D., Muniesa, F. and Siu, L. (eds) (2008) *Do Economists Make Markets? On The Performativity of Economics*, Princeton University Press: Princeton, NJ.

MacKenzie, D., Beunza, D., Millo, Y. and Pardo-Guerra, J. P.(2012) 'Drilling through the Allegheny Mountains: Liquidity, materiality and high-frequency trading', *Journal of Cultural Economy*, 5(3), pp. 279–96.

McKinsey Global Institute (2011) *Mapping Global Financial Markets 2011*, October.

McLeary, M., Radia, A. and Thomas, R. (2014) 'Money creation in the modern economy', *Bank of England Quarterly Bulletin*, 54(1), pp. 14–27.

Malamud, B. D. (2004) 'Tails of natural hazards', *Physics World*, August, pp. 31–5.

Mandelbrot, B. B. (1997) *Fractals and Scaling in Finance: Discontinuity, Concentration, Risk*, Springer-Verlag: New York.

Mandelbrot, B. B. and Hudson, R. L. (2008) *The (Mis)Behaviour of Markets: A Fractal View of Risk, Ruin and Reward*, Profile Books: London.

Marazzi, C. (2008) *Capital and Language: From the New Economy to the War Economy*, Foreign Agents: New York.

Marchionatti, R. (1999) 'On Keynes' animal spirits', *Kyklos*, 52(3), pp. 415–39.

Marcuse, H. (1965) 'Repressive tolerance', in R. P. Wolff, J. Barrington Moore and H. Marcuse (eds), *A Critique of Pure Tolerance*, Beacon Books: Boston.

Martell, L. (2007) 'The third wave of globalization theory', *International Studies Review*, 9, pp. 173–96.

Martignoni, J. (2012) 'A new approach to a typology of complementary currencies', *International Journal of Community Currency Research*, 16, Section A, pp. 1–17.

Marty, M. E. and Appleby, R. S. (1991–4) *Fundamentalisms Observed, Vols. 1–4,* University of Chicago Press: Chicago.

Marty, M. E. and Appleby, R. S. (eds) (1993) *Fundamentalisms and the State: Remaking Polities, Economies, and Militance,* University of Chicago Press: Chicago.

Mattera, O. (2005) 'Jihad, from localism to globalism', *CeMiSS Quarterly,* 3(2), pp. 9–21.

Marx, K. (1867) *Capital, Volume I,* International Publishers: New York.

Marx, K. and Engels, F. (1970) [1850] 'Manifesto of the Communist Party', in *Karl Marx and Frederick Engels, Selected Works in One Volume,* Lawrence & Wishart: London.

Masood, E. (2005) 'A Muslim journey', *Prospect,* 113, August, pp. 42–7.

Massey, D. (2005) *For Space,* Sage: London.

Mattli, W. and Woods, N. (2009) *The Politics of Global Regulation,* Princeton University Press: Princeton, NJ.

May, R. M. and Arinaminpathy, N. (2010) 'Systemic risk: the dynamics of model banking systems', *Journal of the Royal Society Interface,* 7, October, pp. 823–38.

Mehrling, P. (2005) *Fisher Black and the Revolutionary Idea of Finance,* John Wiley: New York.

Mennicken, A. and Miller, P. (2012) 'Accounting, territorialization and power', *Foucault Studies,* 13, May, pp. 4–24.

Merton, R. C. (1973) 'Theory of rational option pricing', *Bell Journal of Economics and Managerial Science,* 4(1), pp. 141–83.

Milanovic, B. (2012) 'Global income inequality by the numbers: in history and now – an overview', Policy Research Working Paper 6259, World Bank Development Research Group, Poverty and Inequality Team, November.

Miles, D. (2010) 'Interpreting monetary policy'. Online, available at: http://www.bankofengland.co.uk/archive/Documents/historicpubs/speeches/2010/speech425.pdf (accessed 20 September 2014).

Minford, P. (2010) 'The banking crisis – a rational interpretation', *Political Studies Review,* 8(1), pp. 40–54.

Minsky, H. P. (1982) *Can 'It' Happen Again: Essays on Instability and Finance,* M. E. Sharpe: Armonk.

Minsky, H. P. (2008) *Stabilizing an Unstable Economy,* McGraw-Hill Professional/ Yale University Press: New Haven.

Minson, J. (2010) 'The sense of existing and its political implications (on François Flahault's "general anthropology")', in M. Zolkos and A. Yeatman (eds), *State, Security, and Subject Formation,* Continuum: London, pp. 157–72.

Mirowski, P. (2002) *Machine Dreams: Economics Becomes a Cyborg Science,* Cambridge University Press: Cambridge.

Mixon, S. (2009) 'Option markets and implied volatility: past versus present', *Journal of Financial Economics,* 94, pp. 17–191.

Mohammadi, A. (ed.) (2002) *Islam Encountering Globalization,* Routledge Curzon: London.

Moore, L. and Juh, S. (2006) 'Derivative pricing 60 years before Black–Scholes: evidence from the Johannesburg stock exchange', *The Journal of Finance*, 61(6), pp. 3069–98.

Moore, N. (2012) 'The perception of the middle', in L. De Sutter and K. McGhee (eds), *Deleuze and Law*, Edinburgh University Press: Edinburgh.

Moore, N. and Bottomley, A. (forthcoming) 'Artisan and the Law', *Law and Critique*.

Mukerji, C. (1997) *Territorial Ambitions and the Gardens of Versailles*, Cambridge University Press: Cambridge.

Myers, M. L. (1983) *The Soul of Modern Economic Man: Ideas of Self-Interest, Thomas Hobbes to Adam Smith*, University of Chicago Press: Chicago.

Naqvi, M. and Southgate, J. (2013) 'Banknotes, local currencies and central bank objectives', *Bank of England Quarterly Bulletin*, 53(4), pp. 317–25.

NEF (2002) *The Money Trail: Measuring Your Impact on the Local Economy Using LM3*, New Economics Foundation: London.

NEF (2014) *Strategic Quantitative Easing: Stimulating Investment to Rebalance the Economy*, New Economics Foundation: London.

Nesvetailova, A. and Palan, R. (2008) 'A very North Atlantic credit crunch: geopolitical implications of the global liquidity crisis', *Columbia Journal of International Affairs*, 62(1), pp. 23–46.

Nier, E., Yang, J., Yorulmazer, T. and Alentorn, A. (2007) 'Network models and financial stability', *Journal of Economic Dynamics & Control*, 31(6), pp. 2003–60.

Nikkinen, J., Omran, M., Sahlstrom, P. and Aijo, J. (2006) 'Global stock market reactions to scheduled US macroeconomic news announcements', *Global Finance Journal*, 17(1), pp. 92–104.

Northcott, M. (2004) *An Angel Directs the Storm: Apocalyptic Religion and American Empire*, I. B. Tauris: London.

Nussbaum, M. C. (2013) *Political Emotions: Why Love Matters for Justice*, Belknap/Harvard University Press: Cambridge, MA.

O'Dowd, L. (2010) 'From a "borderless world" to a "world of borders": "bringing history back in"', *Environment and Planning D: Society and Space*, 28, pp. 1031–50.

OECD (2013) *Measuring Globalisation: OECD Economic Globalisation Indicators 2013*, OECD: Paris.

Oestreich, G. (1982) *Neostoicism and the Early Modern State*, Cambridge University Press: Cambridge.

Ogden, C. K. and Richards, I. A. (1949) *The Meaning of Meaning*, Routledge and Kegan Paul: London.

Ong, A. and Collier, S. J. (2004) *Global Assemblages: Technology, Politics, and Ethics as Anthropological Problems*, Wiley-Blackwell: Oxford.

Orléan, A. (1989) 'Mimetic contagion and speculative bubbles', *Theory and Decision*, 27(1/2), pp. 63–92.

Orléan, A. (2010) 'The impossible evaluation of risk', *Prisme No. 18*, April, Cournot Centre for Economic Studies: Paris.

Pacione, M. (2011) 'Local money – a response to the globalization of capital', *Quaestiones Geographicae*, 30(4), pp. 9–19.

Papoulias, C. and Callard, F. (2010) 'Biology's gift: interrogating the turn to affect', *Body and Society*, 16(2), pp. 29–56.

Parádi-Dolgos, A., Gál, V. and Kovács, T. (2011) 'The penetration of local currencies: a possible solution to the financial challenges of globalization', *Regional and Business Studies*, 3(1), pp. 421–7.

Paz, R. (2001) 'The brotherhood of global jihad', October. Online, available at: http://www.e-prism.org/projectsandproducts.html (accessed 29 September 2014).

Paz, R. (2002) 'Global jihad and the European arena', May. Online, available at: http://www.e-prism.org/projectsandproducts.html (accessed 29 September 2014).

Paz, R. (2003) 'Global jihad and the United States: interpretation of the new world order of Usama bin Ladin', *PRISM Occasional Papers*, 1(1). Online, available at: http://www.e-prism.org/projectsandproducts.html (accessed 29 September 2014).

Perraton, J. (2001) 'Global economy – myths and realities', *Cambridge Journal of Economics*, 25, pp. 669–84.

Perrow, C. (1999) *Normal Accidents: Living with High-Risk Technologies*, 2nd edition, Princeton University Press: Princeton, NJ.

Perrow, C. (2007) *The Next Catastrophe*, Princeton University Press: Princeton, NJ.

Perrow, C. (2010) 'The meltdown was not an accident', *Research in Sociology of Organizations*, 30, Part A, pp. 309–30.

Pfajfar, D., Sgro, G. and Wagner, W. (2011) 'Are alternative currencies a substitute or a complement to fiat money? Evidence from cross-country data', European Banking Center, CentER, Tilburg University, 7 June.

Pistor, K. (2008) 'Global network finance: organizational hedging in times of uncertainty', Columbia Law School Working Paper No. 339, October.

Pollitt, C. and Bouckaert, G. (2004) *Public Management Reform: A Comparative Analysis*, Oxford University Press: Oxford.

Price-Smith, A. T. (2009) *Contagion and Chaos: Disease, Ecology, and National Security in the Era of Globalization*, MIT Press: Cambridge, MA.

Qutb, S. (1964) *Milestones*, Islamic Book Service: New Delhi, India.

Rancière, J. (1999) *Dis-Agreement: Politics and Philosophy*, University of Minnesota Press: Minneapolis, MN.

Randall Wray, L. (2013) 'The lender of last resort: a critical analysis of the Federal Reserve's unprecedented intervention after 2007', Research Project Report, April, Levy Institute, Bard College. Online, available at: http://www.levyinstitute.org/publications/?docid=1739 (accessed 29 September 2014).

Rauch, J. E. (1999) 'Networks versus markets in international trade', *Journal of International Economics*, 48(1), pp. 7–35.

Rawls, J. (1971) *A Theory of Justice*, Oxford University Press: Oxford.

Rawls, J. (1999) *The Law of Peoples*, Harvard University Press: Cambridge, MA.

Reinhart, C. M. (2008) 'Eight hundred years of financial folly', MPRA Paper No. 11864, December 2008. Online, available at: http://mpra.ub.uni-muenchen.de/11864/1/MPRA_paper_11864.pdf (accessed 20 September 2014).

Reinhart, C. M. and Rogoff, K. S. (2009) *This Time is Different: Eight Centuries of Financial Folly*, Princeton University Press: Princeton, NJ.

Reinhart, C. M. and Rogoff, K. S. (2010) 'Growth in a time of debt', *American Economic Review: Papers and Proceedings*, May, pp. 573–8.

Reinhart, C. M. and Rogoff, K. S. (2013) 'Debt, growth and the austerity debate', *New York Times*, 25 April.

Ricoeur, P. (ed.) (1996) *Tolerance between Intolerance and the Intolerable*, Berghahn Books: Providence, RI.

Rieger, E. and Leibfried, S. (2003) *Limits to Globalization*, Polity Press: Cambridge.

Riles, A. (2011) *Collateral Knowledge: Legal Reasoning in the Global Financial Markets*, University of Chicago Press: Chicago.

RIPE (2014) 'Global value chains and global production networks in the changing international political economy', *Review of International Political Economy Special Issue*, 21(1), pp. 1–8.

Robertson, R. (1992) *Globalization: Social Theory and Global Culture*, Sage: London.

Rogoff, K. (2001) 'Why not a global currency?', *American Economic Review: Papers and Proceedings*, 91(2), pp. 243–7.

Rose, N. (2012) 'The human sciences in a biological age', *Institute for Culture and Society Occasional Paper Series*, 3(1), February, University of Western Sydney.

Rose, N. and Miller, P. (2008) *Governing the Present: Administering Economic, Social and Personal Life*, Polity Press: Cambridge.

Rosenberg, J. (2005) 'Globalization theory: a post-mortem', *International Politics*, 42(1), pp. 2–74.

Roy, O. (1994) *The Failure of Political Islam*, Harvard University Press: Cambridge, MA.

Roy, O. (2004) *Globalized Islam: The Search for a New Ummah*, Columbia University Press: New York.

Ruddick, W. O. (2011) 'Eco-Pesa: an evaluation of a complementary currency programme in Kenya's informal settlements', *International Journal of Community Currency Research*, 15, Section A, pp. 1–12.

Ruggie, J. G. (1993) 'Territoriality and beyond: problematizing modernity in international relations', *International Organization*, 4(1), pp. 139–74.

Rumford, C. (2010) 'Guest editorial: global borders', *Environment and Planning D: Society and Space*, 28, pp. 951–6.

Ruthven, M. (2004) *Fundamentalism: The Search for Meaning*, Oxford University Press: Oxford.

Ruthven, M. and Nanji, A. (2004) *Historical Atlas of Islam*, Harvard University Press: Cambridge, MA.

Ryan-Collins, J. (2011) 'Building local resilience: the emergence of the UK transition currencies', *International Journal of Community Currency Research*, 15 (Special Issue D61–7).

Ryan-Collins, J. and Greenham, T. (2012) *Where Does Money Come From?*, New Economics Foundation: London.

Sabel, C. (1991) 'Moebius-strip organizations and open labor markets: Some consequences of the reintegration of conception and execution in a volatile economy', in P. Bairdieu and J. S. Coleman (eds), *Social Theory for a Changing Society*, Westview Press: Boulder, CO, pp. 23–61.

Sacks, J. (2003) 'Global covenant: a Jewish perspective on globalization', in J. H. Dunning (ed.), *Making Globalization Good: The Moral Challenges of Global Capitalism*, Oxford University Press: Oxford, pp. 210–31.

Sageman, M. (2004) *Understanding Terror Networks*, University of Pennsylvania Press: Philadelphia.

Sassen, S. (ed.) (2002) *Global Networks, Linked Cities*, Routledge: London.

Sassen, S. (2013) 'When territory deborders territoriality', *Territory, Politics, Governance*, 1(1), pp. 21–45.

Saunders, D. (2006) 'What does liberalism inherit from early modern religious settlements?', CRESC Working Paper No. 16, April, CRESC: Open University.

Schmitt, C. (1997) [1954] *Land and Sea*, Plutarch Press: Alexandria, VA.

Schmitt, C. (1998) *Political Theology: Four Chapters on the Concept of Sovereignty*, MIT Press: Cambridge, MA.

Schmitt, C. (2003) [1950] *The Nomos of the Earth: In the International Law of the Jus Publicum Europaeum*, Telos Press: New York.

Schmitt, C. (2007) [1975] *Theory of the Partisan*, Telos Press Publishing: New York.

Schneiberg, M. (2013) 'Lost in translation? (a cautionary tale): the Bank of North Dakota and the prospects for reform in American banking', *Research in Sociology of Organizations*, 39A, pp. 277–310.

Scholte, J. A. (2005) *Globalization: A Critical Introduction*, Palgrave MacMillan: Basingstoke.

Schularick, M. and Taylor, A. M. (2009) 'Credit booms gone bust: monetary policy, leverage cycles and financial crises, 1870–2008', NBER Working Paper 15512, November.

Seabrook, L. and Wigan, D. (2014) 'Global wealth chains in the international political economy', *Review of International Political Economy*, 21(1), pp. 257–63.

Sennett, R. (2009) *The Craftsman*, Penguin Books: London.

Serwa, D. and Böhl, M. T. (2005) 'Financial contagion vulnerability and resistance: a comparison of European stock markets', *Economic Systems*, 29(3), pp. 344–62.

Shah, N. (2012) 'The territorial trap of the territorial trap: global transformation and the problem of the state's two territories', *International Political Sociology*, 6, pp. 57–76.

Shefrin, H. (2000) *Beyond Greed and Fear: Understanding Behavioral Finance and the Psychology of Investing*, Harvard Business School Press: Boston.

Shiller, R. J. (2000) *Irrational Exuberance*, Princeton University Press: Princeton, NJ.

Shiller, R. J. (2003) 'From efficient markets theory to behavioral finance', *Journal of Economic Perspectives*, 17(1), pp. 83–104.

Shleifer, A. (2000) *Inefficient Markets: An Introduction to Behavioral Finance*, Oxford University Press: New York.

Sim, S. (2004) *Fundamentalist World: The New Dark Age of Dogma*, Icon Books: Cambridge.

Simmel, G. (1971) *On Individuality and Social Forms*, University of Chicago Press: Chicago.

Simon, H. A. (1985) 'Human nature in politics: the dialogue of psychology with political science', *The American Political Science Review*, 79(2), pp. 293–304.

Sinclair, T. J. (2005) *The New Masters of Capital*, Cornell University Press: Ithaca, NY.

Skidelsky, R. (2009) *Keynes: The Return of the Master*, Allen Lane: London.

Skinner, Q. (1998) *Liberty Before Liberalism*, Cambridge University Press: Cambridge.

Slaughter, A.-M. (2004) *A New World Order*, Princeton University Press: Princeton, NJ.

Smith, G. and Teasdale, S. (2012) 'Associative democracy and the social economy: exploring the regulatory challenge', *Economy and Society*, 41(2), pp. 151–76.

Sornette, D. (2003) *Why Stock Markets Crash: Critical Events in Complex Financial Systems*, Princeton University Press: Princeton, NJ.

Sornette, D. and Woodard, R. (2009) 'Financial bubbles, real estate bubbles, derivative bubbles, and the financial and economic crisis'. Online, available at: http://www.arxiv.org/abs/0905.0220 (accessed 30 November 2009).

Spivak, G. C. (2004) *Death of a Discipline*, Columbia University Press: New York.

Stark, D. (2009) *A Sense of Dissonance: Accounts of Worth in Economic Life*, Princeton University Press: Princeton, NJ.

Stern, J. (2003) *Terror in the Name of God: Why Religious Militants Kill*, Harper Collins: New York.

Stiglitz, J. E. (2010) 'Contagion, liberalization and the optimal structures of globalization', *Journal of Globalization and Development*, 1(2), pp. 1–45.

Stinchcome, A. (2001) *When Formality Works: Authority and Abstraction in Law and Organization*, University of Chicago Press: Chicago.

Stockman, D. (2013) *The Great Deformation: The Corruption of Capitalism in America*, Public Affairs: Washington, DC.

Strandsbjerg, J. (2010). *Territory, Globalisation and International Relations: The Cartographic Reality of Space*, Palgrave: Basingstoke.

Stulz, R. M. (2005) 'The limits of financial globalization', *The Journal of Finance*, 60(4), pp. 1595–638.

Subramanian, A. and Kessler, M. (2013) 'The hyperglobalization of trade and its future', Global Citizen Foundation Working Paper 3, June.

Taleb, N. N. (2004) *Fooled By Randomness: The Hidden Role of Chance in Life and in the Markets*, Random House: New York.

Taleb, N. N. (2007a) *The Black Swan: The Impact of the Highly Improbable*, Allen Lane: London.

Taleb, N. N. (2007b) 'Black swans and the domain of statistics', *The American Statistician*, 61(2), pp. 198–200.

Tan, K.-C. (2005) 'International toleration: Rawlsian vs. cosmopolitan', *Leiden Journal of International Law*, 18, pp. 685–719.

Taylor, P. J. (2003) *World City Network: A Global Urban Analysis*, Routledge: London.

Teschke, B. (2003) *The Myth of 1648: Class, Geopolitics and the Making of Modern International Relations*, Verso: London.

Tétreault, M. A. and Denemark, R. A. (eds) (2004) *Gods, Guns, and Globalization: Religious Radicalism and International Political Economy*, Lynne Rienner: Boulder, CO, and London.

Tett, G. (2009) *Fools Gold: How Unrestrained Greed Corrupted a Dream, Shattered Global Markets and Unleashed a Catastrophe*, Little Brown: London.

Tett, G. (2010) 'Silos and silences: why so few people spotted the problems in complex credit and what that implies for the future', *Financial Stability Review, No. 14 – Derivatives – Financial Innovation and Stability*, July, pp. 139–50.

Teubner, G. (2011) *Networks as Connected Contracts*, Hart Publishing: Oxford.

Teubner, G. (2012) *Constitutional Fragments: Societal Constitutionalization and Globalization*, Oxford University Press: Oxford.

Thompson, G. (2002–5) 'Toleration and the art of governance: how is it possible to "live together" in a fragmenting international system?', in J. Hillier and E. Rooksby (eds), *Habitus: A Sense of Place, 1st and 2nd Editions*, Hampshire: Ashgate, pp. 67–91.

Thompson, G. (2004a) 'Are there any limits to globalization? International trade, capital flows and borders', in N. Karagiannis and M. Witter (eds), *The Caribbean Economies in an Era of Free Trade*, Ashgate: Aldershot, pp. 23–46.

Thompson, G. (2004b) 'Is all the world a complex network?', *Economy and Society*, 33(3), pp. 411–24.

Thompson, G. (2004c) 'Getting to know the knowledge economy: ICTs, networks and governance', *Economy and Society*, 33(4), pp. 562–81.

Thompson, G. (2005) 'Is the future regional for "global standards"?', *Environment and Planning A*, 37(11), pp. 2053–71.

Thompson, G. (2006) 'Global inequality, the "great divergence" and supranational regionalization', in D. Held and A. Kaya (eds), *Global Inequality: Patters and Explanations*, Polity Press: Cambridge.

Thompson, G. (2007) 'Religious fundamentalisms, territories and "globalization"', *Economy and Society*, 36(1), pp. 19–50.

Thompson, G. (2008a) 'Are we all neo-liberals now? "Responsibility" and corporations', *Soundings*, 39 (summer), pp. 67–74.

Thompson, G. (2008b) 'Notes on "methodology and globalization": defending "pragmatic scepticism" and "the number 7" ', *CBS/DBP*, October, mimeographed.

Thompson, G. (2009) 'What's in the frame? How the financial crisis is being packaged for public consumption', *Economy and Society*, 38(3), pp. 520–4.

Thompson, G. (2012) *The Constitutionalization of the Global Corporate Sphere?*, Oxford University Press: Oxford.

Thompson, G. (2014) 'The constitutionalization of everyday life?', paper given at the ITEPE Workshop at CBS, 30–31 January.

Thompson, G. (forthcoming) 'Post-Katrina and post-financial crisis: competing logics of risk, uncertainty and security', in W. Taylor and M. Levine (eds), *The Katrina Effect*, Bloomsbury: London.

Thompson, G. and Kaspersen, L. B. (2012) 'The globalization of the business sector in a small open economy: the case of Denmark and its wider implications', *Socio-Economic Review*, 10(4), pp. 627–53.

Thrift, N. (2004) 'Intensities of feeling: towards a spatial politics of affect', *Geografiska Annaler Series B: Human Geography*, 86(1), pp. 57–78.

Tibi, B. (2002) *The Challenge of Fundamentalism: Political Islam and the New World Disorder*, University of California Press: Berkeley, CA.

Tobin, J. (1998) 'Financial globalization: can national currencies survive?', paper prepared for the Annual World Bank Conference on Development Economics, Washington, DC, 20–21 April.

Triana, P. (2009) *Lecturing Birds on Flying: Can Mathematical Models Destroy the Financial Markets?*, John Wiley & Sons: Hoboken, NJ.

Tsing, A. L. (2004) *Friction: An Ethnography of Global Connections*, Princeton University Press: Princeton, NJ.

Tuckett, D. (2011) *Minding the Markets: An Emotional Finance View of Financial Stability*, Palgrave MacMillan: Basingstoke.

Turner, B. S. (2002) 'Sovereignty and emergency: political theology, Islam and American conservatism', *Theory, Culture and Society*, 19(4), pp. 103–19.

University of Warwick (2010) *The Warwick Commission on International Financial Reform: In Praise of Unlevel Playing Fields*, University of Warwick.

Valverde, M. (2007) 'Genealogies of European states: Foucauldian reflections', *Economy and Society*, 36(1), pp. 158–78.

Vaughan-Williams, N. (2008) 'Borders, territory, law', *International Political Sociology*, 2, pp. 322–38.

Viliante, D. and Lannoo, K. (2011) *MiFID 2.0: Casting New Light on Europe's Capital Markets*, Center for European Policy Studies: Brussels.

Villadsen, K. and Dean, M. (2012) 'State-phobia, civil society, and a certain vitalism', *Constellations*, 19(2), pp. 401–20.

Vujakovic, P. (n.d.) 'How to measure globalisation? A new globalisation index (NGI)'. Online, available at: http://www.fiw.ac.at/fileadmin/Documents/Veranstaltungen/Forschungskonferenz/3._foko/Paper_der_Vortragenden/47.PetraVujakovic.New_Globalisation_Index.pdf (accessed 29 September 2014).

Wagner, D. (2003) 'Christians and Zion: British stirrings'. Online, available at: http://www.informationclearinghouse.info/article4959.htm (accessed 26 June 2014).

Wallerstein, I. (2004) *World System Analysis: An Introduction*, Duke University Press: North Carolina.

Walzer, M. (1981) 'The distribution of membership', in P. G. Brown and H. Shue (eds), *Boundaries: National Autonomy and Its Limits*, Rowman and Littlefield: Totowa, NJ.

Walzer, M. (1997) *On Toleration*, Yale University Press: New Haven, CT.

Weber, M. (1978) *Economy and Society*, edited by G. Roth and C.Wittch, University of California Press: Berkeley, CA.

Weick, K. E. and Sutcliffe, K. M. (2007) *Managing the Unexpected: Resilient Performance in an Age of Uncertainty*, John Wiley & Sons: San Francisco.

Weidmann, J. (2013) 'Stop encouraging banks to buy government debt', *Financial Times*, 1 October, p. 15.

Wickham, G. (forthcoming) 'The "socio" in socio-legal studies: three definitions of society', *Journal of Law and Society*.

Wigan, D. (2009) 'Financialisation and derivatives: constructing an artifice of indifference', *Competition and Change*, 13(2), pp. 157–72.

Williams, B. (2006) 'Tolerating the intolerable', in *Philosophy as a Humanistic Discipline*, Princeton University Press: Oxford, pp. 126–34.

Wolf, M. (2008) 'An embarrassing admission', *Financial Times*, 29 December, p. 12.

Wolf, M. (2009) 'Wheel of fortune turns as China outdoes West', *Financial Times*, 14 September, p. 4.

Woodford, M. (2009) 'Convergence in macroeconomics: elements of the new synthesis', *American Economic Journal: Macroeconomics*, 1(1), pp. 267–79.

Yu, Q. and Lan, X. (2013) 'Handcuff central banks, save the global market', in *The G-20 and Central Banks in the New World of Unconventional Monetary Policy*, *Think Tank 20*, The Brookings Institution: Washington, DC.

Zagorin, P. (2003) *How the Idea of Religious Toleration Came to the West*, Princeton University Press: Princeton, NJ.

Zaloom, C. (2003) 'Ambiguous numbers: trading technologies and interpretation in financial markets', *American Anthropologist*, 30(2), pp. 258–72.

Zaloom, C. (2012) *Out of the Pit: Traders and Technology from Chicago to London*, University of Chicago Press: Chicago.

Zanini, M. (2009) ' "Power curves": what natural and economic disasters have in common', *The McKinsey Quarterly*, June, pp. 1–5.

Zank, M. (ed.) (2002) *Leo Strauss: The Early Writings (1921–1932)*, State University of New York Press: Albany, NY.

Index